D1370440

The Robosapien Companion

Tips, Tricks, and Hacks

JAMIE SAMANS

The Robosapien Companion: Tips, Tricks, and Hacks

Copyright © 2005 by Jamie Samans

All rights reserved. No part of this work may be reproduced or transmitted in any form or by any means, electronic or mechanical, including photocopying, recording, or by any information storage or retrieval system, without the prior written permission of the copyright owner and the publisher.

ISBN (pbk): 1-59059-526-2

CIP data available upon request

Printed and bound in the United States of America 9 8 7 6 5 4 3 2 1

Trademarked names may appear in this book. Rather than use a trademark symbol with every occurrence of a trademarked name, we use the names only in an editorial fashion and to the benefit of the trademark owner, with no intention of infringement of the trademark.

Lead Editor: Jim Sumser
Editorial Board: Steve Anglin, Dan Appleman, Ewan Buckingham, Gary Cornell, Tony Davis,
    Jason Gilmore, Jonathan Hassell, Chris Mills, Dominic Shakeshaft, Jim Sumser
Assistant Publisher: Grace Wong
Project Manager: Sofia Marchant
Copy Manager: Nicole LeClerc
Copy Editor: Liz Welch
Assistant Production Director: Kari Brooks-Copony
Production Editor: Kelly Winquist
Compositor: Diana Van Winkle, Van Winkle Design Group
Proofreader: Linda Seifert
Indexer: Carol Burbo
Artist: Diana Van Winkle, Van Winkle Design Group
Cover Designer: Kurt Krames
Manufacturing Manager: Tom Debolski

Distributed to the book trade in the United States by Springer-Verlag New York, Inc., 233 Spring Street, 6th Floor, New York, NY 10013, and outside the United States by Springer-Verlag GmbH & Co. KG, Tiergartenstr. 17, 69112 Heidelberg, Germany.

In the United States: phone 1-800-SPRINGER, fax 201-348-4505, e-mail orders@springer-ny.com, or visit http://www.springer-ny.com. Outside the United States: fax +49 6221 345229, e-mail orders@springer.de, or visit http://www.springer.de.

For information on translations, please contact Apress directly at 2560 Ninth Street, Suite 219, Berkeley, CA 94710. Phone 510-549-5930, fax 510-549-5939, e-mail info@apress.com, or visit http://www.apress.com.

The information in this book is distributed on an "as is" basis, without warranty. Although every precaution has been taken in the preparation of this work, neither the author(s) nor Apress shall have any liability to any person or entity with respect to any loss or damage caused or alleged to be caused directly or indirectly by the information contained in this work.

For Carla

Contents at a Glance

Contents

PART 1 ■■■ Introduction

PART 3 ■ ■ ■ Programming Your Robosapien

PART 4 ■■■ **Hacking the Robosapien**

PART 5 ▓▓▓ A Look Ahead

About the Author

 **JAMIE SAMANS** was born August 18, 1970, and raised in Bridgeville, Delaware, a small town in the southern part of the state. A history major, he studied medieval intellectual history at Oxford University and received his BA from St. Mary's College of Maryland in 1992. In 1995 he received a law degree from Widener University School of Law and became involved in government relations, primarily working with state legislatures on a wide range of corporate tax issues. In addition to science fiction and robotics, Jamie's interests include building computers, playing guitar, and collecting vinyl records.

He currently lives in the Seattle area with his wife, Carla, and their two rescued pit bulls, Piper and Duce.

Acknowledgments

A few thanks to the people who made this book possible:

My wife, Carla: For putting up with the robot menagerie that took over most of the first floor of our house while this book was being written, the late hours spent in my workshop in the garage, and all of your time spent discussing and helping me organize my ideas for this book. I think you are the most patient woman in the world!

My mother, Charlotte: For teaching me to read and the importance of the written word.

My father, Jim: For showing me as a boy that there was a whole lot more to science fiction than just the *Star Wars* movies, and for always having interesting books laying around for me to "borrow."

Mark Tilden: For meeting me in New York, and for being such an incredible source of information for this book.

Amy Weltman at WowWee: For all of the information and marketing materials you made available to me.

Additional thanks to the crew at Apress, without whom this book *really* wouldn't have been possible!

Sofia Marchant: For keeping me motivated and on schedule. As I have told you before, if not for you I would still be taking interesting pictures and jotting down vague ideas in my notebook.

Liz Welch: For your superhuman attention to detail and your enthusiasm. Who knew that copyediting could be so much fun!

And finally, my dogs, Piper and Duce: For reminding me that as much fun as robots are, playing ball is pretty fun too. And for not chewing up any of the Robosapiens.

PART 1

■■■

Introduction

CHAPTER 1

■ ■ ■

An Introduction to Robosapien

Figure 1-1. *Robosapien comes complete with remote controller, instruction manual, and a cup that it can pick up.*

What is it about Robosapien that makes it so interesting? If you are reading this book, this is probably a question that you have asked yourself at some point. Technically speaking, Robosapien is a biomorphic toy robot. In layman's terms (and according to WowWee Ltd., the company that produces Robosapien), it is a "fusion of technology and personality." Wait a second—I must admit, I paused as I was writing and referred to Robosapien as "it." Is it an it? Is it a he or a she? Or is it something else altogether? As we will see, Robosapien is in many ways an embodiment of its creator, Mark Tilden; however, the answer to a question like that is above all a personal preference. For the sake of consistency I'll refer to Robosapien throughout this book as an "it." I think that if you work your way through this book, you'll understand where I'm coming from, since one of Robosapien's most prominent features is that the robot is what you make of it. Now, with that potentially uncomfortable business out of the way, let's take a look at what I hope to accomplish.

Chances are, whatever it is that interests you about Robosapien will be covered in this book. We'll examine everything from the basics to more advanced topics. My hope is to give you not only an advanced user guide to Robosapien, but also some background information about the theories behind the machine, and to explore the ways to go beyond what comes in the box—using Robosapien as a platform for "hacks" or modifications. Finally, we'll sneak a peek at the new line of Robosapiens due out in 2005—including Robopet, Roboraptor, and the bipedal Robosapien V2.

That's a tall order, but I hope at the very least I can provide you with enough information to aid further, more detailed investigation on your own—to whet your curiosity, as they say. Or even better, to spark your creativity to come up with your own ways to use Robosapien. Curiosity and creativity. These are two words that define my relationship with this funny little robot.

In this chapter, I take a look at Robosapien. What exactly is it? What can it do? To close out Chapter 1, I'll discuss in more detail what I hope to accomplish with this book, and what you, the reader, will need to get the most out of *The Robosapien Companion*.

What Is Robosapien?

Strictly speaking, Robosapien is a battery-operated, remote-controlled robotic toy. Standing 14 inches at the shoulder, and weighing in at 4.8 pounds (including batteries), Robosapien takes up about the same amount of space as a small house cat.

Robosapien uses four D cell batteries, which go into compartments accessed at the bottom of its feet, and the 21-key remote control uses three AAA batteries.

There is a lot more to Robosapien than first meets the eye, particularly from a technical and design standpoint, and we'll examine some of these topics in more detail throughout the rest of the book. But first, we need to figure out exactly what Robosapien is. Is Robosapien a robot, or is it a toy?

Where Does the Term "Robot" Come From?

The term "robot" was first used by the Czechoslovakian playwright Karel Capek (1890–1938) in his 1920 play *R.U.R.* (Rossum's Universal Robots). The play is set on a remote island in the middle of an ocean, at a production facility for robots that are being sold for cheap labor all over the globe. The wife of the factory director uses her feminine charms to convince the lead production engineer, Dr. Gall, to imbue the robots with a soul. Gall complies, and the newly awakened robots quickly realize their mental and physical superiority to the human race and set about wiping out all of humanity. This is a common theme that would show up in subsequent robot fiction throughout the twentieth century.

The word itself is derived from the Czech noun "robota," meaning "drudgery," "servitude," or "labor"; a *robotnik* is the Czech word for "peasant."

In the December 24, 1933, issue of the Czech newspaper *Lidove Noviny*, Capek explains how the term was coined:

> *A reference by Professor Chudoba, to the Oxford Dictionary account of the word Robot's origin and its entry into the English language, reminds me of an old debt. The author of the play* R.U.R. *did not, in fact, invent that word; he merely ushered it into existence. It*

was like this: the idea for the play came to said author in a single, unguarded moment. And while it was still warm he rushed immediately to his brother Josef, the painter, who was standing before an easel and painting away at a canvas till it rustled. "Listen, Josef," the author began, "I think I have an idea for a play." "What kind," the painter mumbled (he really did mumble, because at the moment he was holding a brush in his mouth). The author told him as briefly as he could. "Then write it," the painter remarked, without taking the brush from his mouth or halting work on the canvas. The indifference was quite insulting. "But," the author said, "I don't know what to call these artificial workers. I could call them Labori, but that strikes me as a bit bookish." "Then call them Robots," the painter muttered, brush in mouth, and went on painting. And that's how it was. Thus was the word Robot born; let this acknowledge its true creator.[1]

Of course, Capek's Robots (he consistently capitalizes them in the play) are nothing like the fusion of metal, plastic, and circuitry that we think of as comprising a modern-day robot, though they may have appeared so in his productions. In describing the machines and mechanisms present at the robot production factory, Capek uses terms such as "kneading troughs" and "vats," and a "stamping mill" for forming Robot bodies.[2] From this we can gather that Capek's vision of what makes up a robot is based on biological elements. This makes sense, considering that from a practical standpoint, human actors would be given the task of playing the robot characters on the stage. What Capek's creations do share with our modern understanding of robots is the concept that they are somehow useful. This is a key distinction to make.

Isaac Asimov's "Robot Visions"

The science fiction writer Isaac Asimov (1920–1992) is perhaps most responsible for how we now think about robots in modern times. In his 1942 short story "Runaround," he coined the term robotics, meaning the field of science dedicated to building and studying robots. But much more important, "Runaround" is the first instance we see of Asimov's famed "Laws of Robotics":

- Law One: A robot may not injure a human being, or, through inaction allow a human being to come to harm.

- Law Two: A robot must obey the orders given it by human beings except where such orders would conflict with the First Law.

- Law Three: A robot must protect its own existence as long as such protection does not conflict with the First or Second Laws.[3]

---

1. Taken from Dominik Zunt's excellent webpage on Karel Capek found at `http://capek.misto.cz/english/robot.html`.

2. For more information on Karel Capek and the play *R.U.R.*, please visit Dennis G. Jerz's superb website on the topic at `http://jerz.setonhill.edu/resources/RUR/index.html`.

3. Isaac Asimov, *Robot Visions* (New York: Penguin Books USA Inc., 1991), p. 126.

These laws more than anything make a great backdrop for fiction based on robotic enti-ties. Asimov was prolific, and wrote many short stories and novels set against the backdrop of these three laws, most of which involved some sort of conflict between these laws and revis-ited the "robots taking over the world" (or at least extinguishing humanity) themes we see even as early as the robot's creation in *R.U.R.*

Is Robosapien a Robot, or Is It a Toy?

Based on the writings of Capek and Asimov, I think that in order to be categorized as a robot, a machine must meet two requirements. First, it must be capable of following commands given to it by a human. And second, it must be capable of actually doing something useful.

Robosapien absolutely meets the first criterion. With its remote control, Robosapien is more than willing to execute commands sent to it from a human operator. Moreover, given its several programming modes and various sensors, it is extremely capable of following fairly complex commands. Whether it meets the second criterion is more a matter of interpretation. Capek and Asimov envisioned robots as being able to perform labor and tasks that humans usually do. The question "Can Robosapien do something useful?" is really best responded to by another question: "How do you define 'useful'?" Sure, Robosapien is capable of entertain-ing, and it can pick up small objects. It can also be programmed to act as a sentry and perform other tasks. But you have to ask yourself how useful these functions are. I think for all intents and purposes, right out of the box, Robosapien is not very useful and thus falls more under the category of toy than robot. However, apply some curiosity and creativity, and you will discover that Robosapien is actually designed to be easily "hacked" or modified, which can bridge the gap between toy and tool. Later on in this book, when we begin to explore "hacking" or modifying Robosapien, we'll see some ways to make it more "robot-like." But for now, let's just refer to it as a robotic toy. Throughout the rest of this book, you'll probably find that I refer to Robosapien as a robot more often than not. That is mainly for the sake of convenience, since I really view the stock, unmodified Robosapien as a toy first and foremost.

What Can Robosapien Do?

Yes, Robosapien can do a handstand (with a little help; see Figure 1-2). This is due in large part to its biomorphic design, which we'll discuss in greater detail in Chapter 2.

Figure 1-2. *It can take some patience, but you should be able to get your Robosapien to freely stand on one outstretched claw.*

For now, let's look at some of the key functions and capabilities of Robosapien.

Bipedal Walking

The most obvious feature of Robosapien, once you get past its rather interesting-looking claws, is its ability to walk on two legs. WowWee describes Robosapien as "the first affordable humanoid robot." Its ability to walk on two legs is a bit of a breakthrough—this requires quite a bit of planning and synchronization between his various motors and body parts. Sure, there have been other bipedal robots, and as we'll see in Chapter 6 these have a long history, even going back as far as tin wind-up toys in the form of robots that shuffle around on two legs (see Figure 1-3).

Figure 1-3. *Here's an example of a bipedal wind-up toy robot.*

Additionally, more complex designs, such as The Original San Francisco Toymakers' "Ramon the Robot" (see Figure 1-4) are also capable of bipedal walking. But none of these products have been as proficient at walking as Robosapien.

Figure 1-4. *"Ramon the Robot" is manufactured by The Original San Francisco Toymakers.*

Is Robosapien's walking ability perfect? No. In fact, Robosapien's problem with consistently walking straight is one of the main criticisms about the toy. In Chapter 6 we look at the walking mechanism in greater detail, and I provide some tips and tricks to get your Robosapien walking to the best of its ability.

So What about Those Claws?

Robosapien has two types of hands, both with three fingers. Each hand has a touch-activated sensor, as well as an LED in the palm. The right hand (Figure 1-5), which has rounded fingers, is designed to pick up round or bulky objects such as cardboard tubes, balls, or action figures. The left hand (Figure 1-6), which features straight fingers and a rubbery gripping surface, is designed to grasp and hold smaller, thinner articles such as pencils, napkins, dollar bills, business cards, and paper.

Figure 1-5. *This photograph shows Robosapien's right claw.*

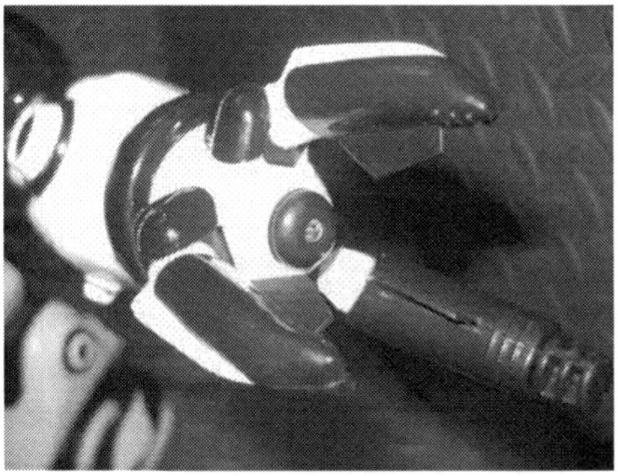

Figure 1-6. *This photograph shows Robosapien's left claw.*

Sixty-Seven Unique Functions

Robosapien is controlled via infrared remote, and it can perform 67 unique functions, including four different ways of walking and two different ways of turning. Both arms can be moved up, down, in, and out. Robosapien bends sideways at the waist—not only does that help it reach objects on the ground, but its unique sideways swinging gait is part of what makes the robot such an accomplished bipedal walker. In addition to these basic commands, Robosapien comes preprogrammed to do some interesting combination moves in the form of kung fu, as well as several "attitude" moves that help to shape Robosapien's personality. Finally, Robosapien has two different demo modes, two diagnostic troubleshooting modes, and a musical dance program. The sidebar "Sixty-Seven Robosapien Functions," lists the functions as described by WowWee.

SIXTY-SEVEN ROBOSAPIEN FUNCTIONS

1. Right Arm Up
2. Right Arm Down
3. Right Arm In
4. Right Arm Out
5. Tilt Body Right
6. Left Arm Up
7. Left Arm Down
8. Left Arm In
9. Left Arm Out
10. Tilt Body Left
11. Turn Right
12. Walk Forward
13. Stop
14. Turn Left
15. Walk Backward
16. Right Sensor Program
17. Sonic Program
18. Left Sensor Program
19. Master Command Program
20. Program Play
21. (SELECT) Advance to GREEN Keys
22. Right-Hand Thump
23. Right-Hand Pickup
24. Lean Backward

25. Right Hand Throw
26. Sleep
27. Left-Hand Thump
28. Left-Hand Pickup
29. Lean Forward
30. Left-Hand Throw
31. Listen
32. Forward Step
33. Right Turn Step
34. Backward Step
35. Right Sensor Program Execute
36. Master Command Program Execute
37. Wake Up
38. Reset
39. Left Turn Step
40. (SELECT) Advance to ORANGE Keys
41. Left Sensor Program Execute
42. Sonic Sensor Program Execute
43. Right-Hand Sweep
44. High 5
45. Right-Hand Strike 1
46. Burp

47. Right-Hand Strike 2
48. Left-Hand Sweep
49. Talk Back
50. Left-Hand Strike 1
51. Whistle
52. Left-Hand Strike 2
53. Bulldozer
54. Right-Hand Strike 3
55. Oops!
56. Demo 1
57. All Demo
58. Power Off
59. Roar
60. Left-Hand Strike 3
61. (SELECT) Return to RED Command Functions
62. Demo 2
63. Dance Demo
64. <, < Combination "Right Walk Turn"
65. >, > Combination "Left Walk Turn"
66. Forward, Forward Combination "Slow Walk Forward"
67. Backward, Backward Combination "Slow Walk Backward"

Interactive Reflex System

All of the commands listed in the sidebar can be arranged together via Robosapien's "interactive reflex system" (or programming modes), and the robot can be set up to react to both touch and sound through its four individual programming modes. Robosapien's four program modes include a "master program," a "sonic program," and left and right programming modes that react to the sensors in its claws and feet (see Figure 1-7).

Figure 1-7. *Touch-sensitive sensors on the front of Robosapien's feet allow it to react when it bumps into things.*

All told, Robosapien is capable of remembering 84 total steps—as long as you don't turn it off. Robosapien's memory is wiped each time you shut off its power. Robosapien communicates through a series of grunts that WowWee has dubbed "international caveman speech." These grunts are not particularly helpful, but they add a lot to Robosapien's unique "personality."

What Does This Book Hope to Accomplish?

I hope with this book to provide you with the means to get the most out of your Robosapien. On its own, this book will give you some background information on the theories and the mechanics behind Robosapien, some simple projects you can do on your own to make Robosapien even better, detailed programming information, and a good hard look at Robosapien's capabilities.

Beyond this, I hope to change your perception of Robosapien, and challenge you to think of it as less of a toy and more of a platform. This is, in my opinion, the secret of a long-lasting relationship with your Robosapien. I feel that, as a toy, Robosapien can get boring pretty fast. Once you have run it through the various routines a few times and mastered the remote control, you may find yourself asking, "Well, what else is there?"

By looking at where Robosapien comes from and what it can do out of the box, and by giving you some ideas about where you can go using Robosapien as a platform for hacks and modifications, I hope to provide you with many more hours of discovering exactly what else there is when it comes to the Robosapien.

What Will I Need to Get Through This Book?

I had originally titled this section "Materials Checklist and Safety Precautions," but that is a bit ambitious. This book endeavors to give you the best experience with your Robosapien out of the box, with no modifications or tools needed. From time to time I'll suggest some easy modifications that you can do to improve your Robosapien's performance, and the last few chapters will concentrate on beginning modifications that will require you to open up the robot and void your warranty. But my goal is to make this book as accessible as possible to everyone, including those of us who are not electronics experts.

A Robosapien Robot

Figure 1-8. *You want me to do WHAT with this screwdriver?!*

The number one item you'll need to work your way through this book is, of course, a Robosapien robot. The author in me hopes that I can make this book so captivating that you could read through it and find it interesting even if you don't own a Robosapien. But the realist in me knows that an accomplishment such as that is probably beyond my (or anyone else's) reach. Although you won't need a Robosapien to work through the chapters on the development of Robosapien and the theories of biomorphic robotics that control it, having one handy will help you understand some of the concepts presented a little bit better. And while no one except the people at WowWee have the version 2 Robosapien (at least at the time of publication), which is called "V2," having a version 1 Robosapien and understanding its abilities can only help you understand the significant upgrades planned for V2.

Your Own Curiosity

Beyond a Robosapien, you'll also need a sense of adventure as well as a sense of curiosity about not only *what* Robosapien can do but *why* it can do it. There is a lot more to Robosapien than just its motors, circuitry, and plastic shell.

Outfitting Your Work Area

Robosapien is designed to go almost anywhere, and for the most part you'll be able to enjoy this book anywhere that Robosapien is capable of going—and even some places where it can't go. However, if you choose to enjoy a chapter or two of this book while relaxing on a raft in your pool, I suggest that you leave Robosapien on dry land!

If you plan on exploring the interior of Robosapien, and doing some of the simple hacking projects I outline throughout the book, a decent work area is essential (see Figure 1-9). It should be well lit and relatively clutter free, and provide you with a comfortable place to sit while working on Robosapien. It should be quiet and out of the way; the last thing you want is to take a break from working on Robosapien only to wake up and discover that your sibling/parent/spouse/cat/dog has accidentally (or otherwise!) disturbed your progress. You should have an area large enough to not only hold Robosapien and your tools, but that also allows you to lay out parts and components as you remove them (should you choose to do so). Finally, I prefer an area where distractions are limited. I use an old desk out in my garage.

Figure 1-9. *The author's robot laboratory is in his garage.*

This space is out of the way, there is plenty of power, and it is close to all of my tools. I cover my work area with a sheet of glass. Most glass shops can cut you a piece to order, and they even round the edges so you don't cut yourself. Glass is not only impervious to hot items like soldering irons and hot-glue guns, but it provides an excellent place to keep diagrams, lists, schematics, and other sheets of paper in full view yet out of the way and protected. Additionally, working on Robosapien involves a lot of small screws and components. When these fall and hit a glass surface they make a noticeable noise, meaning that you won't accidentally drop a part and not hear it fall.

It is important that you have adequate electricity in your work area, both for lighting and for any power tools you may need. One tip someone gave me a long time ago is to run all your tools into one power strip that has a central on/off switch (see Figure 1-10).

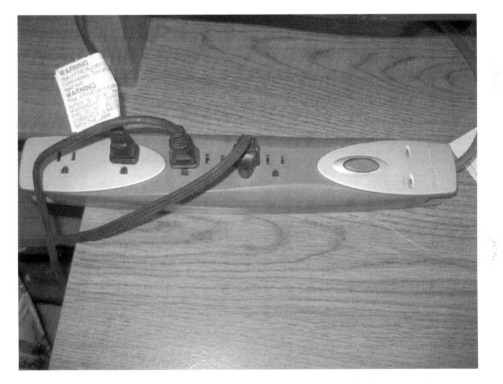

Figure 1-10. *A good power strip is not only convenient but also a good safety precaution.*

This way, if something goes awry and you smell smoke, you can turn everything off quickly and easily and *then* figure out what you have shorted. Speaking of smoke, make sure your work area has decent ventilation. Electrical smoke does not smell good, and some people find that it irritates their throat and lungs. Also, flux used in soldering gives off smoke when it is heated and this can be irritating to some people as well.

You'll need some simple tools (see Figure 1-11).

Figure 1-11. *You don't need a lot of tools to work on Robosapien, but you can never have too many.*

All that is needed to take most of Robosapien apart is a simple Phillips head screwdriver. You should already have one of these, since you also need one to insert Robosapien's batteries in his feet and remote control. Small precision-style flat-head screwdrivers can help you get into places that are glued together, and "Exacto" knives, generically referred to as hobby knives, can help you in a lot of ways too. A good drill, as well as a high-speed rotary tool like a Dremel, can also come in handy. A hot-glue gun can also be useful, as is a variety of tape and glues. A set of wire cutters and a wire-stripping tool can come in handy as well. I also like to use a modeler's tool referred to as a side cutter or a sprue cutter. This tool is designed to cut plastic model components off of the "sprue," or the frame that they come on when you buy the kit. I also use a "miner's style" headlamp, which you can find in most camping supply sections. Since it is worn just above your eyes, it directs the light down directly onto what it is you are working on, and helps you illuminate things, particularly in small, cramped spaces like the interior of Robosapien.

As we'll see in Chapter 13, where I present a pictorial guide to taking the Robosapien apart, everything is very clearly labeled on the inside, and most of the wiring is connected via connectors. Still, when working on anything electronic, a decent-quality soldering iron as well as an inexpensive digital multimeter will save you a lot of time. More on these items later.

Finally, no workspace is complete without a pad of paper and a pen, or better yet, a hacker's journal. Keeping a list of what parts you remove, and the order in which you remove them, can come in handy if you forget where something goes or how to put a piece back together. It is also a great place to keep a running tab of ideas for future projects, things that might only come to you while you have Robosapien partially disassembled.

I don't recommend that you rush out and buy all these tools before you start working on your Robosapien. Start slowly, and just take its shell off a few times to familiarize yourself with the interior of Robosapien before you move on to further disassembly. Gather these tools as you find that you need them, and not only will you not break the bank, but you'll be ready to use them.

Safety Precautions

The most important thing you'll need to protect is your eyes, since they will be open (or at least I hope they will be open) throughout your work. I recommend a good set of goggles that you can keep in your work area. These take a little getting used to, but I think you'll find that putting them on becomes like second nature. I recommend getting a comfortable set. They might cost a bit more, but they'll also be higher quality and more comfortable. You have only one set of eyes, so it is important that you protect them at all costs.

Although nothing we'll work on is capable of starting a fire, it is still a good idea to keep some sort of fire protection near your workspace. For small battery-powered items like Robosapien, a fire extinguisher is probably overkill—a decent container of water is usually all you need. (It also comes in handy if you get thirsty!) If you plan on regularly using really hot tools, such as soldering irons and hot-glue guns, you may want to invest in a small fire extinguisher.

Summary

The Robosapien robot is by all accounts something that is greater than the sum of its parts: a remarkable toy that combines high tech with low tech, complexity with simplicity, and humanistic traits with robotics. It is amazing to learn all that went into creating this robot. Let's start our journey by looking at Robosapien's creator, Mark Tilden, and some of his ideas that have revolutionized not only the toy industry but theories of robotics as well.

■ ■ ■

CHAPTER 2

Robosapien:
A Robotic Family History

(Photo courtesy of WowWee Ltd.)

Figure 2-1. *Robosapien's creator, Mark W. Tilden, appears here with some of his friends.*

In this chapter we'll look into the background of Robosapien: its creator, Mark Tilden (shown in Figure 2-1), and his theories of BEAM robotics, on which Robosapien is loosely based. We'll close the chapter by looking at some of the various types of Robosapiens on the market, and the awards and accolades that Robosapien has received.

Mark W. Tilden

Prior to the release of Robosapien in 2004, Mark W. Tilden was primarily known as the founder and chief proponent of BEAM robotics. Born in 1961 in Stroud, Gloucestershire, England, he moved with his family to Canada when he was two years old. He built his first robot at age three out of wood scraps and rubber bands as a Mother's Day gift. Later projects included a Meccano (a construction toy similar to Erector sets) suit for his cat, numerous school science-fair winners, and in the early 1980s a complex hack on the Tomy OmniBot (see Figure 2-2), an early wheeled toy robot.

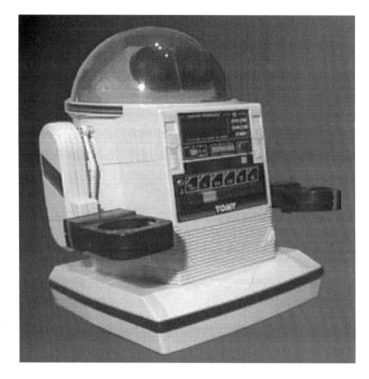

Figure 2-2. *A complex hack on the Tomy OmniBot was one of Tilden's early projects.*

In 1982 I got my first Tomy OmniBot. I opened it up and I found out it was mostly empty space. I filled it with a home built 68000 [an early home automation system based on an 8 MHz processor], and the best visual apparatus I could find. I programmed it from my Atari, I was really hoping I could get this thing to do all this stuff. And I found myself falling into every pratfall that anyone who's ever done artificial intelligence has fallen into. Unless something looks like a man, you cannot tell if it is moving correctly. What sort of body language can you get from a wheel? It's very hard to tell when it is crashing.
—Mark Tilden, February 13, 2005

Tilden attended the University of Waterloo, receiving his master's in systems engineering, and got a job as a design engineer in the Math Department at the university. Still intensely interested in building and hacking robots, in 1989 he attended a lecture by Massachusetts

Institute of Technology (MIT) professor Rodney Brooks. Dr. Brooks developed what is known as *subsumption architecture*, a biologically inspired approach to programming robots for performance in uncertain, or unstructured, environments. The aim of this approach is to build robots that rely on reactive sensors attached directly to motors rather than relying on complicated, processor-based computer brains.

About this time Tilden began laying the foundations for BEAM, eventually founding the International BEAM Robot Games in 1991. These were a series of competitions open to anyone and their robot, as long as the robot was not derived from a kit or bought prebuilt. Robots were judged on sophistication of behavior, novelty of design, efficiency of power source, and quality of hardware innovation.

In 1992 Tilden's theories were beginning to gather attention, and he was invited to speak alongside Dr. Brooks at the Artificial Life III conference in Santa Fe, New Mexico. Never one to travel lightly, Tilden showed up with a menagerie of his robot creations and encouraged the attendees to play with them. "Here it is. Play with it. Make your own conclusions," he told curious onlookers.

Calling himself a "nobody" prior to attending the conference, Tilden walked off with three of the conference's five awards: best innovation concept, best presentation, and the environmentally conscious award. His creations also attracted the attention of a man he later said he thought was "the town derelict"—in fact, he turned out to be Brosl Hasslacher, a theoretical physicist from nearby Los Alamos National Laboratory.

By 1993 Tilden had left his job at his alma mater and was brought into Los Alamos as a research scientist in the Physics Division. He was brought in under what he refers to as "the genius clause" since he did not have a PhD.

So what happened is that I get down there and I basically say two things: I don't have the credentials, so I could have said "Hi, you have to believe me." (Laughs.) So I promised that I would only ever say things if I had something that actually worked. Boy did that do me both good and bad. Good: I was able to build things successfully that are now still working in museums and various places across the country. Bad, because there are an awful lot of people, primarily roboticists, who have their entire reputation based entirely upon virtual presence. "Oh one day the robots will basically take over. Do you have any evidence? Well no, but my toaster is hostile!"

—Mark Tilden, February 13, 2005

While at Los Alamos, Tilden continued his research into BEAM theories, consulting for NASA; DARPA (the U.S. Defense Advanced Research Projects Agency); the U.S. Army, Navy, and Marine Corps; and JPL (Jet Propulsion Laboratory), to name a few. All told, Tilden estimates that he did work for over 30 different governmental agencies.

While working at Los Alamos, Tilden got the opportunity to work on several interesting projects, including a Mars rover, snakelike robots that were to be used to detect land mines (the robot was even capable of continuing the mission if part of it was destroyed by an explosion), and secret projects that he says he can't talk about for another 20 years.

But things were not as smooth as they could have been. Many scientists did not like his biologically derived robotic principles, because, like anything in nature, they can be somewhat unpredictable. This didn't sit well with researchers at NASA, for instance, where "it was all about mitigation of risk."

Basically what happened when I moved down to New Mexico, I was thinking that I would be able to get in tight with the artificial life guys. Because obviously that's what I was doing: I was building self evolving mechanisms that are capable of doing real work in the real world. But I wasn't playing by their rules. That's just it. As soon as you start measuring against their stuff, they suddenly realized: "Ok, well, we can't support you, because unfortunately you are invalidating all of our theory."
                                                        —*Mark Tilden, February 13, 2005*

One late night in 1999, Peter Yanofsky, president and cofounder of WowWee Ltd., a Canadian toy company based in Hong Kong, was flipping through the channels and caught a documentary on the Discovery Channel called *Robots Rising*. In this film Tilden talks about his theories, and there is one memorable scene that features a time lapse of Tilden building a fully working BEAM robot from spare parts—with no plans—in less than 20 minutes. Yanofsky, an inventor himself, immediately saw the potential that Tilden's ideas had for toys. He sent Tilden a ticket to Hong Kong, and the two men met to discuss the potential of incorporating Tilden's robotic theories into toys. Before long WowWee hired Tilden on as a consultant.

Figure 2-3. *By the time he started consulting for WowWee, Mark Tilden already had Robosapien in his sights. (Photo courtesy of WowWee Ltd.)*

Tilden's first major project with WowWee, and his introduction to the toy industry, was the B.I.O. Bugs (see Figures 2-4 and 2-5), which were released in fall 2001. Following this, in summer 2002 he built the first Robosapien prototype and began the two-and-a-half-year journey to get Robosapien to market. We'll come back to Robosapien in a bit. First, let's take a look at some of the fundamentals of BEAM robotics.

Figure 2-4. *The B.I.O. Bug "Destroyer" was one of Tilden's first major projects with WowWee.*

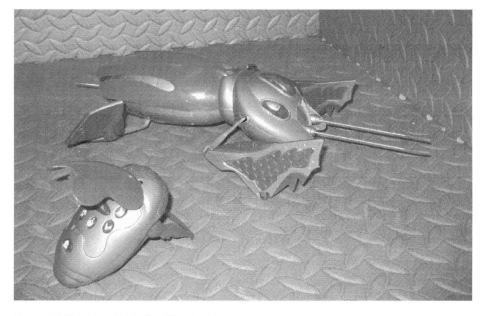

Figure 2-5. *Here's the B.I.O. Bug "Predator."*

The Theory of BEAM Robotics

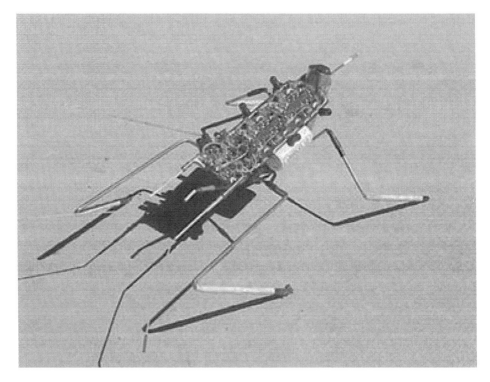

Figure 2-6. *Mark Tilden's Unibug 1.0.*

It is generally accepted that the acronym *BEAM* stands for biology, electronics, aesthetics, and mechanics. Some other versions of the acronym I have encountered include building, evolution, anarchy, and modularity, as well as biotechnology, ethnology, analogy, and morphology. That last one is a little bit of a stretch, I admit.

> *The science behind the idea stems from current concepts in artificial intelligence (AI), artificial life (ALife), evolutionary biology, and genetic algorithms. It seems that building large complex robots hasn't worked well, so why not try to evolve them from a lesser to a greater ability as Mother Nature has done with biologics? The problem is that such a concept requires self-reproducing robots which won't be possible to build (if at all) for years to come. A solution, however, is to view a human being as a robot's way of making another robot, to have an annual venue where experimenters can let their creations interact in real situations, and then watch as machine evolution occurs.*
>
> —*Mark Tilden, from his early BEAM website*[1]

---

1. http://www.nis.lanl.gov/projects/robot/

Entire books have been written on BEAM technology, and classes are taught on it at the university level, so the purpose of this section is to give you more of a basic understanding of the concepts that underpin this somewhat radical theory of robotics engineering. In my opinion, the best book on BEAM technology is *Junkbots, Bugbots, & Bots on Wheels: Building Simple Robots with BEAM Technology,*[2] written by Dave Hrynkiw and Mark Tilden. This book, besides giving a nice, detailed look at the concepts behind BEAM technologies, excels by guiding the reader through a progression of actual robot-building projects, from easy projects at first to more advanced bots. I highly recommend it as a starting point for further research on the topic, if this is an area you're interested in exploring further.

Before we get into the individual concepts that make up BEAM, let's take a look at this concept from a general perspective. The basic principle of BEAM robotics is to take all your preconceived notions about robots and throw them out the window. Throughout the twentieth and early twenty-first centuries, roboticists have built more and more complicated robots as computer (and in particular microprocessor) technologies have gotten better. These highly educated men and women construct intricate programs that tell their robots exactly how to react to any given situation. The problem is that when these robots run into a situation that they are not programmed to react to, they are useless. However, even with this limitation, much of modern robotics development seems to focus almost entirely on complicated brain structures. It is a "top-down" approach to building robots: build the brain and the body will follow. These types of robots are complex and expensive, and usually require significant power resources.

The hallmark of BEAM robotics is to build robots that demonstrate complicated behaviors but that use a minimum of computing power. Simply put, the goal is to design robots that will learn how to operate on their own—bottom-up design instead of top-down engineering.

The secret to BEAM technology is performance to silicon ratio. If you had to basically restart the entire computer robotics industry on a desert island, this would be the technology you would use. This is the secret that [John] Von Neumann, and [Michael] Brady, and [Alan] Turing, and everyone else was looking for. Asynchronous real world control in the smallest number of possible transistors to the maximum possible effect.
—Mark Tilden, February 13, 2005

Think back to subsumption architecture, Dr. Brooks' concept. By elimination of the brain, and by wiring sensors directly to motors, the robot reacts to input. When its sensor hits a table leg, it triggers a motor and its body backs up. In a sense, it *learns*. Take this a step further by applying it to a solar-powered robot. By using photo sensors connected to its motors, the robot will follow a light source and keep itself out of shadows. But because it is solar powered, isn't it in a sense feeding itself as it follows the light? One interesting way I have heard it put is that BEAM has nothing to do with *artificial* intelligence; BEAM robots have *actual* intelligence.

Let's face it, bottom up design is not digital. The art of electronics turned into the business of electronics in 1969. And all these beautiful, simple analog solutions were lost under IBM business workings. Why would you want a calculator that gives you a different answer every time? You put up with more things in a robot than you would with a

---

2. Published by McGraw-Hill, 2002

computer. The digital computer has to sit on a table and do something functional. But something that moves, you put up with it. It's one of the contradictions.... Isaac Asimov was a great fiction writer, but unfortunately was a lousy roboticist.

—Mark Tilden, February 13, 2005

So is a BEAM robot the embodiment of biology, electronics, aesthetics, and mechanics? Not really. Tilden claims that these are simply the elements required to build a successful robot. Let's look at each one on its own.

Biology

Simply put, use nature as an inspiration in building and designing robots. As Tilden has said "simple, elegant ideas that biology uses, and that maybe, in engineering, we can steal." Look outside your window. Things in nature have adapted to their environment in order to survive. In the worst case, organisms that do not adapt die, and at the very least they make their existence much more complicated than it needs to be. Look at elements of biological creatures that help it to successfully adapt to its environment, and apply these same elements to your robots. It follows that like their biological counterparts, robots based on these principles will have an easier time adapting to their environment as well.

Electronics

Obviously, you need some sort of electronics to get a robot to work. The key in relation to BEAM is to keep the electronics as simple as possible. Toward this end, true BEAM robots are entirely analog, as opposed to digital. Digital electronics use pulses of electricity. The power is either on or off. Analog electronics are characterized by a continuous range of values, like a wave. The electronics theory of BEAM ties in closely with the biological theory in the sense that nature is probably more analog than it is digital.

Aesthetics

This is maybe the most elusive of BEAM elements. It is also the simplest. It basically means making sure that your robot looks cool. Not only will this encourage you to keep working on it, but it will make your robot more attractive to others. Furthermore, apply simplicity to this aspect as well. If your robot is clean and well designed, it will be easier to maintain and build. Another aspect of this that ties in with the mechanics aspect of BEAM is that the shape of something defines how it will work.

Mechanics

I think that mechanics is the most important of the BEAM elements. By using good and innovative mechanical design, you can keep your robot relatively uncomplicated. For example, look at Robosapien's spring-based swaying motion. This mechanical technique helps counterbalance Robosapien's movement, greatly aiding its walking ability. Simply put, this eliminates the need for more motors and more elaborate electronic controllers to handle its walking functions.

Think you've got a handle on what BEAM is all about? The best way to learn about BEAM is to actually do it yourself: build some of the simple BEAM robots and all of this will begin to make a lot more sense. See the sidebar "BEAM Resources" for some helpful resources.

BEAM RESOURCES

- *Junkbots, Bugbots, & Bots on Wheels: Building Simple Robots with BEAM Technology*, by Dave Hrynkiw and Mark Tilden (McGraw-Hill, 2002)

- *Robot Building for Beginners*, by David Cook (Apress, 2002)

- http://www.solarbotics.net/—*The* online BEAM resource

- http://www.nis.lanl.gov/projects/robot/— Mark Tilden's original BEAM site, still hosted by Los Alamos National Laboratories

- http://www.beam-online.com/—A good BEAM resource with schematics

Types of Robosapiens

Since its release in spring 2004, up until this writing, Robosapien has continued to evolve. Some changes have been internal, and others simply cosmetic. A comparison of the first Robosapien I bought when they were first released and later models shows many ongoing internal improvements (see Figures 2-7 through 2-11).

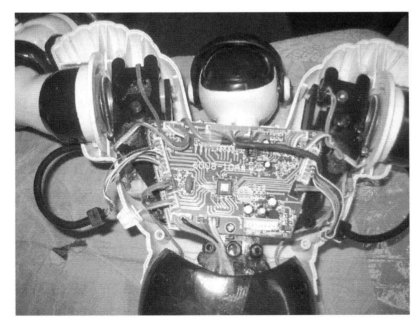

Figure 2-7. *This photo shows the PCB and chest cavity of an early Robosapien.*

Figure 2-8. *This shows the PCB and chest cavity of a later model. Note the different placement of the springs in the shoulders, as well as the differing revision number on the PCB.*

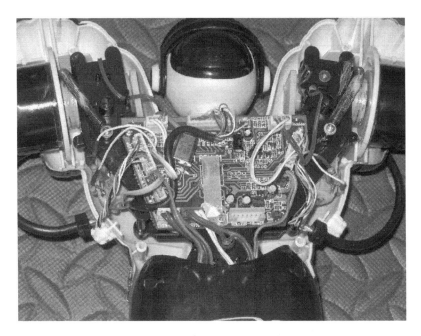

Figure 2-9. *Here's another view from my most recent Robosapien. Again, it's a different PCB revision; note the heat sink over the processor and the shoulder spring placement.*

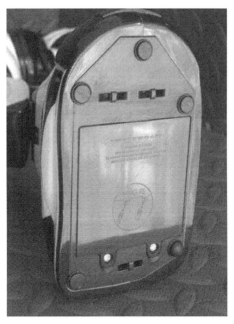

Figure 2-10. *The footpads on the bottom of an early Robosapien looked like this.*

Figure 2-11. *Note the difference in the footpads in this later model Robosapien.*

According to Tilden, these systematic improvements have occurred as the manufacturers understand the robot better and better.

Much more noticeable are some of the cosmetic changes to Robosapien. Well, maybe "cosmetic" is the wrong word, since the shell remains exactly the same—only the color changes. The original Robosapien design (that I have used in most of the pictures throughout this book) uses the standard black-and-white color scheme and has always been available. In summer 2004, The Sharper Image[3] released its "Mark Tilden Exclusive Signature Series Robosapien." This Robosapien is identical to the original (minus the ongoing design changes discussed above) except that it features a new paint job, and a silk screen on one hip of Tilden's signature (see Figure 2-12), and on the other hip a silk-screened Sharper Image brand logo (see Figure 2-13). It is available in chrome and metallic blue.

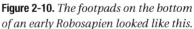

3. http://www.sharperimage.com

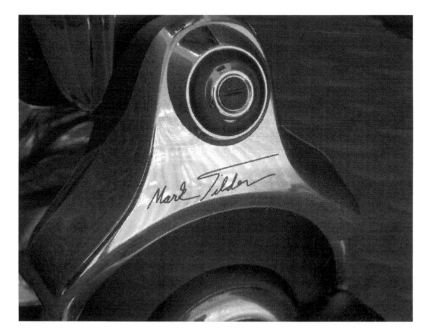

Figure 2-12. *What makes a "signature series" Robosapien?*

Figure 2-13. *The Sharper Image logo appears on the "signature series" Robosapien.*

In addition to the chrome and metallic blue Robosapiens from The Sharper Image, a gold model is available. It was seen predominantly in UK and European markets during the 2004 holiday season. It became available in the United States in early 2005. At this writing these are the only colors available. However, WowWee's 2005 International Toy Fair showroom featured several samples with alternative color schemes, and word is they should be hitting the U.S. market around the time this book is published.

Another type of Robosapien that I would be remiss to not include in this book is the Mini Robosapien (see Figure 2-14).

Figure 2-14. *WowWee's Mini Robosapien is more action figure than robot.*

Identical to its older sibling in form, the $10 Mini Robosapien is more action figure than robot. Its eyes light up and it walks via motorized hip movements; however, it has wheels on the bottom of its feet to help it shuffle along smoothly (see Figure 2-15).

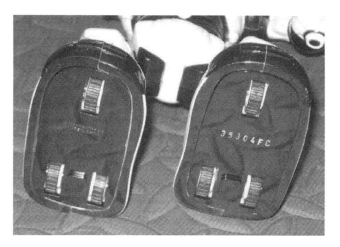

Figure 2-15. *Mini Robosapien has wheels on the bottom of its feet to help it shuffle along.*

It operates on two AAA batteries, and it is either on or off—when it is on it's constantly trying to move forward. It has arms you can pose, and its claws open and close via buttons on its forearms (see Figure 2-16).

Figure 2-16. *The Mini Robosapien's claws open via mechanical pushbuttons on its forearms.*

Inside, there is a single motor that powers the hips, and simple wiring to send power from the batteries to the motor and to the eye LEDs (see Figure 2-17).

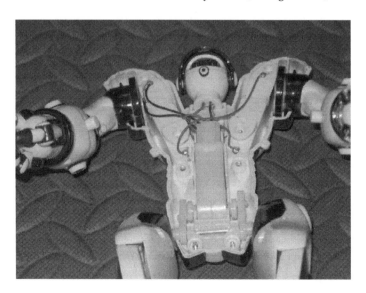

Figure 2-17. *Let's peek inside the Mini Robosapien.*

Figure 2-18. *Robosapien and Mini Robosapien: here's more proof that good looks run in the family.*

Awards and Accolades

To close this chapter on the Robosapien's background, I'd like to mention some of the awards and accolades the toy has received. In 2004 Robosapien took the toy industry by storm, selling over 1.5 million units and winning award after award for its ingenious design, amazing capabilities, and outstanding sales.

One such award, the *Digital World* Innovations Award, honors 15 trend-setting products that have emerged with the convergence of technology and consumer electronics. The 2005 *Digital World* Innovations Awards recognize both benchmark and breakthrough products that set the standard for innovation with unique qualities that distinguish them from the pack. *Digital World's* editors compared hundreds of products before narrowing the field to the 15 winners. *Digital World's* February 2005 issue showcases Robosapien along with the other 2005 Innovations Award winners.

"These are among the most inventive devices available, breaking the boundaries of the computer and consumer electronics worlds while pushing the limits of technology," stated Harry McCracken, editor in chief of *PC World* and *Digital World*. "These are trend-setting products that help define industry standards and raise the bar for creativity in the future. Congratulations to WowWee's Robosapien."

Leading up to the holidays, Robosapien has received more than 30 top honors from the most prestigious toy award programs in the industry such as *The Oppenheim Toy Portfolio*, *FamilyFun*, *Parenting*, *KOL*, *National Parenting Center*, *Creative Child*, and *iParenting*. A large number of these awards come from testing panels made up of kids.

Robosapien has also garnered international attention from both the media and consumers (see the sidebar "2004 Robosapien Awards"). For example, Robosapien was named Hamleys (UK) Toy of the Year and "Boys Toy of the Year" at the 2004 Australia Toy Fair, and was included in the Top 10 in Duracell's 2004 European Toy Survey. Robosapien received South Africa's Best Cutting Edge Toy for 2004 and Toy of the Year from the German Toy Association, and it placed in the Top 10 in the New Zealand Duracell 2004 Toy Test. In addition, the Canadian Toy Testing Council named Robosapien the Energizer Battery-Operated Toy of the Year. Most recently Robosapien took home the prestigious 2004 Hong Kong Award for Industry and Consumer Product Design.

2004 ROBOSAPIEN AWARDS

- *FamilyFun* Toy of the Year Award—Interactive Play (ages 10–12)
- Oppenheim Toy Portfolio Platinum Award
- *Creative Child* Magazine Preferred Choice Award
- *iParenting* Media "Hot" Toy Award Winner
- The National Parenting Center – 2004 Seal of Approval
- *Child* Magazine "Best Toys" – November
- Canadian Toy Testing Council – Three Stars (top rating)
- Hamleys (UK) – "Toy of Tomorrow" award
- Hamleys (UK) – "Toy of the Year" award
- *T3* Magazine (UK) – Five Star Gold Award
- Duracell's 2004 European Toy Survey – Top 10
- Dr. Toy – 100 Best Children's Products for 2004
- Dr. Toy – 10 Best Software/CD-ROM/High-Tech Products for 2004
- Federation of Hong Kong Industries – 2004 Hong Kong Award for Industry
- Consumer Product Design – Grand Prize
- German Toy Association – Toy of the Year
- National Parenting Publications – 2004 Honors Award
- British Toy and Hobby Association – Top 10
- Toy Wishes – All Grown Up – Top 10 Toys for Big Kids
- e-toys 2004 Holiday Hot List
- toytips.com – 5/5 Toy Tips rating; 5/5 Fun Score (kid rating)
- Canadian Toy Testing Council – CTTC/Energizer Battery-Operated Toy of the Year
- #1 on Yahoo's Top 10 List "Toys for All"
- *Parenting* Magazine – Toys of the Year, Ages 8–12 (November)
- South Africa, Toy and Baby Association Toy of the Year Award
- Best Cutting Edge Toy 2004
- New Zealand Duracell 2004 Toy Test – Top 10
- Australian Toy, Hobby, Nursery Fair – Boys Toy of the Year
- #1 Selling Toy – United Kingdom NPD Report
- Australian Toy, Hobby, Nursery Fair – Boys Toy of the Year
- America On-Line KOL Holiday Toy Test – Top Ten, Kids 9–12
- Australia Toy and Hobby Retailer – Toy of the Year

Summary

You don't need to understand BEAM robotics, or know anything about Mark Tilden, in order to enjoy your Robosapien. However, not only is a basic understanding of the background of the robot (and the theories that make it "tick") interesting, but these concepts open up opportunities to further explore your Robosapien. This gives you more to think about and a richer background when you're coming up with programming routines and even potential hacks for your Robosapien. As we'll see in subsequent chapters, Robosapien is a far cry from a true BEAM robot. But as we'll also see, Robosapien would never have been developed if it weren't for Mark Tilden's groundbreaking work in the area of BEAM robotics.

CHAPTER 3

■■■

Robosapien: A Design History

(Photo courtesy of Mark Tilden, WowWee Ltd.)

Figure 3-1. *This is an early computer render of the finalized Robosapien design.*

In February 2005, Mark Tilden and I met in New York City to talk about, what else—robotics and Robosapien. He was in town for the upcoming International Toy Fair, and we met in the heart of midtown Manhattan at Wolfgang's Steakhouse. In between the historic tiled ceilings of what used to be the old Vanderbilt Hotel, and a sizzling platter of perhaps the best porterhouse I have ever tasted, he took me step by step through the design history of the Robosapien robot—from the earliest prototypes, to computer-generated renders that didn't make the cut, to an early look at what is in store in the years ahead. I walked back to my hotel with my appetite for steak, as well as my thirst for knowledge about the development of the Robosapien, fully sated. In this chapter I'd like to share with you some of the photographs that Mark shared with me. I have included the full text of our talk, which lasted almost three hours, in the Appendix to this book. **35**

The original Robosapien prototype was developed during summer 2001 while Tilden was at the Neuromorphic Engineering Workshop in Telluride, Colorado. Creating the first prototype was easy. What proved difficult was transferring the design and internal physics into something that could be mass-produced. With the B.I.O. Bugs and other toys that Tilden had created for WowWee, all he had to do was send a working prototype to the engineers at the factories in China, which they would then duplicate. With Robosapien, it proved more difficult. For one thing, the Chinese engineers, who mostly work on toys, didn't understand some of the advanced physics and concepts of resonance dynamics that go into Robosapien. Another problem was that due to cost constraints, the Robosapien prototype's analog electronics would have to be redesigned using digital circuitry. Of the approximately 20 Robosapien prototypes built, the original "Telluride prototype" is the only one still working today.

There are several stages to the development of Robosapien: the prototype that Tilden built in Telluride, the various prototypes and designs built in China, and finally the shell and personality design. I'll let the pictures speak for themselves.

The Telluride Robosapien

In this section we'll see photos of the original Robosapien prototype, what I refer to as the "Telluride Robosapien," as Mark Tilden builds it by hand.

(Photo courtesy of Mark Tilden, WowWee Ltd.)

Figure 3-2. *Mark Tilden built the first Robosapien prototype at this table in Telluride over a three-week period. If you look closely, you can see the robot's shoulders and arms.*

(Photo courtesy of Mark Tilden, WowWee Ltd.)

Figure 3-3. *Here's the first Robosapien prototype during the early stages of construction. Note the motor at the waist, and the two motors at each shoulder. Motor placement has remained the same even in the mass-produced Robosapiens you find in stores today.*

(Photo courtesy of Mark Tilden, WowWee Ltd.)

Figure 3-4. *In the original, the motor drivers were all mounted directly on the motors themselves.*

(Photo courtesy of Mark Tilden, WowWee Ltd.)

Figure 3-5. *This photo shows an early version of the head. Of particular note is the breadboard on the right with the early "brains."*

(Photo courtesy of Mark Tilden, WowWee Ltd.)

Figure 3-6. *The earliest prototypes had a vision apparatus that allowed the robot to "see" and react to visual stimulus, as you can see in this close-up of the head.*

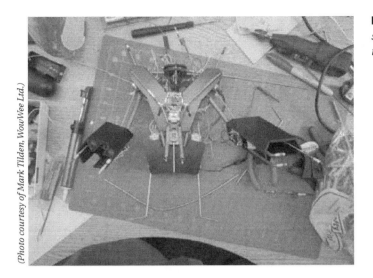

(Photo courtesy of Mark Tilden, WowWee Ltd.)

Figure 3-7. *This photo shows the beginning of the leg construction.*

(Photo courtesy of Mark Tilden, WowWee Ltd.)

Figure 3-8. *One foot is placed. Note the batteries in the feet, as well as the breadboard containing the brain in the foreground.*

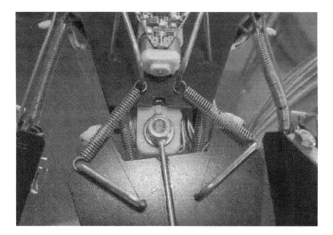

Figures 3-9 and 3-10.
Much of what's shown in these close-ups of the waist and leg spring mechanisms exists even in modern Robosapiens.

(Photos courtesy of Mark Tilden, WowWee Ltd.)

(Photos courtesy of Mark Tilden, WowWee Ltd.)

Figures 3-11 through 3-13. *Organizing the wiring and bringing the brain onboard was finally accomplished, as seen in these two photos. The original Robosapien prototype was completely analog and was based on a 24-transistor nervous network.*

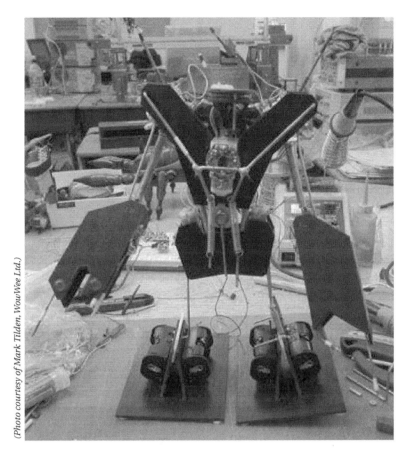

(Photo courtesy of Mark Tilden, WowWee Ltd.)

Figure 3-14. *Here's the completed prototype. According to Tilden, he turned it on and it "figured his way out in a matter of seconds."*

Robosapien Goes to China

Once the prototype was built, it was time to send it to the engineers in China who would rebuild it and get it ready for mass production. Sounds easy enough, right? The problem was that these are people who work on toys, and as Tilden says about the toy industry, "there are three things: there is the package, there is the appearance of the product, and then and only then is there the function. So how it works is pretty much small bananas in terms of selling." Combine this line of thinking with cost constraints, the somewhat counterintuitive BEAM philosophy, and the fact that Robosapien is based on complex physics, and the result is that the engineers had a hard time rebuilding Robosapien. To further complicate matters, the first firm that WowWee contracted with to manufacture the Robosapien went bankrupt just as their engineers were beginning to have some success designing the toy. So they had to start the entire design program anew with a different firm, and even dig various prototypes out of dumpsters!

In this section we'll examine the development of Robosapien in China.

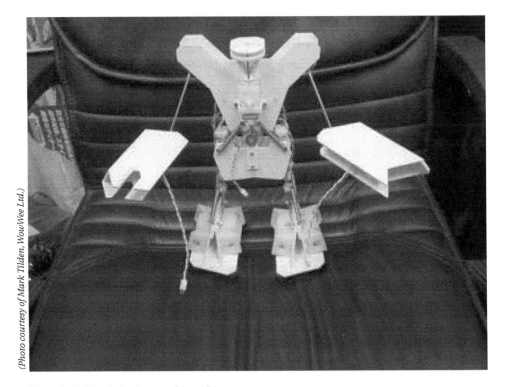

(Photo courtesy of Mark Tilden, WowWee Ltd.)

Figure 3-15. *Here's the first working Chinese prototype.*

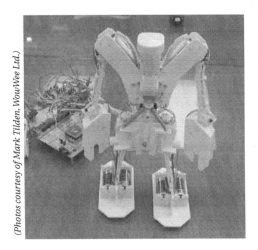
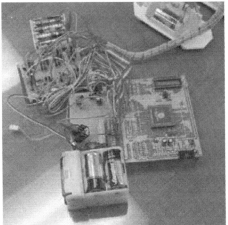

(Photos courtesy of Mark Tilden, WowWee Ltd.)

Figures 3-16 and 3-17. *The problem with the first Chinese-built prototypes was that they had a huge "brain" system. The robot could not carry the "brain"; it actually had to drag the system behind it.*

(Photo courtesy of Mark Tilden, WowWee Ltd.)

Figure 3-18. *This shows an early attempt at getting the brain structure onboard. Note the head: at this point in the development, the vision system was still in play.*

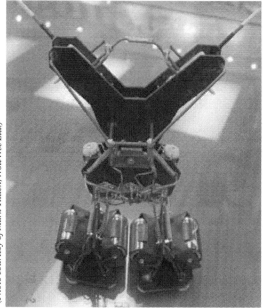

(Photo courtesy of Mark Tilden, WowWee Ltd.)

Figure 3-19. *Mark Tilden built this working, self-contained prototype by hand while trying to explain the finer points of BEAM and reverse kinematics to the Chinese engineers.*

(Photos courtesy of Mark Tilden, WowWee Ltd.)

Figures 3-20 through 3-22. *The second Chinese-built prototype not only had a streamlined, onboard brain system but was also able to walk.*

(Photo courtesy of Mark Tilden, WowWee Ltd.)

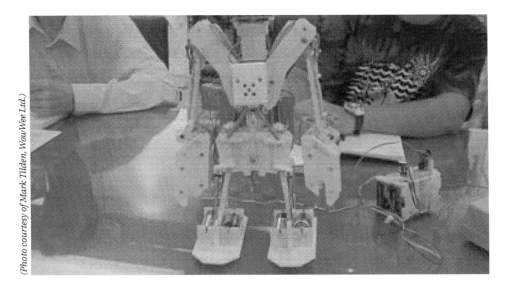

Figure 3-23. *This photo reveals the third Chinese prototype.*

(Photos courtesy of Mark Tilden, WowWee Ltd.)

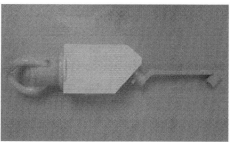 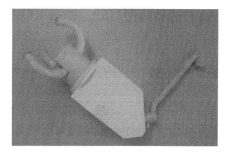

Figures 3-24 and 3-25. *In these early designs, the claw opens and closes based on a nonmotorized, mechanical "cam" system, just like the claws on the mass-produced Robosapien.*

Figure 3-26. *The original was strong enough to lift a full can of beer. This "feature" was removed later for safety reasons.*

(Photo courtesy of Mark Tilden, WowWee Ltd.)

(Photo courtesy of Mark Tilden, WowWee Ltd.)

Figure 3-27. *This "rogue's gallery" features the earliest prototypes.*

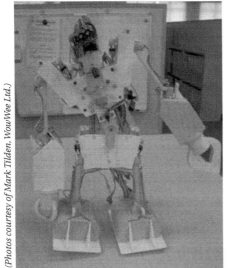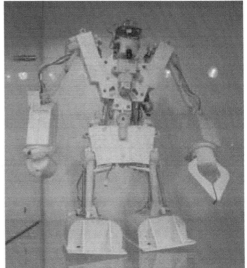

(Photos courtesy of Mark Tilden, WowWee Ltd.)

Figures 3-28 and 3-29. *Things are really coming together in this prototype, with the brain structure and internal frame almost complete. However, literally days after it was built, the company that WowWee had been working with filed for bankruptcy.*

You Can Dress It Up, But You Can't Take It Out

The next stage in the development of Robosapien involved designing the outer shell, creating the unique personality, and beginning mass production of the toy.

(Sketch by Anne Marie Arnold based on Mark Tilden's original drawing)

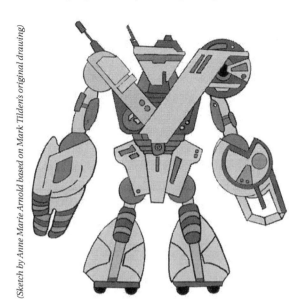

Figure 3-30. *Here's Tilden's own early vision for the Robosapien's exterior. He describes it as "sort of a Bruce Lee meets some sort of Terminator thing. His left hand was supposed to be a sort of universal tool, the right hand was supposed to be a large sort of builder thing. You can see it's very, very close to the original structure and physical mechanism. Which I thought would be ok. Well that's no good for my designers, was it? They were after things that were a lot more sci fi…"*

(Photos courtesy of Mark Tilden, WowWee Ltd.)

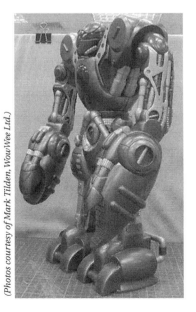 

Figures 3-31 and 3-32. *The drawing and model of an early shell design are shown in these two figures. These are referred to as "look-likes" in the toy industry.*

(Photos courtesy of Mark Tilden, WowWee Ltd.)

Figure 3-33 and 3-34. *Here's another set of "look-likes."*

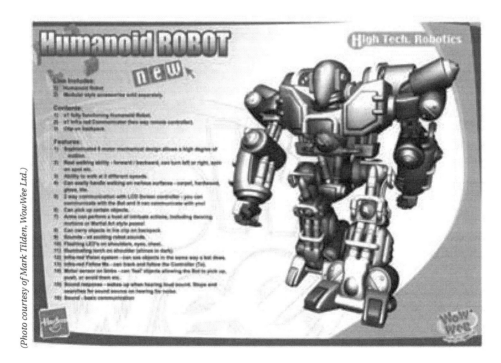

(Photo courtesy of Mark Tilden, WowWee Ltd.)

Figure 3-35. *This graphic shows some of the early concept art for Robosapien, probably designed for marketing purposes.*

WHAT DIDN'T MAKE THE CUT

As with any product manufactured, compromises are made and some features get cut, usually due to cost cutting or just plain feasibility. The early Robosapien concept art shown in Figure 3-35 listed the following planned features for the robot. Take a look at this list (taken directly from Figure 3-35) and see what made it to the final version and what didn't:

Line Includes:

1) Humanoid Robot

2) Modular style accessories sold separately.

Contents:

1) One fully functional Humanoid Robot.

2) One Infra-red Communicator (two way remote controller).

3) Clip on backpack.

Features:

1) Sophisticated 8 motor mechanical design allows a high degree of motion.

2) Real walking ability—forward/backward, can turn left or right, spin on spot, etc.

3) Ability to walk at 3 different speeds.

4) Can easily handle walking on various surfaces—carpet, hardwood, glass, tile.

5) 2 way communication with LCD Screen controller—you can communicate with the Bot and it can communicate with you!

6) Can pick up certain objects.

7) Arms can perform a host of intricate actions, including dancing motions or Martial Arts style poses!

8) Can carry objects in his clip on backpack

9) Sounds - x4 (sic) exciting robot sounds.

10) Flashing LEDs on shoulders, eyes, chest.

11) Illuminating torch on shoulder (shines in dark).

12) Infra-red Vision system—can see objects in the same way a bat does.

13) Infra-red Follow Me—can track and follow the controller.

14) Motor sensor on limbs—can "feel" objects allowing the Bot to pick up, push, or avoid them, etc.

15) Sound response—wakes up when hearing loud sound, stops and searches for sound source on hearing for noise (sic).

16) Sound—basic communication

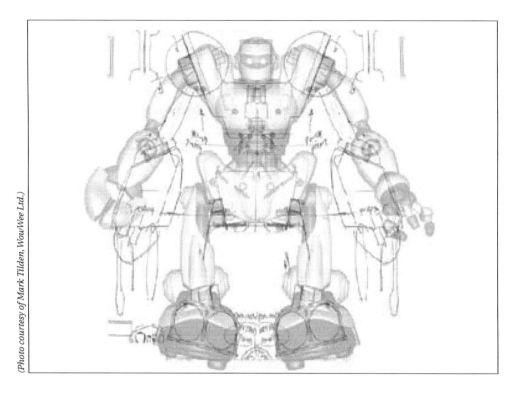

(Photo courtesy of Mark Tilden, WowWee Ltd.)

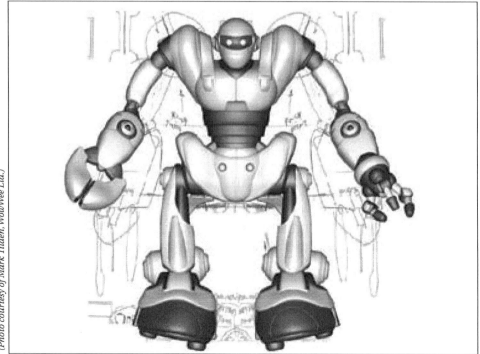

(Photo courtesy of Mark Tilden, WowWee Ltd.)

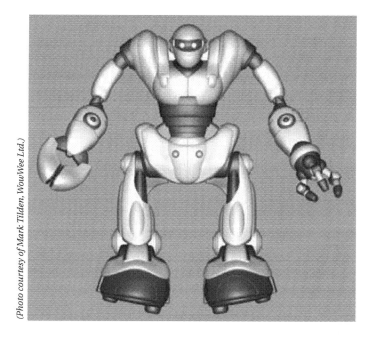

(Photo courtesy of Mark Tilden, WowWee Ltd.)

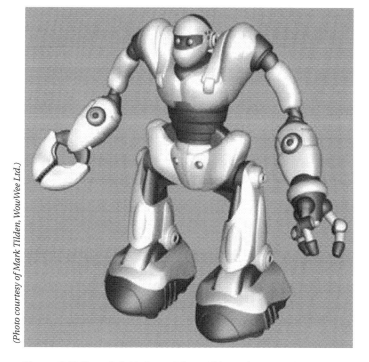

(Photo courtesy of Mark Tilden, WowWee Ltd.)

Figures 3-36 through 3-39. *One of the problems designers faced was making a shell that would not only protect and accommodate Robosapien's internals, but that would also be attractive to buyers. These drawings show the early development of what was to become the final design.*

(Photo courtesy of Mark Tilden, WowWee Ltd.)

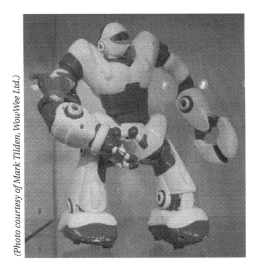

Figure 3-40. *This is one of the first prototypes based on the final design.*

(Photos courtesy of Mark Tilden, WowWee Ltd.)

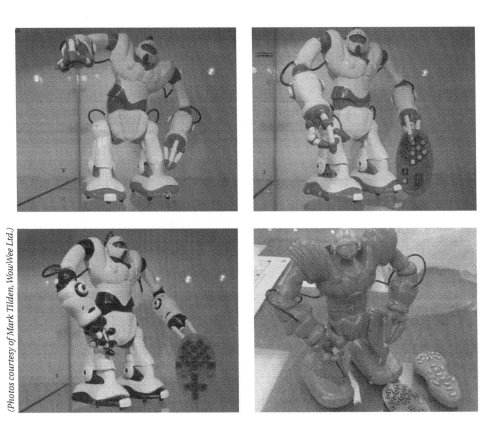

Figure 3-41 through 3-44. *Once a general final design was agreed upon, several more prototypes followed in quick succession, each refining it slightly, until the robot became what we know it as today.*

(Photo courtesy of Mark Tilden, WowWee Ltd.)

Figure 3-45. *With the design finalized, it was time to begin programming Robosapien's personality.*

GIVING ROBOSAPIEN HIS PERSONALITY

"So the robot actually looked pretty good. We had all the major features, and stuff like that, finally what happened was the crush was on...so I had to live at the Wah Shing factory in Shenzhen province.

"I went up there and literally lived with these guys. They knew we were under a crunch. We built our first tool prototype, based upon a 4 bar linkage system, tested the limits of how it actually winds up going. This is the mathematics and theory based upon resonance.... There was one guy there who had actually gone to a western university and had actually heard the word resonance before. So I said, 'ok, you don't have to trust me now, but in a little while, this is going to be very, very efficient.' Cos they were coming back to me and say 'hi yeah, small motor like this cannot move 2 kilogram robot!' And I said, 'yes it can... but you gotta know how.' So I explained it to this one guy, and he believed, and the rest basically went on.

"Great guy by the name of Edward Chan, probably the biggest ego in all of China, but he knows his stuff. And better yet he was able to act as an interpreter. So while I basically danced like a stupid idiot, like what they call 'sen jing gui lo'—crazy white guy—he would translate it into Chinese. And it was the funniest thing in the world, because we were sitting in a lunch room, we have gone 10 days nonstop, I am basically wearing the same clothes by like Day 8. I'd be like 'no, no you idiot, the roar doesn't go "uh uh uh" it goes "ROAAWWRR!!!!"' and then Edward would turn to a programmer and go 'wa.' <laughter>

"And type type type and the next thing you know, the Robosapien was actually doing it, lock it down, lock it down... one after the other... 11 days later, and all this assembler code, we were 4 bytes short of the 12K programming. We squeezed that silicon like you would not believe.

"And we finally basically had this thing put together, and all of a sudden there it was. Unit 0. The first working Robosapien. Then came production." *—Mark Tilden, February 13, 2005*

(Photo courtesy of Mark Tilden, WowWee Ltd.)

(Photo courtesy of Mark Tilden, WowWee Ltd.)

(Photo courtesy of Mark Tilden, WowWee Ltd.)

(Photo courtesy of Mark Tilden, WowWee Ltd.)

Figures 3-46 through 3-49. *What Tilden describes as "a solid acre of girls" is the floor of the Wah Shing plant. At peak production, 508 female workers build one Robosapien every 5 seconds, turning out close to 6,000 Robosapiens in a day.*

Summary

Robosapien's transition from a hand-built, purely analog BEAM robot into a digital toy capable of being mass-produced and marketed was a process that took almost two and a half years. When I had the opportunity to interview Mark Tilden, I was extremely surprised to learn how much "blood, sweat, and tears" went into getting Robosapien ready for the world. I hope that you've found this photo journal of the process and the various prototypes as interesting as I do!

CHAPTER 4

■ ■ ■

Setting Up Your Robosapien

Figure 4-1. *Hey! Let me out of here!*

Now that we've covered some of the theory behind Robosapien, let's roll up our sleeves and get busy with the robot itself! In this chapter, we'll look at Robosapien's packaging and battery usage, and we'll power it up and make sure it operates correctly. We'll also go over the first two Robosapien "secrets" when we cover its diagnostic modes.

The Packaging

One thing you always hear from people who own a Robosapien is how difficult it is to extricate it from the box. The packaging is impressive, and the manufacturer has done a nice job of making it almost impossible to remove the robot. Interestingly, as manufacturing runs continue it seems as if the packaging, rather than getting easier to deal with, is actually becoming more challenging!

I bought my first Robosapien shortly after the U.S. release in spring 2004. In August of that same year, I purchased a limited edition "Mark Tilden Signature Series" Robosapien from The Sharper Image. Finally, in preparation for writing this book, I purchased another Robosapien in January 2005. Obviously the packaging for the Sharper Image Robosapien has different graphics (see Figure 4-2).

Figure 4-2. *The packaging for the Sharper Image Robosapien has different graphics, as you can see here.*

Going beyond the graphics, the packaging is subtly different for all three models.

The size remains the same. At 17.5 inches tall, 13.5 inches wide, and 10.5 inches deep, the box is large. You have absolutely zero chance of remaining incognito when buying a Robosapien. My wife was very embarrassed when I bought my first Robosapien at a Fry's.

Newer models feature a handy carrying handle, ostensibly to help you get your Robosapien up to the cash register. Neither my original Robosapien nor the Sharper Image model features the carrying handle.

Figure 4-3. *The carrying handle on the new packaging helps you get your Robo-sapien to the cash register.*

Figure 4-4. *The original Robosapien packaging doesn't include a handle.*

Figure 4-5. *The Sharper Image Robosapien packaging offers no handle as well.*

Another interesting design change present in the Sharper Image Robosapien is the inclusion of clear plastic inserts to hold the robot's arms in place during shipping (see Figure 4-6).

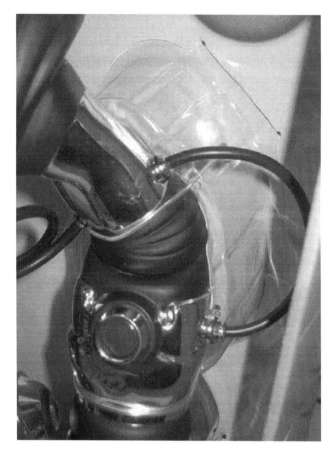

Figure 4-6. *The Sharper Image Robosapien's arm is held in place with a clear plastic insert.*

Neither my original Robosapien purchased in July, nor my newest model purchased in January has these plastic inserts, which incidentally seem far more effective at protecting Robosapien's arms from too much movement during shipping.

Removing Robosapien from the Packaging

Some care must be taken when removing Robosapien from its packaging. As I mentioned before, the manufacturers are very diligent in packaging the toy robot, no doubt to minimize damage during shipping from the factory. Your first impulse will be to carefully remove the robot from the packaging, but once you hit a snag, excitement and adrenaline take over, and more than one Robosapien package has ended up as a pile of tattered strips of cardboard and plastic. Unfortunately, this type of hurried unpacking can often result in damage to Robosapien by placing too much stress on his appendages, so it is worthwhile to take your time and do it right. In this section, I will outline a safe, easy way to remove Robosapien from his packaging.

The first thing you will need to do is gather a few simple tools (see Figure 4-7).

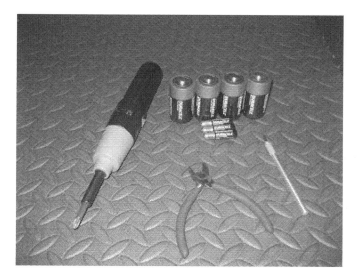

Figure 4-7. *Make sure you lay out the tools and batteries you need before tackling the packaging.*

As you can see, I have a hobby knife, a small set of wire cutters, a Phillips head screwdriver, and the required batteries. These items will be all that you need to get your Robosapien up and running.

Begin with the hobby knife, and cut the pieces of clear tape around the top of the box (see Figure 4-8).

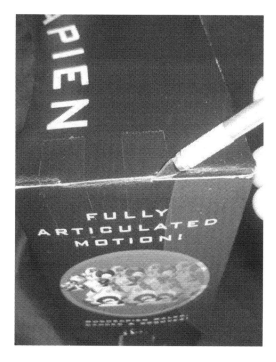

Figure 4-8. *Begin by cutting the plastic tape around the top of the box.*

Next, peel back the cardboard top (see Figure 4-9). Note that newer models seem to have some glue holding the cardboard top in place. Fortunately, it is not very sticky, and the top peels up fairly easily. If it is sticking, use your hobby knife as a lever to help you get through the glue.

Figure 4-9. *After you have cut through the tape, peel back the top.*

Now, you should be able to lift out the cardboard and plastic contained inside Robosapien's graphic exterior. As with the top, newer models of Robosapien may have some glue holding the front of the graphic exterior onto the clear plastic. Once you have completed this step you will be left with an empty shell (Figure 4-10) and a cocoon of clear plastic, tape, wire, and thicker cardboard, to which the Robosapien is attached (Figure 4-11). Take care not to lose the instruction manual during this stage. It is generally packaged in a clear plastic bag between the outer and inner packaging.

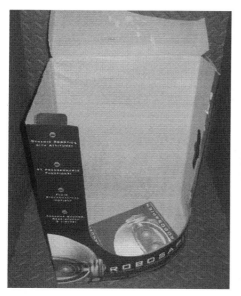

Figure 4-10. *Be careful not to lose Robosapien's instruction manual.*

Figure 4-11. *Next we'll tackle Robosapien's inner packaging.*

You will notice on the back of the inner packaging that the clear plastic "bubble" is held in place by four tabs secured with clear packing tape. Using your hobby knife, cut through this tape (Figure 4-12) and remove the black plastic handle (Figure 4-13).

Figure 4-12. *Prepare to remove Robosapien's clear plastic packaging.*

Figure 4-13. *Remove the handle (found on later models of Robosapien).*

At this point you are ready to remove the entire piece of clear plastic from the packaging (Figure 4-14). Note that it may be glued in some places, particularly on newer models, so take care not to rip the cardboard.

Figure 4-14. *Remove the clear plastic portion of the packaging.*

Well, at this stage in the process, if you've made it this far you can actually touch Robosapien. But we haven't finished yet! Once the clear plastic is removed, you will notice that there is an insidious amount of tape and wire pinning Robosapien against the thick cardboard packaging (Figure 4-15). Note that this is not only on the back of the packaging, but also on the bottom where it holds Robosapien's feet in place. So we still have some work to do. Begin by removing all the tape that covers the wires anchoring the robot to the packaging. Don't forget about the bottom! Use your hobby knife where necessary.

With the tape removed, use your wire cutters to cut through the anchor wires holding Robosapien in place. Make these cuts from the back of the packaging (Figure 4-16). Be sure you do this step over a table or other surface, as there is a chance Robosapien may fall out of the packaging during this stage.

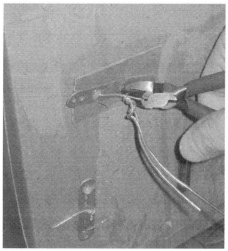

Figure 4-15. *Are you beginning to wonder whether they really want you to get this thing out of the box?*

Figure 4-16. *Cut Robosapien's anchor wires that hold it in the packaging.*

Remove any wires left over from the front of the robot, and Robosapien should come free of the packaging! It will still have wires looped through the bottoms of its feet (Figure 4-17), around the chest, and around the forearms. Remove these, as well as the tag on the right arm (Figure 4-18).

Figure 4-17. *Anchor wires still need to be removed from the bottoms of Robosapien's feet.*

Figure 4-18. *There is not nearly enough packaging with Robosapien. I'm so glad they included this tag.*

We're almost there. On newer models of Robosapien, its left claw is wrapped in clear plastic (Figure 4-19). Go ahead and remove this plastic. This plastic wasn't present on earlier models, and I don't really see a reason for it.

Figure 4-19. *A protective plastic sleeve is found on newer models of Robosapien's left claw.*

You are finally done! Clean up your mess and put the box back together, if you want. Make sure you save the little plastic anchors that kept the wires holding the robot from breaking through the cardboard (Figure 4-20). We'll use these in a project later on.

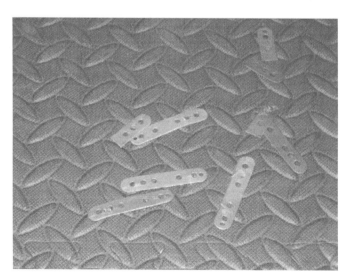

Figure 4-20. *We'll use these later to enhance Robosapien's gripping capabilities.*

Batteries and Rechargeable Batteries

OK, now that we have finally extricated Robosapien from its packaging, it's time to load the robot up with batteries and make sure it operates correctly. As with most battery-operated machines, Robosapien works best when its batteries are fresh. As the batteries lose their charge, Robosapien will have difficulty performing tasks and may even appear to be broken.

■Tip Anytime someone has a problem with their Robosapien, my first troubleshooting step is always to suggest that they try new batteries. Let me repeat. Try *new* batteries—not another set that happens to be rolling around in a drawer somewhere.

Robosapien is designed with something called "regenerative controllers," which is a fancy way of saying it contains circuitry that will store and reuse electrical energy as the robot goes about its movements. Robosapien is also designed so that the weight of the four D cell batteries in the feet provide it with a low center of gravity, and this is integral to its walking ability. Given these two factors, it is worth mentioning the advantages and disadvantages of using different types of batteries in Robosapien.

■Caution Under no circumstances should you mix old and new batteries, or rechargeable batteries with regular alkaline batteries.

There are four types of "household" batteries that the average consumer will run into—alkaline batteries, and three types of rechargeable batteries: nickel-cadmium (NiCad), nickel-metal hydride (NiMh), and rechargeable alkalines.

NiCad Rechargeable Batteries

Let me start by saying that Wow Wee recommends *against* using NiCad batteries in Robosapien or in the Robosapien remote control. According to Mark Tilden, although NiCad will provide a more constant power source, which will translate into more uniform movement, there is a chance that they can overload Robosapien's motor driver circuitry. Under strong load conditions (for example, if Robosapien is trying to raise its arms but they are blocked from moving upward by a wall, pillow, etc.), the chance of overloading the motor driver chip is fairly significant. Another disadvantage to using NiCad batteries is that once they are dead, you can't just throw them away. They contain toxic metals and generally must be returned to the place of purchase for disposal. Also, NiCads will self-discharge at a rate of roughly 20 to 25 percent a month, even when not in use. NiCads in general will last about one-third as long as alkalines before they need to be recharged, and about half as long as NiMh batteries. Finally, NiCads have an output voltage of 1.2 volts, as opposed to 1.5 volts for alkalines.

Given these downsides, it is a good idea to avoid using NiCad batteries in Robosapien. If you have your heart set on it, or if you want to see for yourself if they really do result in more uniform movement for Robosapien (personally I can't see much of a difference), just be careful.

NiMh Rechargeable Batteries

In general, NiMh batteries are replacing NiCad as the rechargeable battery of choice. For one thing, they do not have the special disposal requirements that NiCads do. They are also available with higher capacities, so they will not run out as quickly. They will last about half as long as alkaline batteries. They do, however, self-discharge at about the same rate as NiCads, and they also only put out 1.2 volts (compared to 1.5 volts for alkaline).

If you are set on using rechargeable batteries for Robosapien, then you should strongly consider NiMh. However, there is one major factor that makes these batteries less than ideal for Robosapien: their weight. Depending on their milli-amp-hour (mAH) rating (or capacity), the weight of NiMh batteries will vary. The higher the capacity, the greater the weight. A standard alkaline D cell weighs approximately 145 grams. A super-capacity NiMh D cell rated at 11,000 mAH weighs 170g. Standard off-the-shelf NiMh D cells can vary anywhere from 2,500 mAH up to about 7,000 mAH. These will be significantly lighter than standard alkaline D cells, and require you to adjust your Robosapien's feet so that it will walk correctly. According to Mark Tilden, "to compensate for the lesser weight you have to raise his outside footpads on each foot by at least 2mm (placing #4 washers under his footpads works fine). He will walk a bit shallower but won't stumble. Some [other] adjustment may be necessary."

While they have fewer downsides than NiCads, I feel that NiMh batteries still leave something to be desired.

Rechargeable Alkaline Batteries

The idea behind these batteries is to provide the higher capacity and voltage of alkalines along with rechargeability. The reality is that they are really more of a gimmick, and I recommend against using them in Robosapien. Their capacity begins to drop off sharply after only a few recharge cycles, making these batteries a very poor choice.

Alkaline Batteries

Standard alkaline batteries are what I use in my Robosapien. The WowWee folks claim that based on their tests at the factory they have gotten as many as 28 hours of lifetime from standard Energizer brand alkaline batteries. This is in line with my experience as well.

It seems to me that there are too many downsides associated with rechargeable batteries to warrant their use in Robosapien.

▪Tip Regardless of what type of battery you end up using, place a small sticker on the bottom of Robosapien's foot and mark down the date every time you change or recharge batteries.

Installing Batteries in Robosapien

Installing the batteries is fairly straightforward. Make sure you've got your polarities correct and that your batteries are fresh (not the ones you found bouncing around in the bottom of the kitchen drawer). Robosapien requires three AAA cells in the remote control unit, and four D cells (two in each foot). When installing the D cells, take care that the battery pull straps do not get caught between the battery and the connectors inside the feet (see Figure 4-21).

Figure 4-21. *Install D cell batteries in Robosapien's feet.*

▓**Advanced Tip** According to Mark Tilden, one way to really optimize battery life in Robosapien is to use a 1-farad, low internal-resistance supercap (7v rating) across the battery contacts found at the bottom of the motherboard. This reduces dynamic current loads and will significantly extend battery life.

Digi-Key (http://www.digikey.com/digihome.html) stocks a couple of these that should work well. The first is the PowerStor Aerogel Capacitor. This is a 1F/5V very low ESR cap that measures $8.5 \times 16.8 \times 21.5$mm. The cost is $9 each; Digi-Key P/N 283-2514.

The second is the Panasonic NF Series Gold. The ESR is higher but still low for this application. They are rated at 5.5V and there are 1F and 1.5F versions priced around $5–$6 each. Both are 8×21.5mm. The Digi-Key P/Ns are P6955 and P11063.

Turning On Robosapien

OK, so we've managed to get Robosapien separated from its packaging, and we've got it loaded up with batteries. It's finally time for the moment of truth. Robosapien's on/off switch is located on the lower-right side of its back (see Figure 4-22).

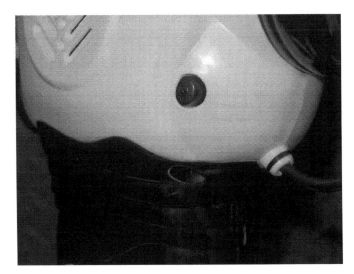

Figure 4-22. *You'll find the power switch on the lower-right side of Robosapien's back.*

When you press down the power switch, Robosapien will spring to life with a yawn, a stretch, a fart, and it will rock forward and backward once and side to side, concluding with an "Uh huh." You may hear a high-pitched whine coming from inside its chest cavity as it stretches—do not be concerned as this is part of the wake-up protocol.

One common mistake people make when turning on their Robosapien is to leave it lying down (since they just put in the batteries). Make sure that it is standing up! Robosapien is ready for your commands from the remote control now, but first let's make sure that it is operating correctly.

Diagnostic Modes

Robosapien comes with two undocumented diagnostic modes that you can use to ensure that the robot's motors and sensors are working correctly. The modes are interesting because Robosapien does a couple of vocalizations during the diagnostic modes that it won't do otherwise.

Before we get started, a note on working with Robosapien: You have probably already noticed that it is somewhat reversed—the controller is set up so that the right and left sides are based not on the robot's right and left, but rather the right and left as you (the operator) are facing Robosapien. So, for example, in the following diagnostic modes, when I say, "Hold in the left sensor," I mean the sensor on *your* left, not Robosapien's.

▓Tip The remote is set up so it's like you are holding the robot in your hands. This turned out to be quite natural for most people, as if you are directing an actor on a stage.

The left side of the controller always operates Robosapien's right side; the right side of the controller always operates its left side. So, if you are standing in front of it, the controller buttons line up directly to the side that will move; if you are standing behind it, the controller buttons line up vertically to the side that will move.

Diagnostic Mode #1

Follow these steps to test Robosapien in Diagnostic Mode #1:

1. Start with the Robosapien turned off with its arms positioned in and down.

2. Hold in one of the left sensors (hand, toe, or heel will work) and turn on the Robosapien via the power button on its back.

3. Immediately after switching on the power, release the left sensor and within five seconds press one of the right sensors four times.

4. Rather than going into the regular wake-up routine, Robosapien will respond with a "Heyyyy," indicating that it has entered Diagnostic Mode #1. The LEDs in the eyes will each light once, first the left, and then the right.

Once you have successfully gotten into Diagnostic Mode #1, follow these steps in this order:

1. Left sensor test: Tap any of its left sensors three times. Robosapien will beep each time its sensor is touched, and the right-eye LED will light for each time you touch a sensor. I recommend touching all three sensors (toe, heel, and finger) to make sure they are each working properly.

2. Right sensor test: Tap any of the right sensors three times. Robosapien will burp each time a sensor is touched, and its left-eye LED will light for each time you touch a sensor. I recommend touching all three sensors (toe, heel, and finger) to make sure they are each working properly.

3. Right arm extend test: Robosapien will automatically extend its right arm out away from its body as far as it will go, opening the claw in the process, and then return it in toward its body. No eye LEDs will light and Robosapien will say "uh huh" to indicate that it is working properly.

4. Left arm extend test: Robosapien will automatically extend its left arm out away from its body as far as it will go, opening the claw in the process, and then return it in toward its body. No eye LEDs will light and it will say "uh huh" to indicate that it is working properly.

5. Right arm up test: Robosapien will automatically raise its right arm up as far as it will go, then lower it completely. Its left-eye LED will light and it will say "uh huh" to indicate that this function is working properly.

6. Left arm up test: Robosapien will automatically raise its left arm up as far as it will go, then lower it completely. Its right-eye LED will light and it will say "uh huh" to indicate that this function is working properly.

7. Sonic sensor test: Robosapien will enter "listen" mode and wait for a loud sound. Its eye LEDs will alternate between left and right. Upon "hearing" a sound through its internal microphone, Robosapien will begin test 8.

8. Walk-forward test: Robosapien will walk forward a few steps.

9. Infrared test: Robosapien will wait for any input from the remote control. Upon receiving this signal (you can press any key), Robosapien will begin test 10.

10. Speaker tone test: Robosapien will emit one or more high-pitched tones from its speaker. The number of tones seems to be dependent on which remote control key you hit during test 9.

11. Reset: After the speaker tone test, Robosapien will commence its usual wake-up routine.

Diagnostic Mode #2

Follow these steps to test Robosapien in Diagnostic Mode #2:

1. Start with the Robosapien turned off with its arms positioned in and down.

2. Hold in one of the left sensors (hand, toe, or heel will work) and turn on the Robosapien via the power button on its back.

3. Immediately after switching on the power, release the left sensor and within five seconds press one of the left sensors four times.

4. Rather than going into its regular wake-up routine, Robosapien will respond with a "Heyyyy" and a whistle, indicating that it has entered Diagnostic Mode #2. The LEDs in its palms will each light once, first the right, and then the left.

Once you have successfully gotten into Diagnostic Mode #2, follow these steps in this order:

1. Right sensor test: Press any one of Robosapien's right-side sensors (toe, heel, or finger). Robosapien will beep when it is touched and its right-eye LED will light up.

2. Manual right arm test: Extend Robosapien's right arm out manually (i.e., with your hand, not with the remote), turning out from the elbow. When you reach the halfway point, Robosapien will burp and its right-eye LED will light up.

3. Manual right arm test (continued): Continue manually extending Robosapien's right arm out away from its body. When its arm is fully extended out, Robosapien's right-eye LED will light up and it will say "whoa, whoa, whoaaaa!" Leave the right arm fully extended (claw open).

4. Left sensor test: Press any one of Robosapien's left-side sensors (toe, heel, or finger). Robosapien will say "ewugh" when it is touched and its left-eye LED will light up.

5. Manual left arm test: Extend Robosapien's left arm out manually (i.e., with your hand, not with the remote), turning out from the elbow. When you reach the halfway point, Robosapien will say "eck" and its left-eye LED will light up.

6. Manual left arm test (continued): Continue manually extending Robosapien's left arm out away from its body. When its arm is fully extended out, Robosapien's left-eye LED will light up and it will fart. Leave the right arm fully extended (claw open).

7. Automatic right arm test: Robosapien will bring its right arm in, move it all the way up above its head, and then bring it down.

8. Automatic left arm test: Robosapien will bring its left arm in, move it all the way up above its head, and then bring it down.

9. Automatic lean right test: Robosapien will lean to the right.

10. Automatic lean left test: Robosapien will lean to the left.

11. Automatic lean forward test: Robosapien will lean forward.

12. Automatic lean backward test: Robosapien will lean backward.

13. Sonic sensor test: Robosapien will wait until its internal microphone detects a sound. When it does, Robosapien will say "uh huh" and its right-eye LED will light up.

14. Infrared test: Robosapien will wait for any input from the remote control. Upon receiving this signal (you can press any key), Robosapien will say "uh uh" and its right-eye LED will light up.

15. Reset: Touch any one of Robosapien's left sensors to commence its usual wake-up routine.

▓**Note** If you are having problems progressing to steps 4 or 7 in Diagnostic Mode #2, try moving Robosapien's outstretched arm up or down an inch or so.

If you made it through these two diagnostic modes, then it is safe to say that your Robosapien is operating correctly and you are ready to move on. Keep these modes in mind if your robot ever starts "acting up"—these two diagnostic modes are great ways to begin your troubleshooting process.

Figure 4-23. *Robosapien is ready to go!*

Summary

Unpacking and setting up your Robosapien carefully takes time, but in the long run it is a worthwhile investment. Many people that I have talked to have been overly frustrated with the unpacking process and have damaged their robots in their haste. Even if you have already unpacked your robot, the sections on batteries and the diagnostic modes should be of interest. I have included a section on troubleshooting in Chapter 14; however, 99 percent of the time a set of fresh batteries and the diagnostic modes will usually solve or at least help pinpoint your robot's problem.

PART 2

Robosapien
Out of the Box

CHAPTER 5

■ ■ ■

Robosapien Anatomy

Figure 5-1. *Without the shell, the Robosapien bears a striking resemblance to some of the early prototypes we looked at in Chapter 3.*

The goal of this chapter is to take a close look at Robosapien from a physical perspective. As Mark Tilden has said about Robosapien, "It has a vitality and an aliveness that is beyond the sum of its parts." To try and understand why this statement is so true, I will look at not only the body, but also the robot's input/output system (i.e., Robosapien's sensor array and vocalizations—or, as WowWee calls it, "international caveman speech"). You will discover that Robosapien contains a lot more of Mark Tilden than just his design ideas.

From an aesthetic standpoint, Robosapien is very well designed and pleasing to the eye. It is, in fact, a 1/5-scale model of Mark Tilden, who is an athletically built 6 foot 3 inches and 350 pounds (see Figure 5-2).

He is exactly 1/5 me, exactly 1/5 of my dimensions. With the exception of the legs. So he's not just my personality, not just my programming, not just my physics, he's actually a little mini me in a lot of ways.

—Mark Tilden, February 13, 2005

Figure 5-2. *Robosapien is based on the physical characteristics of its creator, Mark Tilden.*

Besides the bottoms of its feet, Robosapien has only one other perfectly flat surface on its entire body: the speaker grill on its back.

Something I learned from all my years of biomorphic building is that you don't build things square. Things that are square basically fall down on two axes. And what happens is that Robosapien is basically built entirely upon biological angles. Not the way that you look when you stand, but the way that you basically fall into, the way when you sort of go limp, in something like a Jacuzzi. Your arms don't fall down to your sides, they float right in front of you. And your knees go up as well. And that's exactly what the shape of the Robosapien is based on. All the motor axes, as you can see here, all rotate around a very nice hexagonal frame, all based on very different angles—they're all 30's and 15's and 60's.

—Mark Tilden, February 13, 2005

But there is much more to it than just aesthetics. Starting at Robosapien's belly button and measuring to its elbows, shoulders, legs, it forms a nice hexagon (see Figure 5-3). This provides Robosapien with a consistent center of gravity that greatly aids its walking and movement ability.

Figure 5-3. *Robosapien is designed around a hexagonal shape.*

Physical Anatomy

There are four main elements to Robosapien's physical anatomy: its motors and suspension, its electronics, its head, and its external shell.

Motors and Suspension

Robosapien is based on a seven-motor design. These motors are based on the design Tilden created for the B.I.O. Bugs, and are remarkable for toy motors.

> *One of the things we were so pleased about, the lifetime of a standard toy grade 130 motor is, maximum, about 144 hours. About a week or so. We've never had a failure on a Robosapien... we've gotten as much as 400 hours out of some of our motors.... Our biggest problem was things like springs and plastic pieces failing before the motors did.*
> —*Mark Tilden, February 13, 2005*

The robot has two motors each in its shoulders, hips, and forearms. The seventh motor is located in its lower chest and controls the side-to-side "swaying" motion, which aids the walking mechanics and gives the robot the ability to "lean" over to pick things up and complete other tasks.

Figure 5-4. *This front view of Robosapien shows its two hip motors.*

The combination of its spring-based suspension and the specialized motors is what makes Robosapien so power efficient. The spring system means that the motors do not stop and start abruptly. Rather, the springs help decelerate the motor and then accelerate it in the opposite direction. In a sense, the combination of motors and springs means that as the Robosapien moves it both consumes *and* generates power.

> *The energy that's generated back [through the suspension system], in the Robosapien, the reason it gets so much efficiency—do the calculations: how on earth can it be so efficient? Well, when that motor moves backwards, 50% of the energy is regenerated because of the 3:1 gear ratio. That energy is stored, as a surface charge, on the alkalines. You can't recharge alkalines, but that surface charge is the equivalent of a 100-farad capacitor. So when he gets up in resonance, and is walking and doing really well, even when he is dancing and things like that, you can see all his symmetric functions, right? This arm is going down while this one is going up, because this is generating half the power that this thing needs, locally, coupled by the stored charge on the battery itself.*
> —Mark Tilden, February 13, 2005

Robosapien has two springs at its waist that assist the central seventh motor that controls its side-to-side movement (see Figure 5-5).

Figure 5-5. *Springs in Robosapien's waist aid in the side-to-side motion.*

There is also a spring in each shoulder that wraps around and aids the robot in raising and lowering its arms (see Figures 5-6 and 5-7). Recall that in Chapter 2 we saw some of the variations in shoulder spring placement between Robosapien generations (note the differing connection points in Figures 2-7 through 2-9). I speculate that as improvements were made to the motors (Tilden says they have manufactured 14 million motors, or enough for 2 million Robosapiens), the spring suspension system needed tweaking too.

Figure 5-6. *In this rear view of Robosapien, you can see its shoulder spring system. Also note the wires at each shoulder (they are blue and brown on the actual robot). These connect to limiter switches that give the shoulders three degrees of motion: up, midway, and down.*

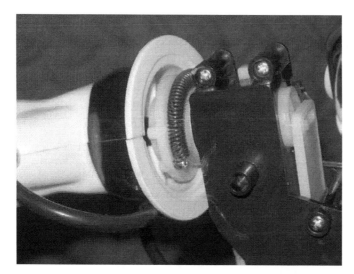

Figure 5-7. *In this front view of a shoulder spring, note how it wraps around the top and attaches on the arm itself. On the right, the shoulder motor is attached to an actuator that turns Robosapien's head when you raise and lower the arm.*

Robosapien also has two springs in each foot. These work not only to enhance the efficiency of the hip motors, but also to aid the two-bar link that keeps the bottoms of the robot's feet parallel with the surface it is walking on (see Figure 5-8). Note that when disassembled as in these photos, the Robosapien will not walk properly. The leg motors actually connect to the inside "thigh" portion of the shell. Without this piece of the shell, the hip motors just spin. Any forward movement that occurs when Robosapien is in this advanced state of "undress" is just the result of it swaying back and forth. More on this later in the chapter when we take a closer look at the shell.

The points where Robosapien uses the spring suspension are also the parts where the motors are doing the most work. For example, the hip motors each have to lift the weight of two D batteries, and the shoulder motors have to lift each arm entirely. The single motor in the waist has to shift the entire upper body weight of the Robosapien, including the arms, from side to side. In the forearms, where the remaining two motors are found, springs can be found in the claw mechanisms (see Figure 5-9). The claw spring mainly keeps Robosapien's grip closed. I suppose you could put a stronger spring in there to improve the robot's grip, but doing this would run the risk of overloading the forearm motors. Additionally, the actual claws are quite difficult to get apart since the part of the claw that attaches to the forearm is glued to the part where the fingers are attached.

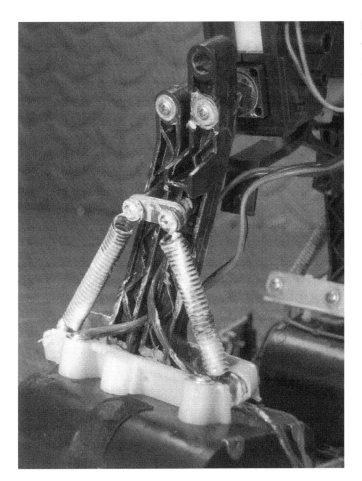

Figure 5-8. *Here you can see the two springs and the two-bar link system in Robosapien's legs.*

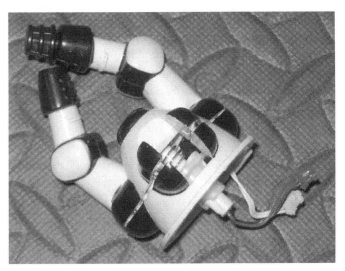

Figure 5-9. *By removing one of the "fingers," you can gain access to the spring system inside Robosapien's claws.*

Robosapien's forearm is an interesting structure (see Figure 5-10). The forearm motors do double duty, as they are responsible for both the rotation at the elbow and the opening of the claws.

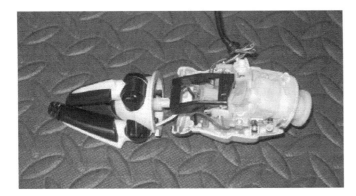

Figure 5-10. *Here you can see Robosapien's forearm, with the claw partially removed.*

Packed into the forearm is a nicely labeled PCB (printed circuit board) complete with connectors. There are connections for the LED in the palm of the claw, the touch sensor on the end of the claw, the motor, and a connection called the "elbow." The elbow connector connects to a tiny switch (see Figure 5-10, lower-right corner) that is triggered when the elbow reaches a certain degree of rotation. Much like the switches in the shoulder (see Figure 5-6), this is what gives Robosapien's elbow three degrees of motion: in toward the body, halfway out, and all the way out with the claw open.

In addition to the PCB, the forearm houses the motor and the actuator responsible for opening and closing the claw. When the motor is activated and spins the forearm at the elbow away from the body, it simultaneously spins a small cam in the forearm. This cam hits an actuator that pushes open the claw. When the elbow is spun back toward the body, the cam spins in the opposite direction and the actuator gets released back toward the elbow. This closes the claw (see Figures 5-11 and 5-12). Mark Tilden told me that it is entirely possible to modify the shape of the cam to change the way the grippers work. For example, you could modify it so that the claw opens when the forearm is in the middle position, and closes when it is at either extreme.

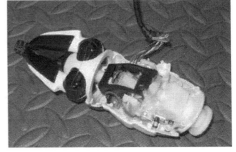

Figures 5-11 and 5-12. *Here we've shown the opening and closing of Robosapien's claw. Note the white plastic cam that rotates and pushes the black plastic actuator into the claw, triggering its opening.*

Newer Robosapiens feature screws in the forearm that make it easy to take it apart. In older models, the forearm is glued together with incredibly strong glue and contains no screws, which makes it very difficult to disassemble. If you take your Robosapien's forearms apart, you will notice that the left and right claws are completely interchangeable.

▨**Easy Hack** Change the LEDs in your robot's palms. Start by disassembling the forearm and removing the claw, including the connectors for the finger sensor and the palm LED. Use a small hobby knife or precision screwdriver to pry off the black bezel that surrounds the LED in the claw (see Figure 5-13). Replace the rather weak stock LEDs with any color you'd like! Note the polarity of both the LED you are replacing and the LED you are using as a replacement. The anode (positive terminal) is usually longer than the diode (negative terminal), and the diode usually has a flat edge on that side of the LED's plastic diffuser. You can also use an ohmmeter to determine polarity, since positive voltage flows out of the black probe when the meter is set to measure resistance. Set the meter to a low-resistance measurement range, like 200 ohms. Touch the probes of the meter to the LED. If the polarity is correct, the LED will glow. If the LED does not glow, switch the meter probes to the opposite leads on the LED. The side of the diode that is connected to the black probe when the LED glows is the anode side. On Robosapien's palm LEDs, the black wire connects to the diode and the red wire to the anode.

Figure 5-13. *Simply pry off the bezel to gain access to the palm LED (a small flathead precision screwdriver works great for this). Note that in this photo, the claw is removed from the forearm; otherwise you can't access the wires leading to the LED as easily.*

Electronics

Continuing with our look at Robosapien's anatomy, the next element is the robot's electronics. One of Robosapien's BEAM characteristics is its extremely simple electronic circuitry. If you recall from Chapter 3, the original Robosapien prototype was completely analog, and based on a 24-transistor design. While BEAM purists might scoff at the fact that Robosapien was converted to digital circuitry (mainly as a method of cutting manufacturing costs), the fact remains that current production-model Robosapiens are still extremely simple from an electronics standpoint. In fact, most basic calculators—not fancy scientific calculators, but the most basic designs—contain more complicated electronics than Robosapien.

Robosapien's circuit board (see Figures 5-14 and 5-15) contains a grand total of two chips: one Hitachi motor driver, which controls Robosapien's nervous network, and a dedicated sound processor based on a modified PIC 20 with a stack depth of 4 and a grand total of 12K of assembler code.

Figure 5-14. *This view of the front side of Robosapien's controller board shows the motor driver chip (center). In newer production models, this chip is smeared with thermal paste and covered with a rudimentary heatsink.*

Figure 5-15. *As you can see in this view of the back side of Robosapien's controller board, the robot's main processor is in the center of the board.*

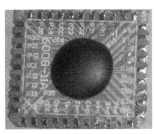
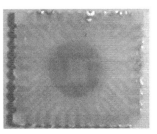

(Photo courtesy of Mark Craig.)

Figures 5-16 through 5-18. *My friend Mark Craig from Scotland was the first Robosapien hacker to completely remove the main processor from the controller board. These photos show the controller board with the processor removed, and the front and back of the chip itself.*

The chip itself, even if you got to it, you'll find out that it's mostly RAM and ROM, it's a very small processor on there, but everything is encrypted. So even if you did extract the code, you can't reverse engineer it. What happens is that in the toy industry, you're always this many days away from death… so the robot had to be protected in a lot of different ways. Interestingly enough, all toys are based upon modified sound processors. In other words, things that sang "Happy Birthday to You" 20 years ago in Hallmark cards.

—Mark Tilden, February 13, 2005

Before moving on to Robosapien's head, it is worth pointing out just how "hackable" the Robosapien's electronics are. Look closely at Figures 5-14 and 5-15. Everything is clearly labeled on both the front and the back of the controller board. All connections, with the exception of the microphone, are connected via solderless, socketed connectors. Look at the back of the board (Figure 5-15); there are even gold-plated solder pads specifically designed to allow hackers easy access to the robot's I/O. Simply put, the robot is specifically designed to be taken apart and modified.

Robosapien's Head

Robosapien's head structure is an important part of its anatomy. The head not only contains the eye LEDs, the importance of which we will see shortly, but it also houses the receiver that picks up the infrared (IR) signals from the remote control.

Figure 5-19. *Robosapien's head contains the eye LEDs as well as the IR receiver (back view).*

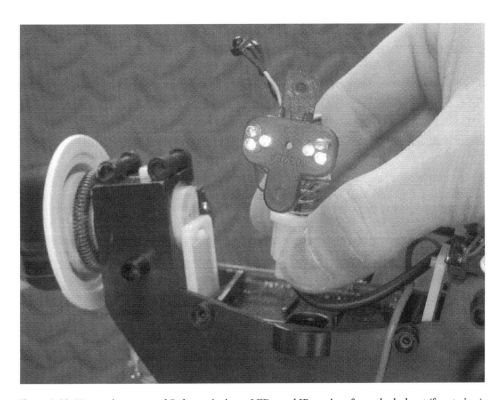

Figure 5-20. *Here we've removed Robosapien's eye LEDs and IR receiver from the helmet (front view).*

One important note about Robosapien's head is that, unlike pretty much every other part of Robosapien, the head is extremely difficult to open up and take apart. It is glued around the edges and inside on four support posts.

The worst condition in toys is called the drop test. One meter drop test. All toys have to be able to take a fall, from a height like this table, onto a solid concrete surface, and pop back up with less than one chance in nine of breaking. We doubled that, we made him so that he could take a two meter drop test, but the problem with that is that to make that work, we found that the head had to be glued together, it was too fragile, even protected by the shoulders, the head would just crack into pieces.

—*Mark Tilden, February 13, 2005*

I can't see any way to get the head apart without damaging it badly (see Figure 5-21). For these pictures I used a couple of small flat-head screwdrivers (and one really large one once I got the bottom partially pried apart), quite a bit of strength, and a lot of patience to get it apart. I *still* managed to accidentally ram a screwdriver under one of my fingernails. If you absolutely must take the head apart, take your time, use caution, and don't expect it to look very pretty once you get it all back together.

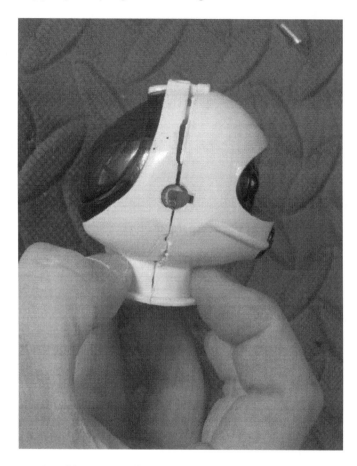

Figure 5-21. *Robospaien sustained some damage when I took apart the head.*

One thing you may have noticed about Robosapien is its animated eyes. As seen in Figure 5-20, each "eye" is actually three separate LEDs. What you might not have realized is that these "eyes" give distinct patterns for the state that the robot is in (see Figure 5-22).

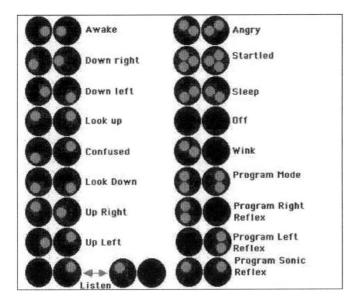

Figure 5-22. *Robosapien's eye LEDs provide a "window into its soul."*

On the controller board (see Figure 5-15) the six outputs for the eyes are labeled as P20 through P25. These can be used very effectively as a digital-level feedback source for hacking projects.

> *You wouldn't believe how I fought like hell to keep the 6 LEDs in the eyes. Because the eyes are the window to that thing's soul. What I mean by that, you pattern match those, and you know exactly what is going on. A beautiful 6-bit interface that tells you exactly what the robot is doing, how he is going on, and what you're doing. It's an 8-wire interface that fits on a 12- wire PIC, if you wanted to do such a thing. And so we made the thing to be hacked in such a beautiful way. And the LEDs of course, you don't have to actually remove them, you can just parasite on to them.*
>
> *—Mark Tilden, February 13, 2005*

External Shell

As we saw in Chapter 3, the design of Robosapien's shell goes far beyond something that merely "looks cool." While this was certainly a big part of it (proven by the fact that Robosapien won the prestigious 2004 Hong Kong Award for Industry and Consumer Product Design), the outer shell is also tasked with protecting and accommodating Robosapien's internals (see Figure 5-23). Additionally, the shell follows one of the BEAM concepts we learned about: the shape of a thing defines how it will work.

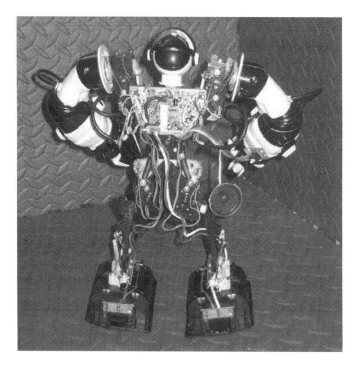

Figure 5-23. *Without a protective shell, Robosapien's delicate internal wiring would probably not last long.*

For example, an examination of Robosapien's arm structure reveals that the upper arm is completely hollow. Between the elbow and the shoulder the plastic shell *is* the structure (see Figures 5-24 and 5-25)—in this sense Robosapien is a bit like a crustacean, just without the tasty meat.

Figures 5-24 and 5-25. *Robosapien's upper arm is completely hollow.*

Similarly, Robosapien is dependent on its shell for walking. Figures 5-26 and 5-27 show the square part of the hip axle. Without the "inner thigh" piece of the shell attached, this axle just spins. Robosapien will still "walk" on some surfaces, like hardwood floors, but any forward motion is the result of the side-to-side swaying from the central waist motor. This provides a good example of how Robosapien's two hip motors and single waist motor combine to produce the robot's unique bipedal gait. Figure 5-28 shows the square-shaped slot in the shell that the hip motor axle connects into.

 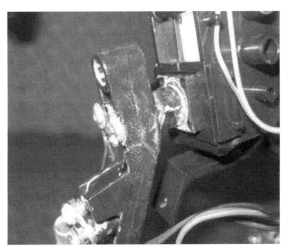

Figures 5-26 and 5-27. *Robosapien's hip with a leg on and a leg off. The square part of the axle fits into a square hole on Robosapien's shell, shown in 5-28. This allows it to walk properly.*

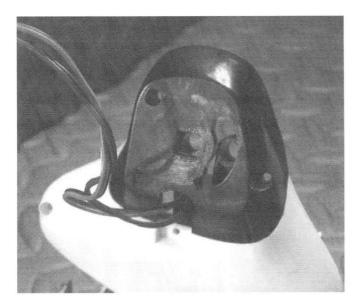

Figure 5-28. *Robosapien's inner thigh shell. Note the square hole for the axle.*

I suppose you could modify the hip axle to make better contact with the two-bar link that makes up the "leg" (see Figures 5-8 and 5-27). Right now, as you have probably noticed in many of the photos in this chapter, there is a tremendous amount of grease. Better contact might be achieved by cleaning off all the grease, roughing up the surfaces a bit, and screwing the hip joint down nice and tight. That said, there isn't much plastic there at the joint, and I imagine that eventually it would fail. Using the inner-thigh shell in this manner to aid the walking dynamic adds quite a bit to Robosapien's structural integrity.

Input/Output System

Now let's turn our attention to Robosapien's input/output system. In this section I cover the robot's sensor array and its language: international caveman speech.

Sensors

Robosapien has sensors in seven locations. The robot has six impact or "touch" sensors: one on a finger of each claw (see Figures 5-29 and 5-30), and one on the heel and toe of each foot (see Figures 5-31 through 5-33). These are designed so that they will be triggered when manually pushed, or when Robosapien "bumps" into something. Robosapien also has a microphone in its chest that picks up auditory input (see Figure 5-34).

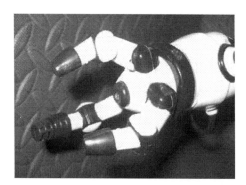 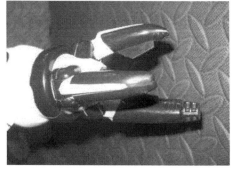

Figures 5-29 and 5-30. *Robosapien has a reactive impact sensor on each claw.*

Figures 5-31 through 5-33. *Here we're showing the "toe" and "heel" sensors on Robosapien's feet. Figure 5-33 shows the sensor without the plastic shell. Note the hacker-friendly solder pads marked "CN1" and "CN2" on the far left of the sensor PCB.*

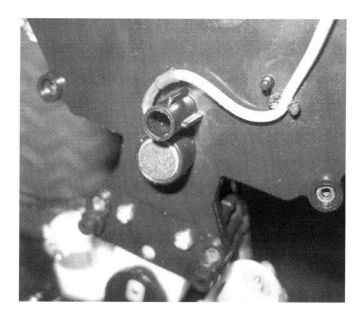

Figures 5-34.
Robosapien's sonic sensor is a small microphone placed in the center of the robot's chest cavity.

You might think, "Seven sensors, wow! That's quite a few..." but the reality is that these translate into only three. All of the impact sensors on each side are essentially "tied together" as one input for programming purposes. As you will see in Part 3 (which covers programming the Robosapien), the robot has three reactive program modes: left, right, and sonic. The result is that all of the touch sensors on the robot's left side (finger, heel, and toe), for example, will trigger the same reactive program.

The touch sensors also have a built-in safety feature. Usually Robosapien will go into "sleep mode" after five minutes without receiving an IR input. However, if both the left and the right sensors are held in for one minute, Robosapien triggers a safety mode. After one minute with both left and right sensors activated, the robot first runs its "reset" command. If this fails to free up at least one of the sensors, then Robosapien runs its shutdown routine. This comes into play if Robosapien has fallen over or is stuck up against a wall—in either case both sensors will be pressed in, and by attempting to free itself and/or shutting down, Robosapien lessens the chance that its motor driver will be overloaded by something like trying to repeatedly raise its arm when pinned against the floor.

With Robosapien's sonic sensor, the robot will react to sounds in its environment. It will not react to voice or other complex sounds—it is simply an on or off sensor. Any loud noise, even tapping against the robot's shell, will trigger the sonic sensor. The sonic sensor will not work if one of the robot's motors is running, which is a good thing since the robot's motors and movements can be noisy. It takes about a second after the last motor movement for the sound sensor to become active again.

"International Caveman Speech"

Aside from the digital feedback provided by Robosapien's eyes, the robot's primary means of communication is its speech capabilities. WowWee has termed this "language" *international caveman speech*. It's really not a language at all, since the robot knows only one word. You have probably noticed that when you shut it down (or when it shuts itself down), its right arm falls to the side and shakes, and the robot utters the word "Rosebud." This is in fact a homage to the 1941 Orson Welles film *Citizen Kane*. Tilden explained it in an interview with *The New York Times Magazine*: "If you remember, you wait the entire movie, and you find out that Rosebud was the name of his favorite toy. So just imagine the poetic symmetry. Just before Robosapien dies, he has a dream of another toy."[1] But what it lacks in vocabulary, it more than makes up in attitude.

Imagine for a minute that you are head of a large toy company that wants to sell millions of robots all over the world. You have dubbed this robot "a fusion of technology and personality." How do you make this personality universal? How do you make it so someone in say, Germany, can understand and get the same enjoyment from the robot as someone in Japan? One way would be to release language-specific variations of the robot. The other way would be to come up with a method of nonverbal communication.

International caveman speech is a language comprised of grunts, groans, kung fu–style "hi-yahs," and sounds usually more suited to, ahem, biological creatures. To say that Robosapien's burping and farting is proof of the biological aspect of the BEAM technology would be a bit of a stretch, I'm afraid. To say that it is a brilliant cost-cutting and marketing move is more accurate.

Tilden recorded all the noises himself—yet another aspect of Robosapien that reflects its creator. The United Kingdom–based *Observer* broke the story in December 2004:

> *In a hotel room in Hong Kong the maid walks in to find a large, bearded man under a tent made out of pillows and a duvet, clutching a torch and burping into a voice recorder. The man is Mark Tilden, 6ft 3in and weighing 350lb, who has consumed huge quantities of Thai food and Pepsi ("because Chinese and Coca-Cola doesn't make you burp very well") to help him bring up wind. What the maid, in her shock, does not realise is that she is witnessing the birth of the most sought-after toy in the world."* [2]

Yet, however much you might like Mark Tilden and Robosapien, the fact is, the speaker volume is rather loud, and there is no apparent way to adjust the volume levels. One method, suggested on WowWee's Robosapien webpage (http://www.Robosapienonline.com), is to simply put tape over the speaker grille on Robosapien's back. While rather inelegant, I must say that this method works fairly well. I am of the opinion, however, that in about the same time it takes to get out the tape and cut a piece that looks halfway decent on the robot, you can solder in a volume control, or even an on/off switch (see Figure 5-35). See Chapter 14 for a step-by-step guide on installing a volume control in your Robosapien.

---

1. "A Robot for the Masses," by Francisco Goldman, *The New York Times Magazine*, November 28, 2004.
2. "The Burping Robot Who Gave Mars a Miss," by David A. Smith, *The Observer*, December 5, 2004.

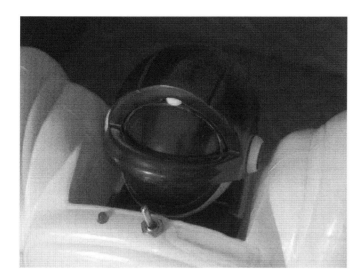

Figures 5-35. *It's easy to install a voice on/off switch and indicator LED on Robosapien. The area behind the robot's head makes an excellent spot for small hacks and modifications.*

Summary

Robosapien's unique anatomy is a combination of BEAM characteristics, elegant (and functional) design, and marketing savvy. The robot is truly more than the sum of its parts, as the next sections on operating the Robosapien will show.

CHAPTER 6

■■■

Controlling and Walking Your Robosapien

Figure 6-1. *Here's Robosapien in action. (Photo courtesy of WowWee Ltd.)*

Chapter 7 covers all of Robosapien's 67 commands in detail. This chapter covers operating your Robosapien, and I take a look at the remote control from a more general perspective, as well as some of the mechanics behind the robot's unique bipedal walking mechanism. Finally, I provide some suggestions on how to tune your Robosapien's walking ability.

The Remote Control

As we saw in Chapter 5, Robosapien receives commands through an infrared (IR) receiver situated under the helmet at the very top of its head (see Figure 6-2). This means that in order to receive signals from the remote control, the robot has to be able to "see" it. This is where infrared comes into play.

How It Works

When Robosapien receives an IR command, the signal travels down a wiring harness that snakes down through the robot's neck, finally connecting to the top of the controller board in Robosapien's chest cavity.

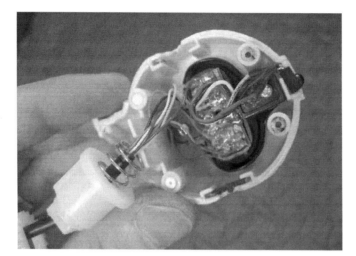

Figure 6-2. *The IR receiver in Robosapien's head is situated at the very top, so that the robot can receive IR signals equally well from the front, back, and sides.*

Once the signal reaches the controller board, it travels over the robot's internal bus and is processed by the microcontroller, which then sends the appropriate signals to the motor driver. Finally, the motor driver sends out the signals to the various motors.

> *One of the things that basically makes me nuts, you have to be able to press the buttons really fast, but you can in fact make the Robosapien walk by basically moving his shoulders at the same time.*
>
> —*Mark Tilden, February 13, 2005*

Robosapien's remote control is the device that is responsible for sending these signals to the robot (see Figure 6-3).

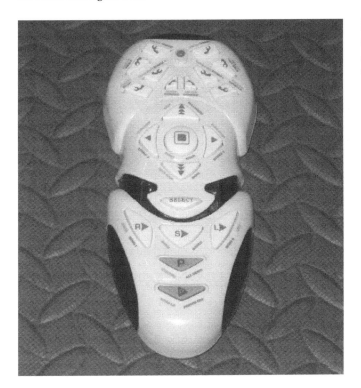

Figure 6-3. *This photo shows the standard Robosapien remote control.*

Dissecting the Remote Control

Much like the robot itself, the Robosapien remote control has seen subtle changes to its internals over the many months that Robosapien has been manufactured (see Figures 6-4 through 6-6). None of these changes, as far as I can tell, have had any impact on the operation of the remote control itself.

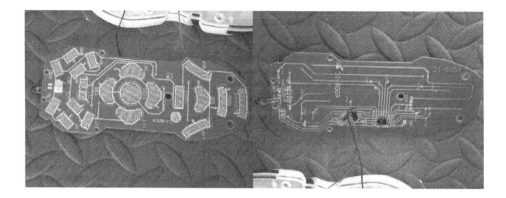

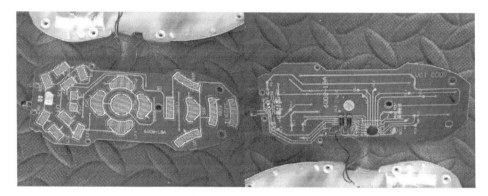

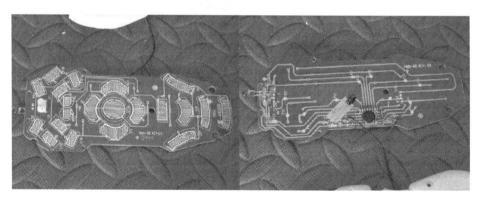

Figures 6-4 through 6-6. *In these photos of Robosapien remote controls, note the differing PCB revision numbers, and some of the differing components and PCB screening. They are arranged from top to bottom, oldest to newest.*

It is worth pointing out that, like the circuitry inside the robot, the remote control's PCB is also very clearly labeled and features gold-plated soldering pads for those who choose to modify it or just to explore it in greater detail. The external build of the remotes have remained the same, with the exception of the Sharper Image Robosapien remote, which matches the shell of the robot that it comes with (either chrome or metallic blue).

Figure 6-7. *The Sharper Image Robosapien's remote matches the finish of the robot it is packaged with. It also has a discreet Sharper Image logo above the "Program Play" key at the very bottom of the remote.*

Infrared and Robosapien: A Primer

The remote control contains 21 keys and is capable of emitting 67 known functions. It uses "consumer IR," which is the same infrared standard that electronic components such as televisions and stereos use. There are a couple of plusses and minuses to using this type of IR.

First, the bad news. The biggest problem comes when you have multiple Robosapiens. Unlike remote controls that operate on radio frequency, where you can change channels, Robosapien's IR means that if you send a command to one robot, all other Robosapiens in the vicinity will react to that command. This is great if you have several Robosapiens and want them to all do exactly the same thing. As the owner of four Robosapiens, I can tell you that the robot's dance routine performed in quadraphonic sound and motion is quite a sight. However, this eliminates the ability to use two robots independently of one another. We will look at a low-tech solution to get around this in Chapter 9.

Another minus to IR is that all types of light interfere with it to one extent or another. Direct sunlight, fluorescent lights, and electronically dimmed lights are three of the main culprits. To battle this interference, WowWee claims to have equipped Robosapien with a special visor. I don't see how this helps anything: the visor even has a square cutout in it so it never obstructs the IR receiver at the top of the robot's head (see Figures 6-8 and 6-9).

Figures 6-8 and 6-9. *Robosapien's visor is supposed to help with infrared interference, but I doubt that it does much in that regard. The robot's infrared receiver fits into the square on the top of the head.*

Another issue worth mentioning is that the IR that Robosapien uses is not compatible with the Infrared Data Association (IrDA) standard, which is used in a lot of personal digital assistant (PDA) devices and laptop computers. IrDA is a nonprofit organization that tasks itself with setting standards for IR serial computer connections. The IrDA standard, generally referred to as just "IrDa," is designed to send data at faster speeds, but at far less range than consumer IR. IrDA's maximum range is about 6 feet, and it can send data at speeds of 2,400 to 115,200kbps. In comparison, consumer IR has a range of about 30 feet. One of Robosapien's IR commands is a mere 8 bits. This is why IrDA is most often implemented in devices that need to "sync" or otherwise send large amounts of data over a short distance. Robosapien benefits from the longer range of consumer IR and simply doesn't need the large bandwidth that IrDA supplies.

Now for the good news. The fact that Robosapien uses consumer IR means that you can teach the robot's commands to a "learning" remote to control Robosapien. I set up a special Robosapien page on my Sony RM-AV3000 remote (see Figure 6-10). Note that it is unlikely that Robosapien's commands will interfere with any of your audiovisual components, but there is a small chance that your components will interfere with Robosapien! Every time I turn the volume on my NAD brand amplifier up or down, it sends Robosapien wildly spinning.

Another advantage to the IR that Robosapien uses is its portability. Using an IR dongle that attaches to a computer's universal serial bus (USB) or serial port, you can control Robosapien via a PC.

We tried for the longest time to find some stable IR platform that we were going to give away software for. But there is no standard! Sony Clie's were great because they have a full-size screen, beautiful interface, already had a programmable this, that, and the other thing, they are based on Palm 3 so there was no license involved, pretty easy to work on, then all of a sudden Sony canceled them. So the software just sort of sat there in limbo. But fortunately some hackers on the web started coming up with their own sort of things. Some people found that a universal programmer worked pretty well. But they weren't sequenceable. People came up with their own blaster technology... the fact is, there is no reason why you couldn't have some sort of programmable, sequenceable controller, recording a Robosapien move and then playing back for hours. One of the things that's cool about the mechanism, if you press something like say, the lean forward, lean backward... there's a point where you can actually press and move the motors faster than the robot does. Hidden secret #13. <Laughs> You can, through an IR port, move him faster than he can move himself. We put the IR into one of the only direct interrupts that goes into the processor. So if you are feeding that thing precise controlled IR codes, you can give him much more degree and resolution of motion than he is capable of on his own.

—Mark Tilden, February 13, 2005

We'll discuss interfacing Robosapien with computers and PDAs in a bit more detail in Chapter 11.

Figure 6-10. *I set up my Sony RM-AV3000 remote control to work with Robosapien.*

Walking Your Robosapien

Robosapien's bipedal walking is what makes—and to a certain extent breaks—the robot. It is one of the main things that make the robot seem more "human." Imagine for a minute if Robosapien only got around on wheels. How boring! The robot would have a lot less personality (one writer compared the robot's walking to that of "an infant Popeye"), and a lot less "wow" factor.

(Photo courtesy of WowWee Ltd.)

Figure 6-11. *Robosapien's bipedal walking ability is a big part of the robot's success.*

The fact that Robosapien walks on two legs is fairly amazing. Sure, toys have "walked" for over 100 years. But for some reason—perhaps it is the fact that they are generally rigid and less articulated—a wind-up walking toy skittering across a floor or a passive toy using gravity to waddle down an incline do not impress the way Robosapien does.

But walking is also Robosapien's Achilles heel (how's that for a nice analogy?). The number one complaint people seem to have with Robosapien is that it will not walk straight. And in truth, it has a tremendously hard time with that. Later in this section we will look at why this is and also some ways to improve your Robosapien's walking ability. First, let's examine some of the science and the history behind it.

Bipedalism and Robotics (and Toys!)

As we saw in Chapter 5, Robosapien's walking motion is a combination of suspension that keeps the robot's feet parallel to the ground, and motors that move its legs at the hip and its waist back and forth. Essentially, as Mark Tilden said (who would know better, right?) the robot is "an upwards walking pendulum." The first walking toys, which appeared in the nineteenth century, were not mechanical; rather, they were what is referred to as passive toys. They were designed to be pulled by a string or to walk autonomously down a slope using gravity. The first known patent for a walking toy was U.S. Patent Number 376,588, awarded in 1888 to George T. Fallis (see Figures 6-12 through 6-14).[1]

---

1. Fallis, G. *United States Patent No. 376,588: Walking Toy*, 1888.

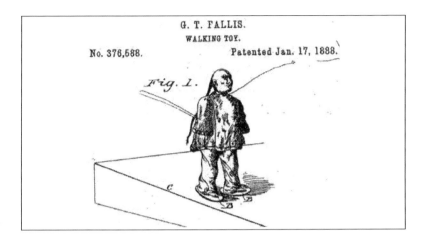

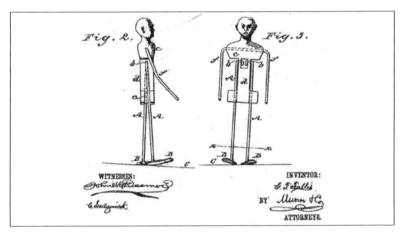

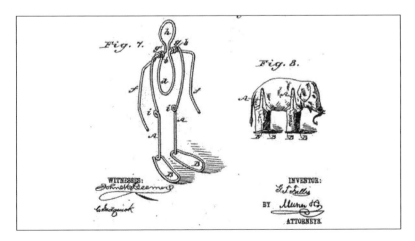

Figures 6-12 through 6-14. *Here are diagrams from George T. Fallis's 1888 patent.*

Much like that of Robosapien, Fallis's design relied on counter-swinging arms, oversized and relatively heavy feet, and a side-to-side rocking motion to give the toy its gait.

In 1912 two men, Balduin Bechstein and Paul Uhlig, expanded on Fallis's design. The result was London Patent Number 7,453.[2]

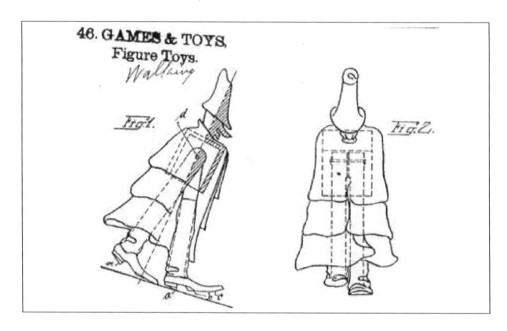

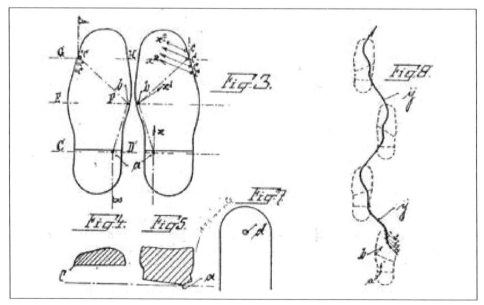

---

2.   Bechstein, B. and P. Uhlig. *London Patent No. 7453: Improvements in and relating to toys*, 1912.

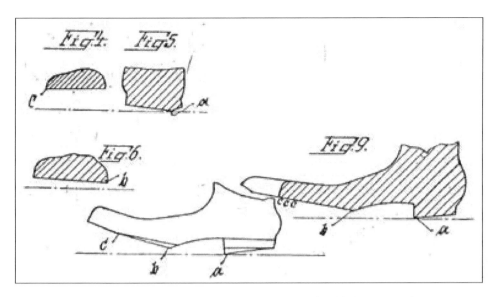

Figures 6-15 through 6-17. *Here are diagrams from Bechstein and Uhlig's 1912 London patent.*

Bechstein and Uhlig's design still had no knees, but the legs were hinged at the toy's shoulders. The design focused more on strategically placed ridges on the toy's feet, which gave it its side-to-side motion. Essentially it was a balancing act where one step fell into the next. Note in Figure 6-16 that the placement of the ridges in Bechstein and Uhlig's toy design is fairly consistent with the placement of the rubber pads on Robosapien's feet!

These patents were all but ignored by scholars studying walking gaits for the next 70 years. The trend during this time was to use motors to precisely control knee, hip, and ankle movement. The problem was that this methodology was not very energy efficient and required complex programming and motor timings to pull off. This runs parallel to the "top down" engineering applied to much of twentieth-century robotics, where the brain is designed first with the body as an afterthought.

In the late 1980s an engineer named Dr. Tad McGeer from Simon Fraser University in British Columbia drew upon some of these ideas when he developed what is known as the theory of "passive dynamic walking."[3] This theory operates under the assumption that when a person walks, they essentially let their legs swing on their own, only using slight amounts of control and power to maintain their gait. McGeer applied this concept to robotic walkers (with knees no less!) with great success. Mark Tilden cited McGeer's work in the 1994 paper he coauthored with Brosl Hasslacher while he was at Los Alamos titled "Living Machines."[4] It makes sense that Tilden, whose BEAM theories went against the grain of traditional robotics research, would be attracted by McGeer's work in passive dynamic walking, and today we can see the influence in Robosapien. See the sidebar for further study in the area of bipedal robots and walking gaits. Most of those articles are not for the weak of heart!

---

3. McGeer, T. (1990) "Passive Dynamic Walking." *International Journal of Robotics Research.* 9(2): 68–82.

4. Hasslacher, B., Tilden, M. W., "Living Machines," Robotics and Autonomous Systems: The Biology and Technology of Intelligent Autonomous Agents. Editor: L. Steels. Elsivier Publishers, Spring 1995. (LAUR-94-2636)

FURTHER READING ON THE SCIENCE BEHIND BIPEDAL ROBOTS

- "Passive Dynamic Walking," Human Power and Robotics Lab, Cornell University (lab of Andy Ruina): `http://ruina.tam.cornell.edu/hplab/pdw.html`

- Brosl Hasslacher and Mark Tilden's "Living Machines" paper: `http://cipres.cec.uchile.cl/~rbeam/living_machines.pdf`

- Tad McGeer's "Passive Dynamic Walking" paper: `http://ruina.tam.cornell.edu/research/topics/locomotion_and_robotics/ history/papers/mcgeer_1990_passive_dynamic_walking.pdf`

- Droid Logic: `http://www.droidlogic.com/`

Improving Robosapien's Walking Ability

The science and history behind bipedal walking in robots is fascinating, and I highly recommend seeking out and reading some of the articles and papers I have cited. Much of this research deals with mathematics and physics that are far beyond the scope of this book. However, while those may give you a broader understanding of *how* Robosapien walks, it is unlikely that any of them can help you if you are having a specific problem with your Robosapien.

The most obvious problem with Robosapien's walking ability is that the robot almost never seems to walk perfectly straight. It nearly always ends up veering to one side, usually to the left in my experience, and it seems that the robot is happier walking in circles than following a straight line. As I have mentioned, I have four Robosapiens, all from different manufacturing time periods, some with different motors and even different types of footpads (see Figures 2-10 and 2-11 in Chapter 2), and none of them will walk in a perfectly straight line.

In examining the way that Robosapien walks, the most important thing to understand is that a large number of variables go into every step the robot takes. Think back to Chapter 5, where you learned that Robosapien is a 1/5-scale model of its creator Mark Tilden. However, the robot's walking speed is not to scale; if that were the case, the robot would walk extremely slowly, to the point of being very uninteresting. Robosapien ends up walking roughly five times faster than the equivalent human. Now imagine for a second if you walked five times faster than normal—you'd probably have trouble walking in a straight line too!

Another variable to consider is the power Robosapien's motors are getting. Remember that the waist motor and both hip motors contribute to the robot's gait—three motors in total. Now, as we saw, each motor is also assisted by the spring suspension system that helps to accelerate and decelerate the motors. Because the robot's movement and suspension is based on dynamic resonance, the resonance actually increases the longer that the motors and suspension are operating. Also remember that the combination of the suspension and motors stores a surface charge on the batteries. Although this helps a lot in terms of power consumption, it also means that the motors are getting huge variances in power with each and every step. If you pay close attention to your Robosapien when it is walking, you can actually see that sometimes one leg or the other doesn't travel as far forwards as it should, or travels too far. These variations can at times make it almost looks as if the robot is limping. Additionally, as the batteries get older, they are less able to continue providing the same voltage that they do when they are new.

You also have to take the surface Robosapien is walking on into consideration. The robot will walk differently on thick carpet than it will on thin carpet and it will walk differently on concrete than it will on hardwood floors. All of these things have to be considered when examining Robosapien's ability to walk. Of course, the fact that Robosapien can walk at all on so many diverse surfaces is amazing in itself.

A classic example of what I call biomorphic intelligence: walk your Robosapien from linoleum, onto carpet, onto something else, right, and across anything you want. He can walk over Legos. If you know anything about the algorithms normally associated with walking robots, like zero motion point and stuff like that, all of it is based on one thing: you got a flat foot on the ground, and the ground is flat. You'll never see Asimo walking on carpet, you'll never see him walking on an irregular surface. Robosapien? Up to something as deep as 1 inch shag, go go go go go!

—*Mark Tilden, February 13, 2005*

WowWee addressed this issue through an email from their customer service department shortly after the robot was released (see the sidebar). The contents of the email have been broadly disseminated on the Internet.

THE OFFICIAL WOWWEE RESPONSE ON WALKING DIFFICULTIES

Here are the contents of an email that WowWee's customer service department sent out to anyone who wrote them to inquire about their Robosapien's difficulties walking in a straight line:

As the Robosapien walks on feet instead of wheels, he does tend to travel slightly to the left or right when walking over long distances just due to variations in floor texture. Your Robosapien was tested on smooth and carpeted surfaces before being shipped, but we understand that these do not represent everybody's floor surface. He'll walk a bit differently everywhere.

If you think your Robosapien is not walking straight, please check the following:

Be sure his arms are balanced when walking. Moving his arms left or right, or up and down will affect how straight he moves. Press SELECT - WAKEUP to reset his arms to the best straight-walking position.

Be sure he is walking on level surfaces. He has a natural tendency to walk downhill on uneven floors. He will have trouble walking straight on shag carpeting or irregular brick surfaces.

Make sure his footpads are clean and not restricted by gum, cloth, or hair. Likewise check his ankle and hip shells to make sure something is not caught in them restricting movement. Make sure he has not lost one of his footpads due to excessive play. They can usually be just squeezed back in, or mounted solidly with a touch of superglue around the base.

SIMPLE FIX

If all of these are fine, then the simple way to adjust your robot's walking ability for your floors is by putting a bit of slick masking tape over the outside back heel footpad opposite to the direction he's turning. If the turning is less severe, then apply the tape to the inside heel footpad.

After you have determined which footpad has to be slicker, a neater and more permanent solution is to rub a thin superglue film over it (taking every precaution necessary when dealing with superglue). Reapply after the first coat dries, and let dry again.

We hope this will help make the robot behave better for your particular floors.

Sincerely,

Robot Tech Support,

WowWee Ltd.

In summer 2004 I tried to do an extremely comprehensive tuning on Robosapien's walking using these guidelines. Basically I set up a "field" (see Figure 6-18) and set Robosapien walking, measuring the spot where the robot's left foot stepped off the field. During this testing I jokingly referred to my garage as my "Bipedal Robotic Testing Laboratory."

Figure 6-18. *I used this setup to try to make some sense out of Robosapien's walking patterns.*

I used clear tape to cover different variations of the rubber pads on the bottoms of the feet to see if I could properly tune the robot to walk straight. I wanted to figure out the effects of taping each of the rubber pads, as well as combinations of them, and how—or if—this steered the robot. After I had the tape placed over the footpads I would start Robosapien in the corner of the rug (where the white masking tape markings are, see Figure 6-18), set it to walking, and then measure where the robot walked off the rug.

I did at least 20 repeats of each test (over 500 walks in all), continuously keeping track of where the robot went out of bounds (see Figure 6-19).

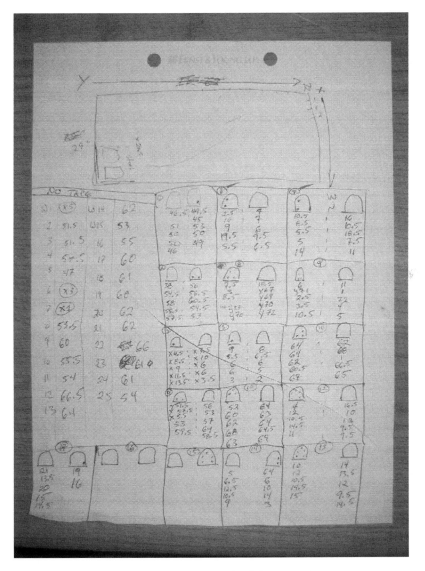

Figure 6-19. *Here's a page from the notes I took while attempting to tune Robosapien's walking ability.*

What I discovered is that there was no consistency at all to my results, not even a slight trend. One thing I noticed is that Robosapien has a "warm-up" period that affects the way its motors work. After Robosapien was walking for a while, it seemed to do a much better job than it did right after I turned it on. Another factor that I noticed is that the robot would occasionally drag one foot slightly, a sort of stumble, which ended up severely throwing off the walking "trajectory." I concluded that the way Robosapien's motors in its leg and waist work are in fact not very uniform and that floor surface also plays a factor.

Eventually, using this method I was able to get Robosapien to walk straight most of the time, but only after it had done a pretty significant amount of walking and the motors were "warmed up." Taping the footpads made practically no difference at all, in the sense that just as soon as I got one configuration working reasonably well, it would stop working and the exact opposite configuration would seem to work. When the motors were "cold," the results were not consistent at all, other than the robot always turned to the left (in my case) in hugely varying degrees. The only conclusion I came to is that Robosapien is a toy, and not meant to really be a precision walker that can complete missions on distant moons or other environments where absolute precision is necessary.

When I interviewed Mark Tilden I told him about my experiment and the results.

This is a big thing they found with all the girls doing our [quality control] tests. The robot had to sort of operate within certain performance parameters. And many robots were doing things like "oh it walks off, it's obviously defective" and then they'd test it again and be like "No, it walks straight..." I'm sorry, but the robot is based upon a law of indeterminism, which is not wholly measurable in all possible instances. You gotta remember, at any one particular instance, he only has less than half a square centimeter actually on the ground. He only has both of his footpads on for the amount of time it takes him to rock from one side to the other. And that turns out to be an extremely critical time. The robot is basically like a bottle of ketchup, if you balanced it just on the edge, before it falls over. It's hard to demonstrate on this table. If you've ever taken an empty beer can and spun it slowly so it basically pirouettes... the Robosapien operates on exactly the same principle, but doesn't fall over.

—Mark Tilden, February 13, 2005.

Mark had this advice for getting the Robosapien to walk in more of a straight line:

If you want sort of predictability, when you actually set him to walking, hold him down solidly by the shoulders, set him to walking, and lightly let him go. Because his initial conditions, that is, the very first step he takes, determines what he'll do eventually. By holding him down, you get the battery up to a certain operational level, and by doing this you get a much greater predictability.

—Mark Tilden, February 13, 2005.

I've found that this works reasonably well. Also, by utilizing Robosapien's "slow walking" capability (press forward on the remote control twice), the robot seems to do a much better job of walking in a straight line.

Summary

The bottom line is that there are simply too many variables associated with getting Robosapien to walk in a straight line. Just when you think you have it sorted out, the battery drains sufficiently to throw off your tuning, or the motors warm up and begin operating with more efficiency. Have fun with the robot and always remember that it is a toy, and a fairly amazing one at that.

CHAPTER 7

■■■

Robosapien Commands

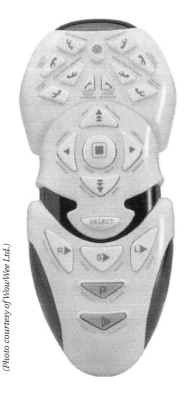

Figure 7-1. *Here's Robosapien's 21-key remote control.*

(Photo courtesy of WowWee Ltd.)

In this chapter I will cover all of Robosapien's preprogrammed commands in detail (see the sidebar "Sixty-Seven Robosapien Functions"). So grab your remote, turn on your Robosapien, and let's look at what the robot can do from a movement and functional standpoint.

Robosapien's remote control is divided into three segments: top, middle, and bottom (see Figure 7-1). The top section controls the robot's upper body, the middle controls its movement, and the bottom segment contains the buttons for programming Robosapien. The robot's commands are divided into three levels, or command modes: red, green, and orange.

SIXTY-SEVEN ROBOSAPIEN FUNCTIONS

1. Right Arm Up
2. Right Arm Down
3. Right Arm In
4. Right Arm Out
5. Tilt Body Right
6. Left Arm Up
7. Left Arm Down
8. Left Arm In
9. Left Arm Out
10. Tilt Body Left
11. Turn Right
12. Walk Forward
13. Stop
14. Turn Left
15. Walk Backward
16. Right Sensor Program
17. Sonic Sensor Program
18. Left Sensor Program
19. Master Command Program
20. Program Play
21. (SELECT) Advance to GREEN Keys
22. Right-Hand Thump
23. Right-Hand Pickup
24. Lean Backward
25. Right-Hand Throw
26. Sleep
27. Left-Hand Thump

28. Left-Hand Pickup
29. Lean Forward
30. Left-Hand Throw
31. Listen
32. Forward Step
33. Right Turn Step
34. Backward Step
35. Right Sensor Program Execute
36. Master Command Program Execute
37. Wake Up
38. Reset
39. Left Turn Step
40. (SELECT) Advance to ORANGE Keys
41. Left Sensor Program Execute
42. Sonic Sensor Program Execute
43. Right-Hand Sweep
44. High 5
45. Right-Hand Strike 1
46. Burp
47. Right-Hand Strike 2
48. Left-Hand Sweep
49. Talk Back
50. Left-Hand Strike 1
51. Whistle
52. Left-Hand Strike 2

53. Bulldozer
54. Right-Hand Strike 3
55. Oops!
56. Demo 1
57. All Demo
58. Power Off
59. Roar
60. Left-Hand Strike 3
61. (SELECT) Return to RED Command Functions
62. Demo 2
63. Dance Demo
64. <, < Combination "Right Walk Turn"
65. >, > Combination "Left Walk Turn"
66. Forward, Forward Combination "Slow Walk Forward"
67. Backward, Backward Combination "Slow Walk Backward"

Introduction to Command Modes

The remote control contains 21 keys. One key is SELECT (see Figure 7-2), which works sort of like a Shift key on a keyboard, and gives you access to two additional functions for each key. Because of the SELECT button, each button on Robosapien's remote is capable of three different commands.

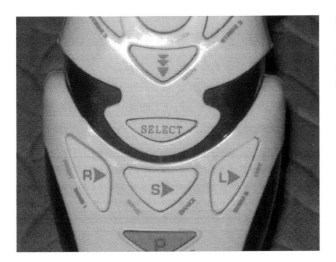

Figure 7-2. *The SELECT key makes each button on Robosapien's remote capable of three commands instead of just one.*

Robosapien's movements are divided into three command modes covering basic movement (red), combination moves (green), and "attitude" moves (orange). Press SELECT once and the remote control's indicator LED (see Figure 7-3) glows green; press it twice and the LED glows orange. Red commands—so called because the rubber remote control keys are labeled with red paint and because the indicator LED flashes red when these buttons are pressed—are accessed by simply pressing the button. The green and orange commands are painted on the remote next to the key in their corresponding color.

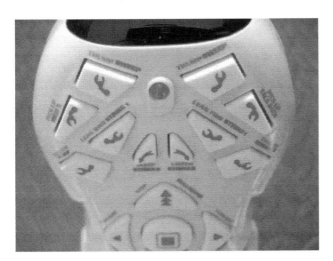

Figure 7-3. *Robosapien's remote control contains an LED that indicates which command mode the remote control is currently in.*

Using the Remote Control

Robosapien's remote is set up so that the right side of the remote controls the robot's left side, and the left side of the remote controls the robot's right side. After nine months of using Robosapien I don't give it a second thought anymore, but it was a bit confusing at first. It is particularly confusing if you are operating the robot and it is facing away from you, since in this arrangement, the left side of the remote controls the robot's right side, and vice versa. As I mentioned in Chapter 4, the robot was set up this way: it is designed to be operated facing you. So if you send your Robosapien off on a mission to thump your dog who is sleeping on the other side of the room, remember this or else you may swing with the wrong arm and miss!

When working through these commands, make sure your Robosapien is properly situated. Unless otherwise specified, prior to running these commands run the "Reset" command (SELECT then Stop). This resets Robosapien's arms and ensures that you are trying the command from the same reference point as I am.

Movement: Red Commands

The "red" commands control the Robosapien's basic movement (and programming, which we will study in detail in Part 3 of this book).

Right Arm Up

Pressing this button once raises Robosapien's right arm slightly. It raises the robot's arm until it hits the limiter switch (see Figures 7-4 and 7-5) found in Robosapien's shoulder. Pressing the Right Arm Up button a second time raises Robosapien's arm all the way up. A plastic tab at Robosapien's shoulder keeps the arm from going all the way around (see Figures 7-6 and 7-7).

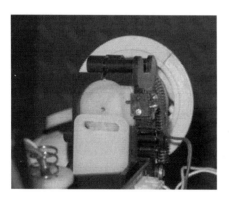

Figures 7-4 and 7-5. *Robosapien has a limiter switch in the shoulder that sends feedback when the arm is raised to a certain point. Note how when the arm is raised the actuator spins and presses in the small switch.*

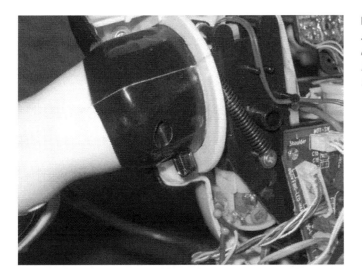

Figure 7-6. *Note the small black plastic tab directly under the screw hole in Robosapien's underarm area.*

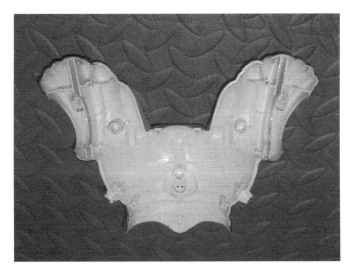

Figure 7-7. *The under-arm tabs shown in Figure 7-6 rotate into the front of the shell when the robot's arms are raised. In this photo you can see the springs (under the Phillips head screws) where the tab is stopped to keep the arm from rotating all the way around Robosapien's back.*

Right Arm Down

Starting from the "reset" position, pressing this button moves Robosapien's arm slightly down. Then the shoulder springs pretty much ease it back up into the original position. When Robosapien's arm is fully raised, the Right Arm Down button moves the robot's arm down until the limiter switch shown in Figure 7-4 is triggered. Pressing the button again will move the arm down until it either hits the front of the robot's leg or the shoulder springs stop it from moving anymore.

Right Arm In

Pressing the Right Arm In button rotates the robot's right arm at the elbow and moves Robosapien's arm in toward its body. The elbow operates much like the shoulder in the sense that there is also a limiter switch here (see Figure 7-8) that tells Robosapien when its forearm is halfway between all the way in and all the way out.

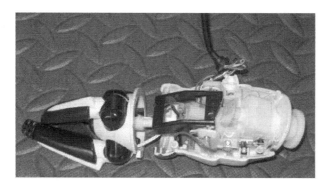

Figure 7-8. *In the bottom right of the arm, you can see the limiter switch in Robosapien's forearm.*

Right Arm Out

With the right arm in the "all the way in" position, pressing the Right Arm Out button rotates the robot's arm out away from its body until the switch seen in Figure 7-8 is triggered. Pressing it a second time rotates the arm all the way out away from the body. When this is done, as we saw in Chapter 5, a cam spins and an actuator opens Robosapien's claw. The claw remains in an open position until the arm is rotated back toward the robot's body. Figure 7-9 shows the plastic tab that resides in Robosapien's upper arm. This stops the forearm from rotating 360 degrees.

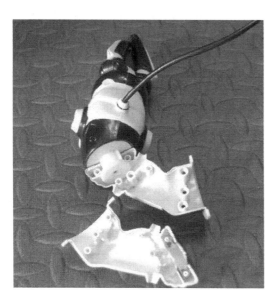

Figure 7-9. *Robosapien has a small plastic tab in its elbow that stops the arm rotation.*

Tilt Body Right

Pressing the Tilt Body Right button makes Robosapien lean over toward the right. Because of the spring suspension in the waist area, the robot quickly snaps back into a full upright position. By pressing this button repeatedly, you can "freeze" Robosapien in a leaned-over position. This is useful, as we will see, if you are trying to program your own manual pick-up routine.

▓Tip On a hard surface like a wood or tile floor or a tabletop, it is possible to get Robosapien to creep forward (well, it's more of a slow shuffle) by just pressing the Tilt Body Right and Tilt Body Left buttons in a rhythmic pattern. Try it!

Left Arm Up

Left Arm Down

Left Arm In

Left Arm Out

Tilt Body Left

For the left arm and Tilt Body Left commands above, please see the corresponding sections for the right arm and Tilt Body Right commands; everything works the same way but with the opposite buttons.

Walk Forward

Simply enough, by pressing the Walk Forward key Robosapien walks forward with its trademark swagger. The robot will continue moving forward for five minutes after the last IR signal is received. If it doesn't receive another signal within five minutes, however, it will put itself to sleep. Also, if any of its touch sensors are triggered (heel, toe, or a finger), it will stop dead in its tracks.

Slow Walk Forward

This command is accessed by pressing the Walk Forward button twice. As we saw in Chapter 6, this results in a much straighter walk. WowWee calls this "slow walk," yet in this mode Robosapien's hip motors seem to be moving twice as fast. This results in shallower steps, which slow Robosapien down somewhat, about 25 percent.

▓Note How fast is Robosapien? On hardwood floors Robosapien travels about 4 inches per second in regular walking mode. This equates to 20 feet a minute. At this speed, it would take Robosapien roughly 4 hours, 24 minutes to travel 1 mile. If I were to point Robosapien east from my house in Seattle, it would take the robot about 525 days to cross the United States and reach New York City. Assuming a 28-hour battery life, Robosapien would need 451 battery changes during the journey.

Turn Right

Pressing this button makes Robosapien shuffle back and forth and turn in place in a clockwise fashion.

Right Walk Turn

Pressing the Turn Right button twice results in what WowWee calls the "right turn walk." Basically, this shuts down Robosapien's left hip motor, so the robot walks using only the waist motor and the right hip motor. This causes it to walk in a wide clockwise circle.

Turn Left

Left Walk Turn

Walk Backward

Slow Walk Backward

For these four commands, please see their opposites discussed earlier: Turn Right, Right Walk Turn, Walk Forward, and Slow Walk Forward.

Stop

As you can very well imagine, the Stop command is very useful for a robot whose brain only has 12KB of memory. When you press this button, Robosapien immediately stops whatever it was doing and says "uhh." Pressing this button is also a quick way to bring the robot out of sleep mode or listen mode.

SELECT

This button provides access to Robosapien's green and orange command modes.

Right Sensor Program

Sonic Sensor Program

Left Sensor Program

Master Command Program

Program Play

The five buttons above provide access to Robosapien's various programming modes, which we will explore in great detail in Part 3 of this book. At the red command level, pressing these buttons enters programming input mode. The Program Play button ends programming input mode for the sonic, left, and right sensors and plays back in full whatever you have programmed into the robot's master program.

Combination Moves: Green Commands

The next command mode we are going to examine is the green command mode. These functions are accessed by tapping the SELECT button (the LED at the top of the remote will glow green indicating that you have entered the green command mode) prior to entering the desired command. Green commands are listed in green paint next to the respective remote control button. With a few exceptions, these commands are almost all combination moves, meaning that they consist of two or more of the red commands. However, they still have their own unique IR code. This is important for programming purposes, because it allows you to string together longer routines.

Right-Hand Thump

This command is a combination move consisting of Right Arm Out, Right Arm Up, Right Arm In, and Right Arm Down. It is very fluid and looks really nice. Robosapien concludes the performance with a grunt!

Right-Hand Pickup

This combination move consists of Right Arm Down, Right Arm Out (opening claw), Tilt Body Right, Right Arm In (closing claw), and Right Arm Up. It allows Robosapien to pick up and hold objects, if they are placed correctly and if they are of a shape that Robosapien can grasp. The move is designed so that Robosapien will not bang its fingers against the floor while performing it—this would not only trigger the robot's finger sensor, bringing the move to a halt (or launching a reactive program, if you have one loaded), but it would also run the risk of eventually damaging Robosapien's fingers. As such, Robosapien will not be able to pick up anything that is positioned lower than about two inches.

Another limitation on Robosapien's ability to pick up objects has to do with the placement of the object. In order for Robosapien to pick something up, it has to be in a certain position (see Figure 7-10) relative to the robot.

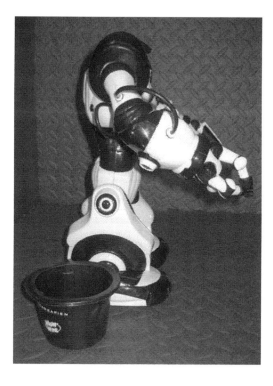

Figure 7-10. *In order for Robosapien to pick up an object, such as its cup, the object must be placed on the outside back edge of the robot's foot.*

Given the lack of precision in Robosapien's movements, this means that it is extremely difficult (but not impossible) to walk the robot over to an object and have it pick that object up. It is easier to put the robot in a standing position, and manually bring the object to Robosapien to pick up.

■Tip If you are having trouble positioning objects for Robosapien to pick up, turn off the lights! The LEDs in Robosapien's palms will reliably illuminate the "target spot" on the floor for the pickup ability.

IMPROVE ROBOSAPIEN'S GRASPING ABILITY

This is an easy hack that will improve the grasping ability of Robosapien's claws by making them more "claw-like." These will especially help Robosapien pick up softer items like socks or other laundry items, or even your little sister's favorite teddy bear.

Step One: Prepare Your Tools and Work Area

To complete this project you will need at least two anchors from Robosapien's packaging (see Chapter 4), a rotary tool (equipped with a cutoff wheel), a hobby knife, a good-quality pair of scissors, a bit of strong glue, and one of Robosapien's claws. You can do the modification to either claw, but remember that the right claw is designed to pick up bulky items and the left claw to pick up thinner items. Also note that the tips of the right claw are hard rubber, while the tips of the left claw are hard plastic. I have completely removed the claw for purposes of this guide, but I have also done this hack with the claw attached. Your choice! Shown here are all of the tools you will need to enhance Robosapien's claw:

Step Two: Shape the Claw Attachments

Start by looking over the anchors that came as part of your Robosapien's packaging. In older robots, these were made of thick, black plastic. Newer models seem to have lighter-grade plastic anchors that are much easier to work with. Pick a nice clean, undamaged anchor and pull off any glue that is still stuck to the anchor. Using the following picture as a guide, take your scissors and try to approximate the shape of the claw shown here. The top example shows a finished claw attachment; the bottom example shows one in progress.

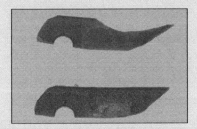

You can use a hobby knife to help you round edges and further smooth the plastic as you are shaping it. Once you have completed one claw, use it as a template to shape the second claw. They don't have to be exactly identical, but they should be close to the same length.

Step Three: Prepare Robosapien's Fingers

In this stage of the project, we will prepare Robosapien's "fingers" to accept the claw attachments. Note that we will only be putting the attachments on two of the robot's fingers. Leave the finger with the touch sensor alone. As you can see here, Robosapien has "notches" on the inside tips of its fingers on both hands.

Using these notches as a guide, take your rotary tool and grind a slot in the finger tip as shown below. This photo shows the finished slot:

Continued

You can also use the seam in the white part of the finger to help guide your cut. If your rotary tool has variable speed, make sure you set it to a low speed. The cutting wheel will cut through the plastic like a hot knife through warm butter, and using a slower speed gives you more control. You can use your hobby knife to clean up the slot as much as you like, Alternatively, if you've made the slot a little bit too wide, leave the melted plastic bits in place to help fill things in.

Step Four: Fit the Attachments

With the slots made in the fingers, it is now time to fit the claws you made. Chances are your slots are too shallow for the attachments you made in Step 2. No worries; simply shave down the attachments you made so that they fit properly in the slots or cut the finger slots deeper. This photo shows a properly placed claw attachment:

With the claw attachments properly sized and fitted to the slots, take your glue and put some on both sides of the attachment you made. If the slot you made is much too wide, you can use white glue instead to help fill in the gap (let it dry for several hours). Press the attachment into the slot and if you used the special glue let it set for a few minutes. *Et voilà*—you have finished!

These photos show this mod on both the right (top) and left (bottom) claws:

Right-Hand Throw

This combination move consists of Right Arm Up (it ignores the limiter switch), Tilt Body Left, Right Arm Down, Right Arm Out (to open the claw; it begins this movement as soon as the limiter switch is triggered on the way down), and Right Arm In. The effect, if

Robosapien is holding an object in its right hand, is to throw it, although the robot isn't capable of throwing anything very far. More or less, this move results in Robosapien bouncing the object off the ground in front of it.

Left-Hand Thump

Left-Hand Pickup

Left-Hand Throw

For these left-side commands, please see the corresponding sections on them for Robosapien's right side, above.

Sleep

This command puts Robosapien to sleep. The robot stretches, yawns, and begins snoring. When the robot is in sleep mode, all of its sensors are inactive; however, it will remember any programming you have entered if you wake it back up. If after two hours Robosapien has not been woken up, it will run the power-off routine. You can wake the robot up from sleep mode by either running the wake-up command or just pressing the Stop button.

This is the first command we have looked at where Robosapien moves both of its arms simultaneously.

Wake Up

This command runs Robosapien's wake-up routine (even if the robot is not asleep). Robosapien stretches, farts, and works out some robotic kinks in its joints by leaning forward, backward, and to both sides. The robot ends the wake-up routine in the "reset" position, wide awake and ready to receive your commands.

Figure 7-11. *Rise and shine! Robosapien performs a big stretch as part of its wake-up routine.*

Listen

Placing Robosapien in listen mode makes the eye LEDs bounce back and forth from side to side. When in this mode, Robosapien will not respond to any remote control commands except Stop, which brings the robot out of listen mode. While in listen mode, Robosapien responds to a loud noise or a tap on its shell with either its default grunt, or whatever you have programmed into the sonic sensor program. If it receives no sound input (or a Stop command from the remote control) for two hours, Robosapien will shut itself down.

Reset

This command resets Robosapien into the robot's default position.

Figure 7-12. *Here's Robosapien's "default" position, following a Reset command.*

Forward Step

This command, which makes Robosapien moves forward four steps, is particularly useful as part of program routines.

Right Turn Step

This command makes Robosapien spin in place for a short period of time. Unlike the red command Turn Right, which spins Robosapien infinitely, this command spins the robot approximately 45 degrees (on a hard surface). On a softer surface like carpet, it is not a very useful command.

Left Turn Step

See description for Right Turn Step, above.

Backward Step

Use this command to make Robosapien take four steps backward.

Lean Forward

Pressing this button makes Robosapien move four motors simultaneously! Both hips rotate forward, and the robot rotates both of its arms in.

Lean Backward

This is identical to Lean Forward, except in reverse.

Left Sensor Program Execute

Sonic Sensor Program Execute

Master Command Program Execute

Right Sensor Program Execute

These four buttons execute Robosapien's various programs, which is handy if you have forgotten what you programmed into the robot. If you have not programmed anything into Robosapien, it responds to each program execute command with a different grunt. We will look at programming Robosapien in much more detail in Part 3 of this book.

Attitude: Orange Commands

Robosapien's third and final command mode is the orange command mode. These commands are largely responsible for giving Robosapien its unique personality. These commands are accessed by hitting the SELECT button twice (the LED at the top of the remote will glow orange indicating that you have entered the orange command mode) and then hitting the appropriate button on the remote. The orange commands are listed on the remote in orange paint next to the appropriate button.

Like the green command mode, the orange commands are primarily combination moves; however, they tend to be much more complex, and are usually accompanied by some sort of vocalization in Robosapien's international caveman speech. Also, like the green commands, these have their own unique IR code, meaning for programming purposes they only count as one command.

Right-Hand Sweep

When this command is selected, Robosapien bends at the waist to the right and sweeps its right arm forward and up. Perfect for knocking things over at the dinner table.

Right-Hand Strike 1

This is the first of Robosapien's karate moves. Mark Tilden is actually a black belt in karate, although I am not completely sure about the accuracy of some of these moves. This move is an inside strike accompanied by a lusty "hoy-yah!"

Right-Hand Strike 2

Another karate move, this time an open hand strike punctuated by an enthusiastic "hi-yah!" The robot completes the move with an appreciative sounding "ooooh," seemingly quite impressed with its own martial arts prowess.

Right-Hand Strike 3

This is Robosapien's final right-side karate move, and the most threatening. The robot reaches out to the right, steps forward while twisting its arm, and then rocks side to side aggressively. If I was 14 inches tall I would run for the hills!

Left-Hand Sweep

Left-Hand Strike 1

Left-Hand Strike 2

Left-Hand Strike 3

These four commands are all the opposite of the corresponding right-side commands. Note that the international caveman speech vocalizations are slightly different.

High 5

Robosapien does its best to "fit in" with this command, reaching up for a high five and then doing its best Fonzie impression with a cool "heyyyy." Don't leave Robosapien hanging!

Figure 7-13. *"Heyyyy..."—Robosapien's "high 5" command.*

Burp

I always heard that in Germany, it was considered good manners to burp after a meal. However, Robosapien doesn't eat, and the robot is not German. So what gives? The actual burp, if you recall from Chapter 5, is the result of combining Mark Tilden, spicy Thai food, and too much Pepsi.

Talk Back

I have no clue what Robosapien is trying to say; I suppose that's one of the drawbacks of international caveman speech. It almost seems as if the robot is apologizing about something. Maybe it was the burp.

Whistle

As it turns out, Robosapien is quite the "ladies robot." Who knew? Don't overuse this command, or I guarantee you will be doing the volume control mod featured in Chapter 14 faster than you can say "but I don't want to sleep in the guest room tonight, honey." And please, no computer nerd jokes about hardware, software, or floppies!

Bulldozer

Press this command and Robosapien becomes almost unstoppable! It shuffles forward, taking 15 quick steps. It is worth pointing out that when the robot is in "bulldozer" mode, its touch sensors are disabled. This mode is perfect if something is standing in Robosapien's way, and it is heavy enough to trigger Robosapien's touch sensors, but light enough for the robot to push it forward out of the way.

Roar

This is my favorite Robosapien command. It's perfect for most occasions, especially for scaring curious cats that get too close. When this command is triggered, Robosapien raises both arms and lets out a fearsome roar. It is also useful to express anger and frustration.

Figure 7-14.
"Rrrraaawwrrrr!!!"

Oops!
And you thought the burp was bad. Honestly, I don't want to know what Mark Tilden's involvement with this sound was. Rumor has it that it was recorded the morning after the Thai food and Pepsi binge.

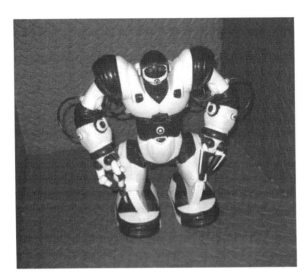

Figure 7-15. *Oops!*

Demo 1
This command sends Robosapien through all of the karate, thump, and sweep moves, and ends with a terrible roar! Well, almost... It would seem that Robosapien isn't in very good shape, since it ends the routine with an "ouch."

Demo 2
This demo mode puts Robosapien through most of the "attitude" moves. It starts with a Reset, then a Wake Up, then Bulldozer, then Roar, then Whistle, then High 5, then Talk Back, then Oops, and it finally finishes off with a Burp. Always a crowd pleaser!

Dance Demo
The Robosapien instruction manual says "he's got the moves!" Mark Tilden, talking about how Robosapien is in many ways an embodiment of himself, had this to say about the dance demo: "Robosapien... dances like a really sad, awkward, white, science guy. That's me!"[1]

In truth, Robosapien's dance routine is very impressive, even if it doesn't know "the robot" dance move.

---

1. "The Burping Robot Who Gave Mars a Miss," by David A. Smith, *The Observer*, December 5, 2004.

All Demo

This mode starts off with the Dance Demo, then Demo 1, and finishes with Demo 2. This is over two nonstop minutes of robotic goodness.

Power Off

As we learned in Chapter 5, during the Power Off routine, Robosapien utters the only word it knows in any language (unless you count "hi-yah" as a word). Robosapien leans to the right, shakes its outstretched claw, as if it was dropping a snow globe, and says "Rosebud." A fitting homage to a great American movie, and a nice piece of poetic symmetry: a toy talking about another toy.

Summary

Robosapien's 67 preprogrammed commands can be a lot of fun. But after a while, they can get a bit repetitive, and you will get tired of seeing the same old things over and over. This is where the robot's various programming modes come into play. Using the program modes expands Robosapien's repertoire, and allows you to add some of your own personality to the robot.

PART 3

Programming Your Robosapien

CHAPTER 8

■■■

Program Modes

Figure 8-1. *Robosapien has a lot of flexibility in its programming modes. You can make programming your Robosapien as simple, or as complex, as you like.*

One of the things that really sets Robosapien apart from other remote-controlled toys in its price range is its ability to be programmed with up to 84 steps. Of course, like most things with Robosapien, its programmability has some shortcomings, which we will also look at in this chapter. Probably the biggest shortcoming is the fact that Robosapien does not "remember" any programming after you have turned off the robot. In fact, WowWee acknowledges this in the manual, where it provides space to write down your favorite programs (see Figure 8-2).

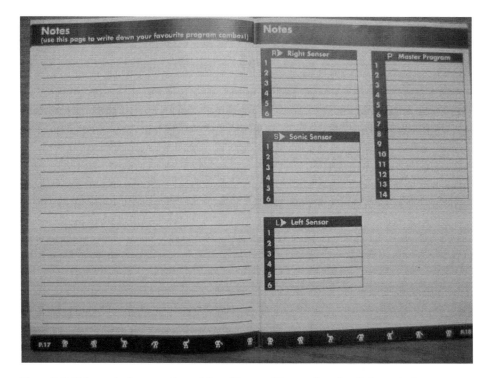

Figure 8-2. *Robosapien's manual provides a "low-tech" way of storing Robosapien's programs.*

▧**Tip** Make a programming journal. Admittedly, the fact that Robosapien has no onboard memory to store programs that you have created can be frustrating. An easy solution to this dilemma is to make your own programming journal. Either make photocopies of the of the "Notes" section provided in Robosapien's manual on pages 17 and 18 (see Figure 8-2), or use a word processing or spreadsheet program and create your own template. Put these in a binder and write down your programming steps as you explore Robosapien's capabilities. You will never lose track of a programming sequence again.

Even so, the robot's programmability is a key feature, and something that will give you hours of enjoyment if you apply some creativity and your own curiosity. Like almost all of Robosapien's features, the programming modes can be as simple or complex as you want them to be.

Robosapien has three reactive programming modes: touch sensor programming for both the left and right sides, and sonic sensor programming. By "reactive" I mean that these programming modes react to some sort of stimulus, either touch or sound. Robosapien also has a manual master command programming mode that allows you to enter in routines and play them back manually. This chapter takes a look at each of Robosapien's program modes and how to operate them (see Figure 8-3). Once we have looked at the programming modes in detail, you'll learn how to combine them to make your own complex program routines.

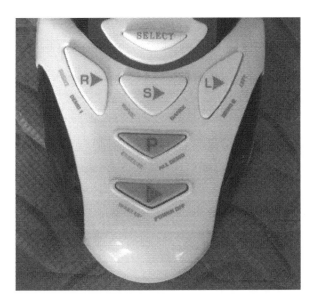

Figure 8-3. *The five buttons used to access Robosapien's various programming modes are located at the bottom of the remote control, underneath the SELECT key.*

Touch Sensor Programming

As we saw in Chapter 5 (which covered Robosapien's anatomy), the robot has six touch sensors: one on each heel, one on each toe, and one on each of the claws (see Figures 5-29 through 5-33). Using Robosapien's right and left sensor programs, you can program these to respond whenever they are touched. Note that the touch that triggers these sensors can be either a direct touch from a human or an inadvertent touch that comes as a result of walking into a wall or other object.

Despite having six touch sensors, however, Robosapien has only two programming modes that these sensors will trigger. Essentially, all of the right-side sensors are linked together, and all of the left-side sensors are linked together. This means that if you have programmed something into the left sensor program, it will be activated when any of the touch sensors on the robot's left side are activated, and the same goes for the right sensor program and the robot's right-side sensors. The effect of this is that Robosapien really has only two programmable touch sensors, although they can be triggered in multiple spots (see Figure 8-4).

Robosapien's default program for its touch sensors is a simple "ooh!" for the right-side sensors or "ouch!" for the left-side sensors. Additionally, when the touch sensors are in default mode, activating any of the robot's touch sensors has the same effect as hitting Stop on your remote control; Robosapien will stop what it is doing and wait for further commands.

The user can program up to six individual commands into Robosapien's left and right sensor programs. However, these six steps can consist of combination and attitude moves, which we learned about in Chapter 7, so these programs can end up being quite long.

Figure 8-4. *Robosapien is more likely to trigger its finger sensors than its toe sensors when it runs into things. This is probably why the finger, toe, and heel sensors were linked together on each side. Note how beat up the bottom of the author's closet door is, undoubtedly from countless robots crashing into it!*

To program Robosapien's touch sensors, follow these steps:

1. Make sure that the robot is turned on and is not in sleep mode. Usually a quick Stop command will make sure that the robot is awake and ready to be programmed.

2. With the controller in "red command mode" (i.e., the LED on the remote control is not illuminated), press either the right or the left sensor program button. The robot will give a low beep indicating that it has entered program mode. When it is in program mode, the left- or right-eye LED will blink, corresponding to the side that you are programming.

3. Now enter up to six commands, but don't take too long—after five minutes with no IR input from the remote control, even in program mode, Robosapien will put itself to sleep. In fact, you can enter the commands quite quickly, as fast as you can hit the buttons on the remote control. As you enter each command Robosapien will give a low beep to acknowledge the entry. There is no need to keep a count of how many you have entered, as Robosapien will say "ooh!" in international caveman speech after you have input the sixth command, and then play back the routine that you just entered. Note that pressing SELECT to access green and orange commands does not count as a step for purposes of programming.

4. If you would like your program to contain fewer than six commands, hit the Program Play key (the bottommost key; see Figure 8-3), and Robosapien will exit program mode with a lusty "wuah" and play back the commands that you just programmed into your robot.

So you have one of Robosapien's touch sensors programmed; now what? To play back what you have programmed, hit SELECT once and enter into green command mode (make sure the LED on the remote control is glowing green). Then press the corresponding right or left program button to play back what you have programmed into the robot. Alternatively, you can just hit one of the touch sensors for the side you have programmed to make sure that everything works.

Robosapien will "remember" what you have programmed into its touch sensors for as long as it is on, even if it puts itself to sleep. The robot erases its memory when you turn it off or when it shuts itself down automatically. If you have programmed a routine that you would like to remember, I hope you followed my earlier suggestion and entered it in your program journal!

To clear a program, you have a choice of either turning the robot off and on, which wipes its memory, or you can clear it manually. To manually clear the program, make sure you are in red command mode and press the key for the program you want to clear, as if you were entering the program mode. At this point you can either enter your new program, which will automatically overwrite what you had entered previously, or you can just hit the Program Play button to completely clear Robosapien's memory.

We look at some advanced programming examples in Chapters 9 and 10, including how to program Robosapien's touch sensors so that the robot has a low level of autonomy.

Sonic Sensor Programming

Robosapien's sonic sensor is located in the robot's chest cavity and consists of a small microphone (see Figure 5-34 in Chapter 5 and Figure 8-5).

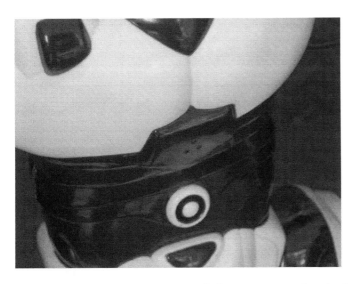

Figure 8-5. *Robosapien's sonic sensor receives audio input through a small three-hole speaker grill in the robot's chest shell, directly above the navel area.*

The sonic sensor operates in much the same way as the robot's touch sensors. Once you have programmed a routine to the sonic sensor program, as soon as the robot "hears" a loud noise—meaning as soon as the microphone picks up a signal—the robot will play back what you have programmed. Similar to the touch sensors, Robosapien's sonic sensor program can be either directly or indirectly activated. By this I mean that you can manually trigger the sonic sensor by clapping your hands or tapping on Robosapien's shell, or you can wait for an external sound to trigger the sonic sensor program. As we will see in Chapter 9, this makes Robosapien an excellent sentry!

Like the touch sensors, which are set up by default to make a noise and stop Robosapien when they are triggered (if nothing is programmed), there is also a default for the sonic sensor. When Robosapien's sonic sensor is activated but nothing is programmed, the robot will respond with a default "yeck." However, unlike the touch sensors, which are always turned on, Robosapien's sonic sensor must be activated. In order to activate the sonic sensor, you have to put Robosapien into listen mode. This is a green-level command and is accessed by hitting SELECT (the remote control LED will glow green) and then Tilt Body Left. When Robosapien is in listen mode, its eyes dart back and forth—well, they alternate between the right-eye LED and the left-eye LED and give the illusion of darting back and forth. The necessity of activating the robot's listen mode to make its sonic sensor operational is probably a good thing, as most people would get very tired of Robosapien saying "yeck" every time a sound triggers the microphone. The microphone is quite sensitive.

▨**Note** When Robosapien has entered listen mode, it will not respond to any commands from the remote control except Stop, which immediately ends listen mode. This means that you cannot walk the robot around or send it any other commands while it is listening. The noise from its motors would probably trigger the sonic sensor anyway, even if it could respond to remote control commands and move while in listen mode.

Another way that Robosapien's sonic sensor program is similar to its touch sensor programs is the fact that the sonic sensor program can hold only six steps. To program Robosapien's sonic sensor program, follow these steps:

1. Start by hitting the Stop button to make sure that the robot is turned on and not in sleep mode.

2. Next, make sure you are in red command mode on the remote control by confirming that the remote's LED is not lit, and press the Sonic Sensor Program button. Robosapien will give a low beep indicating that it is in program mode, and both of its eye LEDS will flash slowly.

3. Enter up to six commands using your remote control, and Robosapien will give a low beep to confirm that it has received each input.

4. As when programming the touch sensor programs, Robosapien will say "ooh!" after you have entered the sixth command and then replay the entire routine that you have entered. Follow the same procedure you would for the touch sensors if you would like to program the sonic sensor program with fewer than six commands: hit the Program Play key and Robosapien will exit program mode with a "wuah" and play back the commands that you just programmed into it.

5. Once you have programmed a routine into Robosapien's sonic sensor program, don't forget to activate the sensor by putting the robot into listen mode.

To test your routine, make a loud noise or tap on the outside of Robosapien's shell to activate the sonic sensor. Alternatively, you can enter into green command mode and issue the Sonic Sensor Program Execute command (press SELECT, then the Sonic Sensor Program button). If you use this method to test the sonic program, the robot does not have to be in listen mode.

Figure 8-6. *When programming Robosapien, don't forget that some of the robot's demo moves involved stepping forward to some degree or another. Robosapien thanks you in advance!*

To clear the program for the sonic sensor, turn the robot off and then back on. You can also clear it manually by pressing the Sonic Sensor Program button, as if you were programming a new routine, but instead of entering commands simply press the Program Play button. Of course, at this point you can just program in a new routine too.

I find Robosapien's sonic sensor mode to be the most useful, since it simply requires an audible sound in order to be triggered, instead of having to either manually activate a touch sensor or try to steer the robot into something so the sensor gets activated. We will look at it in more detail in Chapter 9.

Master Command Programming

Robosapien's master command programming mode is where you can really begin to see the potential of the robot's ability to be programmed. Unlike the touch sensor programs and the sonic sensor program, which can each hold up to six commands, Robosapien's master command program can hold up to 14 steps. Fourteen? But didn't I say that Robosapien can be programmed with up to 84 individual steps?

Yes, I did, and here is where the master command program gets really interesting: each one of the 14 commands can be a six-step routine that you have programmed to either of the touch sensors or the sonic sensor. Do the math: 14 multiplied by 6, and there you have your 84 steps.

■Note The master command program can link in anything that you have entered into the touch or sonic sensor programs, but not vice versa. This means that when you are programming Robosapien's touch sensor or sonic sensors, you cannot add the master command program or any of the other sensor programs as a step. If you try, Robosapien will not accept the command and give you an annoyed "yech" in international caveman speech. According to Mark Tilden, this is so that the robot can't be "tricked" into an endless program that would eventually burn out its motors or motor driver circuit.

Robosapien's default program in master command mode is a simple "uh huh" in the robot's international caveman speech. To activate it, simply press Program Play while you are in red command mode and have not programmed anything into the master command program.

Unlike the touch and sonic sensor programs, which require some sort of input to be triggered, the master command program must be started manually. Follow these steps to program your Robosapien's master command mode:

1. Press Stop once to make sure the robot is turned on and ready to be programmed. Make sure you are in red command mode (i.e., no LED lit on the remote control). It's also not a bad idea to issue the Reset command (SELECT, then Stop) to position your Robosapien in its default position.

2. While still in red command mode, press the Master Command Program button. Robosapien will perform a low beep to indicate that it is ready to receive the programming routine, and both of its eye LEDS will flash slowly. If you have been working your way through this chapter, the low beep should be a very familiar sound by now!

3. Enter up to 14 individual commands. Robosapien will confirm each command with a low beep. You can also enter sonic or touch sensor program routines as a single step; I will discuss this feature in greater detail in a bit.

4. As you saw when programming the touch and sonic sensor programs, when you have entered the final step, in this case the fourteenth, Robosapien will respond with an "ooh!" and then replay the routine you just entered. If you wish to program fewer than 14 steps, hit the Program Play key to let Robosapien know that you have finished entering commands. As with the other programming modes, the robot will reply with a "wuah!" and replay the steps you just entered.

5. To play back the master command mode program that you have entered, press the Program Play button on Robosapien's remote.

To clear the master command program, either power down Robosapien or press the Master Command Program button immediately followed by the Program Play button. As it does in the other programming modes, Robosapien will hold your routine in memory until you turn it off or it powers itself down.

▓**Note** Robosapien's All Demo command, which plays back the robot's three demo programs, lasts for 126 seconds. By programming the All Demo command as each of the 14 steps in Robosapien's master command program, you can hit Program Play and keep your robot busy for over 29 continuous minutes. I do not recommend doing this, as the inevitable heat buildup inside the robot has a good chance of either damaging the motor driver and/or having an adverse effect on one or more of Robosapien's motors. At best it will put a serious drain on the batteries.

Extend the Programming Capabilities: Combining Program Modes

We have seen how to program all of Robosapien's individual program modes: touch sensors, sonic sensors, and the master command mode. In this section I to look at some of the finer points of linking these programs together as part of the master command program.

As I mentioned earlier, any (or all) of the 14 steps in Robosapien's master command program can be a routine that you have already programmed into either the sonic sensor program or one of the touch sensor programs. When programming Robosapien's master program in this way, you can mix in the sensor programs in any order, and even mix them in with regular commands.

To program this functionality into Robosapien, you need to first program the left, right, and/or sonic reactive programs with the routines you want. Then, as you are programming the master command program, just hit the red command level sonic, left, or right sensor program button as one of your programming steps. It will only count as one of the 14 steps allowed by the master command mode.

By programming Robosapien in this way, you can store up to 84 commands in the robot's memory. However, Robosapien will pause and wait for the input required to trigger the reactive program (i.e., the touch and/or sonic input). So while you could, for instance, program Robosapien's sonic sensor to play the All Demo command six times in a row when triggered (almost 13 minutes), and then program the master command program to play the sonic program 14 times, this will not result in 177 continuous minutes of robotic goodness. Rather, when it receives a sonic input, it will play the All Demo command six times, then wait for another loud noise to trigger it again. Robosapien will repeat this pattern until all 14 steps of the master command program have completed. This type of programming is called "conditional reflex programming," and we will study it in more detail in Chapter 9.

Figure 8-7. *Robosapien loves to dance—just not for several hours with no breaks.*

It is also possible for Robosapien to simply play back the routines you have programmed into its reactive sensor programs, without waiting for touch or sound input. To do this, rather than using the red command level sonic, left, or right sensor program buttons as one of your programming steps, go into green command level as you are programming and enter the Program Execute command. This still counts as a single command for programming purposes, and using this method, it is possible (though not advisable) for Robosapien to play the All Demo command 84 times in a row without stopping. If you aren't sick of the song in the Dance Demo already, you will be if you try this.

One final note on combining program modes: When you have programmed the master command program to include reactive sonic sensor programs, there is no need to program in a "listen" command—Robosapien can detect that the next step involves the sonic sensor and goes into listen mode automatically. This holds true whether the sonic sensor is the first step in the master command mode program, the last step, or if it is mixed in with other commands. Very handy, and it saves you a programming step by not having to program in "listen."

Summary

Robosapien gives you a lot of flexibility in terms of programming, once you get acquainted with some advanced programming tips, such as conditional reflex programming and using the program execute as a single step in the master command routine. With practice, these will become second nature to you and you will become very adept at programming Robosapien and amazing your friends! Read on for more advanced examples, and some ideas that I hope will pique your curiosity to explore Robosapien's programming further on your own.

CHAPTER 9

■■■

Advanced Programming Examples

Figure 9-1. *Robosapien has a smaller brain than an iRobot Roomba robotic vacuum, but is much more programmable.*

In Chapter 8 we learned all about Robosapien's different program modes. In this chapter, I would like to look at some advanced—and some not-so-advanced—ways of implementing the different programming modes and having fun with your Robosapien.

> *Something to emphasize is the symmetry of the RS programming structure. As the sound sensor requires 0.7 of a second to stabilize following the last motor movement (the sonic sensor can only operate when all robot motors are stopped), and the sonic program button is conditionally reactive, it made sense to make the two touch subroutines on that layer conditionally reactive as well.*
>
> *—Mark Tilden, March 7, 2005*

In April 2004, just months before Robosapien's worldwide launch, much of the work on Robosapien was complete and the factories in China were already beginning their manufacturing runs. It was during this time that Mark Tilden sat down and wrote a 37-page document on the Robosapien titled "Robosapien Website Content 4-12-04." It is a great piece of writing, a primer for Robosapien in the words of its creator. Parts of this document would end up being edited and would become the manual that is included in the box with each Robosapien. Another part would become the Robosapien "Frequently Asked Questions" section found on WowWee's Robosapien website.[1] And yet another portion would become part of a series of "secrets" and programming tips that WowWee would periodically post on their website.

Since Robosapien's release, rumors have swirled about whether the robot has any "Easter eggs" or hidden secrets and, if so, the extent of these secrets. Some have said the robot has 28 hidden secrets; others have put the number at 23.

> *One of the problems with the secret functions is you don't know why the robot needs them. Half of them are designed, basically, for the safety of the robot, the other half are designed for crazy bastards looking into something.*
>
> *—Mark Tilden, February 13, 2005*

Many of the claims have been outlandish. For example, one person claimed that the robot contains another song in addition to the music played during the Dance Demo (not true, according to Tilden, "not enough memory ROM"). If you read my interview with Mark, reprinted in full in the Appendix, you will get an idea of what most of the "secrets" are. I don't think there was ever a real list or compendium of them and other than the diagnostic modes we covered in Chapter 4, I don't think any of these "secrets" were specifically planned. Rather, they are cool things about the robot—things that were put in for safety reasons, relics of features and capabilities that eventually had to be cut from the final product, and programming tips such as those presented in this chapter.

The five examples in this chapter were all originally published on WowWee's website as Robosapien "secrets" and are reprinted here with permission. With one exception, they are all originally from Mark Tilden's original "Website Content" document so I have also added some comments from this document that didn't make it into the version published on the Web. You will notice that they are not numbered sequentially; I present them in this way because so many of them are based on the theory of conditional reflex programming, and I felt it was a good idea to discuss this theory first. You also might notice some inconsistencies in command names compared to what we have been using so far in the book.

---

1. http://64.254.158.14/robosapien/more.html

The goal was to make the Robosapien as complex as you needed him to be. If you consider the RS brain, it is a fast response, easily programmed, minimal sensored, multipurpose sequencer with multiple reconfigurable input-output motor drive ability. Coupled with a 6-bit word-output (the eye LEDs) and internal timeouts, it's the best general-purpose biomorphic controller you can buy.

—Mark Tilden, March 7, 2005

Robosapien Secret #2: Conditional Reflex Programming

A "conditional reflex" is defined by WordWeb as "an acquired response that is under the control of (conditional on the occurrence of) a stimulus."[2] The term comes from the great behavioral psychologist and Nobel Prize winner Dr. Ivan Pavlov, who wrote a book called *Conditioned Reflexes*, originally published in his native Russian in 1926 and translated to English in 1927. Perhaps you have heard the phrase "Pavlov's dog"? Dr. Pavlov based his theory of conditional reflexes on experiments he did with dogs. His experiments involved conditioning dogs with a bell at their feeding time, then later discovering that they would reflexively salivate upon hearing the bell, whether or not food was present.

Fortunately, Robosapien doesn't drool (or for that matter eat, unless you count batteries). But it is possible to use concepts of conditioned reflexes to program your Robosapien. This is useful if you want to set up your Robosapien for interactive tasks and games where the robot waits for user input instead of just carrying on by itself.

Conditional programming was so people could work static reactive experiments. The multiposition arms were set so that the robot could be used to pick up and place objects on a step-high surface. When combined with programming, the robot now has stop-and-wait abilities. [Think] Rube-Goldberg applications to machine shop to a Three Stooges–like sketch routine. (Hackers Secret: by changing the shape of the internal arm cam, the robots hands can open in the middle position and close at both extremes, improving the RS's ability to pick and ace things on a step.)

—Mark Tilden, March 7, 2005

What follows is WowWee's tutorial on conditional reflex programming:[3]

---

2. http://www.wordwebonline.com/en/CONDITIONALREFLEX
3. See http://64.254.158.14/robosapien/pdf/RS_ConditionalSecret.pdf for the original of this document.

Conditional Reflex Programming

During master program P> playback, the robot can be set to "wait" for specific sensor inputs before advancing to the next program instruction. This works for all reflex sensors. When in Program Mode ("Beep, beep, beep"), you can press any of the reflex buttons (R>, S>, or L>), and that sensor will then be entered as a single "step" in the master program.

The master program can link in the reflexes, but not the other way around. If you try, the robot will give you an "Eeh!" noise, telling you that you've tried an illegal programming function. When a touch reflex is in "conditional mode" during program playback, the robot ignores all other signals except a touch on that specific sensor (or a STOP command from the remote).

The master program P is only 14 steps long, but can conditionally link in the Reflex sensors, each of which are 6 steps each for a total of 84. Each of the reflex sensors will behave just as they do normally, but only when it is their turn in the program.

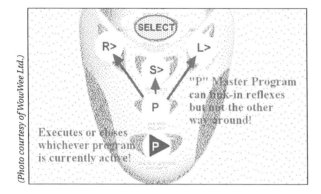

(Photo courtesy of WowWee Ltd.)

Figure 9-2. *Here's Robosapien's programming layout.*

During program playback, the robot can be set to "conditionally" wait for specific sensor inputs before advancing to the next instruction. This works for all reflex sensors, both sound and touch.

Pull My Finger

A "touch" example is the "Pull My Finger" conditional program below. After the robot's power-on wakeup has finished, enter this...

1. Press R>

2. Select – Select – OOPS

3. Select – STOP

4. Press P>

5. STOP

6. Press L>

7. Select – Select – BURP

8. Select – STOP

9. Press P>

10. STOP

11. Press P

12. Select - STOP

13. Left Forearm IN

14. Right Forearm OUT

15. Right Shoulder UP

16. Right Forearm IN

17. Right Forearm OUT

18. R>

19. Right Forearm IN

20. Left Forearm OUT

21. Left Shoulder UP

22. Left Forearm IN

23. Left Forearm OUT

24. L>

25. Select – Select – HIGHFIVE

After entering the command, the robot will automatically execute your comedy routine. Press STOP to end, or P> to see again.

This routine will wait for someone to touch it, then the robot will offer his right hand. When the victim touches the sensor finger, the robot will pull his hand away, "retort" appropriately, then reset for the left side to await another victim.

Figure 9-3. *Robosapien waits for a touch after being programmed with the "Pull My Finger" example. Note the robot's right-eye LED is lit, indicating that it is waiting for a right-side sensor input.*

Reflex Karate Chop

This reflex programming example was never published. When programmed in this way, Robosapien will karate-chop anything it walks into:

1. Press R>.

2. Press SELECT – SELECT – Strike 2.

3. Press P>.

4. Press Stop.

5. Press Walk Forward.

Robosapien walks until it receives a right-side finger, toe, or heel touch, then stops and chops. This move is best used against 12-inch toys, stacked soda cans, water bottles, Kleenex boxes, and other lightweight objects. You need to find a balance between objects that are heavy enough to trigger Robosapien's touch sensors without falling over, but still light enough that the robot can knock them down.

Robosapien Secret #1: Autonomous Wandering

This advanced programming example (and its variations, which we will explore later) takes conditional reflex programming to the next level. Using these examples you can give Robosapien a low level of autonomy, meaning that the robot will wander around on its own without any input from the user. This is an outstanding feature in a robot at Robosapien's price point; most robots capable of autonomy cost several times what Robosapien does.

In theory, this sounds great, but in practice I find that the robot tends to get "stuck" on the strangest things while wandering autonomously (see Figure 9-4).

Figure 9-4. *Robosapien gets stuck on the rough drafts of the first several chapters of this book while wandering around my office.*

Additionally, ledges and stairs can pose a serious threat to Robosapien while in any of the autonomous modes. It turns out that the reason why other robots that have autonomous modes are so much more expensive (such as the Sony Aibo) is because they have more advanced sensors, usually IR-based, that can determine distance, drop-offs such as ledges and stairs, and other hazards.

Still, in an uncluttered area, with not a lot of corners or weird angles that Robosapien can get caught on, the robot's autonomous functions are a lot of fun. Another thing worth noting is that Robosapien does the autonomy programs best on a hard floor surface. Many of these moves require quarter turns and so on, and on a carpeted floor the robot just isn't as responsive.

The autonomy mode is designed so that people could easily experiment with subsumptive reaction programming in an autonomous machine. It works in any walking mode including turning, which can be used to create a reactive soccer mode where spinning robots kick only those balls that touch their sensors.

—Mark Tilden, March 7, 2005

The following is WowWee's tutorial on autonomous walking:[4]

Autonomous Wandering

Your robot has a secret that will allow him to wander about so that when he touches something with his heels, fingers, or toes, he will perform a reflex task, then carry on. Using this, he can push boxes, play simple soccer, karate chop anything in his path, or wander around picking things up when he finds them, without you having to control him.

It works like this. Normally, his touch sensors (R> and L>) are set to default ("Ooo", and "Ouch") so when he walks into something he will just stop.

However…

If his sensor reflexes are not default, then when he touches something while walking he will execute that reflex program (different from left or right), then return to the walking mode he was in before the reflex played.

Basic Object Avoiding

For example, after power-on wakeup has finished, type in this…

1. Press R>
2. BACKWARD
3. LEFT TURN button (above the L> button)
4. Press P>
5. STOP
6. Press L>
7. BACKWARD

---

4. See http://64.254.158.14/robosapien/pdf/RS_AutonomySecret.pdf for the original of this document.

   8. RIGHT TURN button (above the R> button)

   9. Press P>

   10. STOP

   11. Select – STOP (arm reset)

   12. When finished, press FORWARD

He will now wander for five minutes, backing up and turning away every time he touches or kicks something. By giving him an occasional forearm motion by the remote he will continue to wander, otherwise he'll just go to sleep if he does not hear an IR command after five minutes.

Maze Mode

A basic backup when he hits something will definitely take him out of harm's way, but it takes time and will not allow him to get out of corners. The following reflex program allows him to do just that, and lets him quickly wander around hallways or furniture.

   1. Press R>

   2. Select – LEANFWD

   3. Select – BACKWARD

   4. Select – BACKWARD

   5. Select – LEFT TURN button (above the L> button)

   6. Select – LEANBWD

   7. Press P>

   8. Press STOP

   9. Press L>

   10. Select – LEANFWD

   11. Select – BACKWARD

   12. Select – BACKWARD

   13. RIGHT TURN button (above the R> button)

   14. Select – STOP

   15. Press P>

   16. Press STOP

   17. Press Select – STOP (arm reset)

   18. When finished, press FORWARD

The right side will hug walls, while the left will make him steer clear of them.

By changing the direction of his reflex action, he can turn into something, rather than away from it. For example, he can kick his accessory cup around quite effectively with the following program…

1. Press R>

2. Select – Right turn button (above the R> button)

3. Press P>

4. Press STOP

5. Press L>

6. BACKWARD

7. Select – Left turn button (above the L> button)

8. Press P>

9. Press STOP

10. Select – STOP (arm reset)

11. When finished, press FORWARD

Now he can kick around his accessory cup or other things with less chance of losing them. A few coins in the bottom of his cup will keep it from sliding too far ahead of him while he kicks it.

Figure 9-5. *Robosapien is actually very good at "dribbling" the accessory cup soccer-style.*

He can also push boxes (equal to or larger than a tissue box) and other things around. Anything he can touch with his sensors is fair game.

1. Press R>

2. Select – RIGHT TURN button (above the R> button)

3. Select – LEANFWD

4. FORWARD

5. Select – LEANBWD

6. BACKWARD

7. LEFT TURN button (above the L> button)

8. Press STOP

9. Press L>

10. Select – LEANBWD

11. Select – Select - BULLDOZER

12. Select – BACKWARD

13. Select – BACKWARD

14. RIGHT TURN button (above the R> button)

15. Select – STOP

16. Press STOP

17. Press Select – STOP (arm reset)

18. When finished, press FORWARD

He will now push boxes and other objects about in two different ways.

Figure 9-6. *Mini Robosapien's box makes an excellent accessory for box pushing.*

Wandering Ninja

Take a swing, at everything. A cardboard paper towel tube will fit tightly in his right hand allowing him to thrash things safely but with amusing results.

1. Press R>

2. Select – RIGHT STRIKE 1

3. Select – BACKWARD

4. Select – FORWARD

5. Select – Select – ROAR

6. BACKWARD

7. Left turn button (above the L> button)

8. Press STOP

9. Press L>

10. Select – LEFT STRIKE3

11. Select – RIGHT STRIKE3

12. Select – BACKWARD

13. Select – BACKWARD

14. Select – Right turn button (above the R> button)

15. Select – STOP

16. Press P>

17. Press STOP

18. Press Select – STOP (arm reset)

19. When finished, press Forward

Sleeping pets beware.

Figure 9-7. *My dog, Duce, never saw it coming.*

Find and Grab Mode

Set him to pick stuff up and throw it around. His accessory cup works well.

1. Press R>

2. Right shoulder up

3. Right turn button (above the R> button)

4. Select – RIGHT PICKUP

5. Select – Select - BULLDOZER

6. Select – RIGHT THROW

7. Select – STOP

8. Press STOP

9. Press L>

10. Left shoulder up

11. Left turn button (above the L> button)

12. Select – LEFT PICKUP

13. Select – BACKWARD

14. Select – LEFT THUMP

15. Select – STOP

16. Press STOP

17. Press LEFT TURN, LEFT TURN

He will now walk in circles looking for objects, pick them up, and toss them. Has also been known to work with small laundry articles.

Figure 9-8. *Getting Robosapien to actually "find and grab" was akin to finding a needle in a haystack. Look! The robot missed the cup by mere millimeters again!*

Party Mode

For a more sophisticated example that will entertain people at a party, type in this...

1. Press R>

2. Select – Select – HIGH5

3. Select – BACKWARD

4. Select – Select - TALKBACK

5. Select – BACKWARD

6. Select – RIGHT TURN button (above the R> button)

7. Select – STOP

8. Press STOP

9. Press L>

10. Select – BACKWARD

11. Select – Select - DANCE

12. Select – BACKWARD

13. LEFT TURN (above the L> button)

14. Select – Select - WHISTLE

15. Select – STOP

16. Press STOP

17. Press FORWARDS

He will now entertain any that touch him with a hello and grunts, or a song, dance and a whistle, before backing up and turning away. He will also do the same thing if left in a spin-in-place mode or walk turn mode by pressing either turn button twice.

Five-Minute Burp-Fart Fest

For a less sophisticated example that will entertain people at a party, type in this...

1. Press R>

2. Select – Select - BURP

3. Press STOP

4. Press L>

5. Select – Select – OOPS

6. Press STOP

7. Press BACKWARD

As soon as he hits a wall, he will randomly "entertain" for 5 minutes.

The time it takes to run a reflex program does not take away from the time taken for wandering. If you put a LISTEN command in the touch reflexes, then the robot will wait for up to two hours for a sound letting it walk again. In a noisy place like a small room with a loud TV or stereo, the following program can possibly keep your robot wandering for many hours.

1. Press R>

2. BACKWARD

3. Select – LISTEN

4. Left turn button (above the L> button)

5. Select – LISTEN

6. Select – STOP

7. Select – LISTEN

8. Press STOP

9. Press L>

10. BACKWARD

11. Select – LISTEN

12. Right turn button (above the R> button)

13. Select – LISTEN

14. Select – STOP

15. Select – LISTEN

16. Press STOP

17. Press Select – STOP (arm reset)

18. When finished, press FORWARD

The right side will hug walls, while the left will make him steer clear of them. Many such combinations are possible. Variations are encouraged. Have fun.

Notes

- While wandering, your Robosapien will continue wandering for 5 minutes unless he gets a refresh signal from his IR controller (press a forearm action button quickly every few minutes, for example).

- If you do want him to stop walking after playing a touch reflex, put a STOP command at the end of your reflex program. He will execute any touch reflex, but then completely stop moving after he hits this command in your program.

- He does not respond to touch sensors when he's executing a touch reflex, but he does respond to any LISTEN sonic triggers in your reflex program.

- This mode works for all walking modes of the robot, not just forward. He can walk in large circles at night and scan whatever he touches with his flashlight hands, for example, using WALK-TURN (Select – TURN).

- Select – STOP puts his arms into the best position for sensing objects in front of him. If his forearms are inwards, his shoulders will get caught on walls. If out too far, then he will trigger on anything his fingertips touch.

- Press R> - P> and L> - P> to clear his touch-reflex sensors to default.

Robosapien Secret #11: Automatic Robot Sentry

Up to this point, all of the advanced programming examples we have looked at have utilized Robosapien's touch sensors. In this example, we will leave the touch sensors alone and use the robot's sonic sensor. Robosapien makes an excellent sentry, since this task doesn't require any precise movements. In fact, it is really a nice use of the robot, be it as a guard for your room, your office, what have you. I made excellent use of it last Halloween, when trick-or-treaters came to the front door and triggered the robot every time.

Figure 9-9. *Robosapien excels as a sentry. Combined with the wireless camera hack in Chapter 15, the robot is a decent security tool.*

The following is WowWee's guide for setting up your robot as a sentry:[5]

Automatic Robot Sentry

In "Listen" mode, your Robosapien will wait for over 2 hours before getting bored and shutting down. You can "link in" the listen modes up to 14 times using the regular P program; the following is an example of how to make your robot "guard" a hallway for hours and always stay in place.

1. Press S>

2. Select – Select – Left Turn (Strike3 on the right controller side)

3. Select – Listen

4. Select – Select – Stop (Roar)

5. Select – Listen

6. Select – Select – Right Turn (Strike3 on the left controller side)

7. Select – Backwards

8. STOP

9. Press P

10. Press S> 14 times or until the robot says "Ooo! Uh-Huh!"

Robosapien will now enter a mode where he will wait against a wall and strike anything that passes by, occasionally stepping back into place against the wall. He will do this 42 times before finally stopping. Press STOP to deactivate. Press P> to play again.

Change the S> reflex to the following for more in-your-face action:

1. Press S>

2. Select – Select – Stop (Roar)

3. Select – Forwards

4. Select – Forwards

5. Select – Select – Left Turn (Strike3 on the right controller side)

6. Select – Select – Right Turn (Strike3 on the left controller side)

7. Backwards

8. STOP

9. P>

Robosapien will now awaken, come forward and attack, then return to his place at the wall.

Many such programs are possible.

Have fun!

---

5. See http://64.254.158.14/robosapien/pdf/RSSentrySecret_117_04.pdf for the original of this document.

Robosapien Program Feature #18: Song and Dance Programming

OK, so maybe you should take Robosapien off security detail and leave that up to your dogs and/or alarm system. Robosapien is, after all, an entertainment robot, so it makes perfect sense that the robot is an excellent entertainer. The programming examples set forth in this section provide some great ideas on how to set your Robosapien up to "rap" and even dance. Sammy Davis Jr. had nothing on Robosapien!

Work through these examples a few times and you will begin to get the hang of how "rhythmic" Robosapien's international caveman speech and movements can be. With a little practice, you will be able to come up with examples that are much better than the demos included in Robosapien's internal memory.

The following combines WowWee's guide for song and dance programming and some of Mark Tilden's more advanced rapping techniques:[6]

Song and Dance Programming

Your Robosapien has some limited singing and dancing skills. Power on your robot, wait until he finishes his wakeup, and then enter the following…

1. Press P

2. Select – Select – TALKBACK

3. Select – R>

4. Select – S>

5. Select – L>

6. Select – R>

7. Select – S>

8. Select – L>

9. Select – Select – TALKBACK

10. Select – R>

11. Select – L>

12. Select – R>

13. Select – L>

14. Select – R>

15. Select – Select – BURP

The robot will automatically execute an amusing short "rap" song. Press STOP to end, press P> to play again.

---

6. See http://64.254.158.14/robosapien/pdf/RS_RapSongProgram.pdf for the original of this document.

The default reaction sounds under the R>, S>, and L> can be reconfigured a variety of ways with the Robosapien's other personality noises. For example, enter the following:

1. Press P

2. Select – L>

3. Select – L>

4. Select – S>

5. Select – S>

6. Select – S>

7. Select – L>

8. Select – L>

9. Select – S>

10. Select – S>

11. Select – S>

12. Select – R>

13. Select – R>

14. Select – L>

15. Select – Select – STOP

The robot will automatically sing another "song." Press STOP to end, press P> to play again.

Dancing

Once you have a beat you like, you can now program the reflexes with motions that will allow the robot to dance.

With the last program still under the master program P, enter the following:

1. Press R>

2. Right Shoulder UP

3. Select – LEANFWD

4. Left Shoulder UP

5. Select – LEANBWD

6. Right Shoulder DOWN

7. Left Shoulder DOWN

Press STOP, or wait for the routine to finish, then enter the following...

1. Press S>

2. Select – LEANBWD

3. Select – LEANFWD

4. Select – LEANBWD

5. Select – LEANFWD

6. Left Forearm OUT

7. Right Forearm OUT

Press STOP, or wait for the routine to finish, then enter the following...

1. Press L>

2. Select – LEANFWD

3. Tilt RIGHT

4. Select – LEANBWD

5. Tilt LEFT

6. Right Forearm OUT

7. Left Forearm OUT

Press STOP, or wait for the routine to finish, then press P>. The robot will now go through a 40 second long dance routine. To hear your original song again without erasing your reflex dance moves, press

- Select – P

If you want to change the beat or length, you can change your song without affecting your dance moves by pressing P and entering a new song (like the first song above for example).

In this way, you can easily enter a basic beat and edit dance moves in any pattern. Add LISTEN commands through your reflex steps to make the robot dance in beat to loud songs from your stereo. Add walk and turn commands to make him cover some dance-floor territory.

Many combinations are possible. Variations are encouraged.

Here is another example of what you can accomplish by changing what is programmed into the reflexes, resulting in a much longer song and dance routine. Start by programming in one of the original "songs" from above:

1. Press P

2. Select – L>

3. Select – L>

4. Select – S>

5. Select – S>

6. Select – S>

7. Select – L>

8. Select – L>

9. Select – S>

10. Select – S>

11. Select – S>

12. Select – R>

13. Select – R>

14. Select – L>

15. Select – Select – STOP

Now it's time to program the reflex sensors:

1. Press R>

2. STOP

3. STOP

4. Tilt LEFT

5. STOP

6. STOP

7. Tilt RIGHT

8. STOP

9. Press S>

10. STOP

11. Select – LEANFWD

12. Select – LEANBWD

13. STOP

14. Select – LEANFWD

15. Select – LEANBWD

16. STOP

17. Press L>

18. STOP

19. STOP

20. Select – Select – RIGHT SWEEP

21. STOP

22. STOP

23. Select – Select – LEFT SWEEP

24. STOP

Press P> to play back this advanced song and dance routine.

Robosapien Secret #20: Ninja Bots

This guide was the last to appear on the WowWee website, and was not included in Mark Tilden's original "Website Content" document. Among the serious Robosapien hacking community online, this guide drew some grumblings. The idea of using old toilet paper tubes to "mod" Robosapien was abhorrent to some of the people doing some of the advanced hacks, and also to those who had been anxiously awaiting the release of the latest "Easter eggs." It seems like very few actually got the humor. In this section I have used all of the original pictures Mark Tilden took for the WowWee guide.[7]

Ninja Bots

Bought two Robosapiens but can't get them to fight because the controllers are on the same frequency? Here's a simple modification using household materials that allows your robot to fight, with a friend or against another robot in automatic mode.

- Take a standard toilet-roll tube and cut it down the middle.
- Squeeze it onto Robosapien's head as shown below.

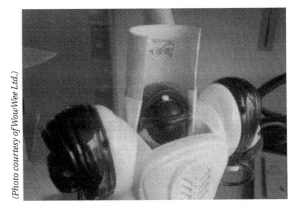

(Photo courtesy of WowWee Ltd.)

Figure 9-10. *In the finished "mod," note the Chinese toilet paper tube!*

---

7. See http://64.254.158.14/robosapien/pdf/RSFightingSecret_207_04.pdf for the original of this document.

The robot will now only be controllable from behind. Two or more robots can be controlled this way without interfering with each other.

■**Note** Be sure to always point the remote directly at the back Robosapien's head when playing.

ADDITIONAL:

- The right hand is designed to tightly hold on to a standard paper-roll tube without dropping it. When used in conjunction with Robosapien's fighting moves, it makes a very satisfying "bop" noise when it connects.

Figure 9-11. *Here's the front view.*

(Photo courtesy of WowWee Ltd.)

- Extend the range of your robot's reception by putting tinfoil around the inside of the tube.

- Print out and put a face on your tube with team names or expressions.

Figure 9-12. *Here is the sample Robosapien "face" included in the document.*

(Photo courtesy of WowWee Ltd.)

- An example "face" is shown in Figure 9-12.

- Use the same trick to make your Robosapien an automatic sentry who will attack any incoming aggressor (like another robot), but won't listen to your remote from the front.

With the tube in place, and standing behind your sentry, type in the following…

1. Press S>

2. Select – forward

3. Select – Select – STRIKE3 (left)

4. Select – Select – STRIKE3 (right)

5. Select – Select – STOP

6. Select – backwards

7. P>

8. STOP

9. P

10. Press S> 14 times or until Robosapien says "Ooo, Uh Huh!"

The robot will now attack anything that touches it for up to 14 times. Press STOP to end, press P> to play again.

Try programming S> with different fight move combinations to improve your robot's skills and tactics. You can program R> and L> also.

Have fun.

(Photo courtesy of WowWee Ltd.)

Figure 9-13. *Robosapien looks like it is ready to attack something on Mark Tilden's desk.*

(Photo courtesy of WowWee Ltd.)

Figure 9-14. *This picture is interesting if only to see a part of Tilden's work area.*

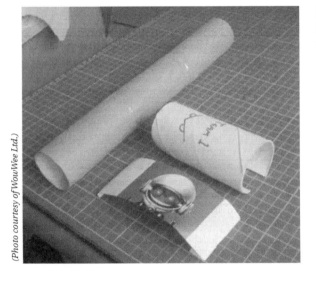

(Photo courtesy of WowWee Ltd.)

Figure 9-15. *The first rule of writing a good "how to" guide is to lay out your materials!*

Summary

It amazes me that there is this much functionality out of what amounts to only four programming modes and three sensors. Robosapien's ability to be programmed, and the complexity with which you can program the robot, definitely seems to be one feature of the robot that a lot of people have not yet explored. In the next chapter, we look at some of the online Robosapien resources, as well as some adaptations of the programming examples we have looked at in this chapter.

CHAPTER 10

■ ■ ■

Online Robosapien Resources and Community Submitted Programs

Figure 10-1. *This "community" of Robosapiens doesn't have online access.*

In Chapters 8 and 9 we learned how to program Robosapien and we also looked at some of Mark Tilden's programming ideas. In this chapter, I take a look at the "Robosapien community" that has developed on the Internet, and some of the programming ideas that people have adapted and begun to share online.

As I sit and write this almost a year after Robosapien's worldwide release, I am a little surprised that there hasn't been a virtual explosion of online activity relating to Robosapien. Don't get me wrong; the community is robust and thriving. But with an estimated two million Robosapiens in circulation, I'm just surprised that there isn't more volume.

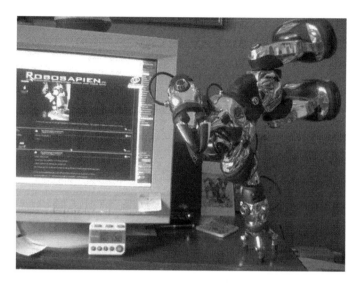

Figure 10-2. *One of my Robosapiens learns a new trick from the Robosapien.tk website.*

I believe that a big part of the problem is that there is no way to easily store and share program routines. My suggestion to start your own programming journal is a good one. But if you want to share your programs with others online, you still have to go get your journal, sit down at a computer, and type them in. Another part of the problem is (I hope) why you are reading this book: people get their Robosapiens and fail to explore all of the robot's capabilities. Let's face it; it's a great robot, and a fantastic toy, but how many people really make the most of Robosapien's abilities? Or are even aware that a lot of them are there?

I think we would see a lot more online interactivity if there was a way to transfer, store, and share Robosapien program routines.

> *One of the things people always say is "Oh, when are you giving us a robot with a USB port?" Not until next year, sorry. The brain for the Robosapien costs us 70 American cents. USB, just the interface, is a buck seventy. Just the ability to add USB, not even including all the software, is more than twice the cost of the entire brains of the Robosapien.*
>
> *—Mark Tilden, February 13, 2005*

In a perfect world, Robosapien would come with a cable that plugs into your computer's USB port. By connecting the robot to your computer, you would launch a software application that would give you access to all of Robosapien's memory and programming modes. You could upload and download program routines, edit and save routines offline, and share the files with other Robosapien enthusiasts via the Internet. Since I am dreaming, let's also give Robosapien rechargeable batteries that would charge via the USB connection.

A lot of people kept on saying, "Why didn't you make it rechargeable? You're that cheap?"
<Laughs>

—*Mark Tilden, February 13, 2005*

Unfortunately, that sort of thing would add a lot of complexity to the robot, and probably make it cost prohibitive. Not only would Robosapien need a bigger brain, more memory, and internal software to handle the program routine files, but an application would have to be developed that would run on the Robosapien owner's computer. This would add a whole new level of customer support, compatibility issues, and so forth. WowWee's decision makes a lot of sense. But I can dream, can't I? As we will see in Chapter 11 (which covers PC and PDA control of Robosapien), my dream can be a reality if you are willing to obtain some additional hardware and software—which, like anything, comes at a price.

So for now the Robosapien online community remains low tech, but no less vibrant and interesting.

The Robosapien Online Community

In this section we look at some of the Robosapien resources available on the Internet.

Online Resources and Forums

Five of the best websites are described in this section. For complete URLs, please see the sidebar.

ONLINE ROBOSAPIEN RESOURCES QUICK LINKS

- http://robosapienonline.com/

- http:/www.robosapien.tk (also http://home.planet.nl/~pruim006/)

- http://www.i-cybie.net/forums/forum-view.asp?forumid=18

- http://www.therobosapien.com/

- http://www.gadgetmadness.com/archives/20040830-ultimate_review_robosapien_
  programmable_toy_battle_robot_from_thinkgeek.php

Robosapienonline.com

This is WowWee's official Robosapien website. It hasn't been updated in many months. It is still a great resource, though, if you are in the market for a Robosapien (or have recently purchased one) and want to learn more about the robot's basic features. One of the best things it has going for it is the Robosapien FAQ (see the sidebar).

ROBOSAPIEN FAQ[1]

Can I operate two Robosapiens at the same time?

Robosapien is not a radio control product. It works on infrared light waves (just like a television controller)—so there is only one option for controlling him. Therefore, if multiple Robosapiens are near each other, the signal from one controller could activate all of them. The receiving range is approximately 20 feet, which means that for truly individual play, multiple Robosapiens would need to be 30 feet apart.

Where is Robosapien's power switch?

It's located just below his right shoulder blade. Press in to power him on; if he has previously shut down automatically, you will need to press the button twice (out and back in). Robosapien will respond with his "Wake Up" routine.

Why does Robosapien seem to operate in the opposite direction from the controller?

The remote is set up so it's like you are holding the Robot in your hands. This turned out to be quite natural for most people, like you are directing an actor on a stage.

The left side of the controller always operates Robosapien's right side; the right side of the controller always operates his left side. So, if you are standing in front of him, the controller buttons line up directly to the side which will move; if you are standing behind him, the controller buttons line up vertically to the side which will move.

Try working the remote upside down if that is more comfortable for you.

Why won't Robosapien respond to the controller?

Robosapien is "blinded" by sunlight or electronically dimmed lighting.
Try lowering his visor, or remove him from the interference source.
Robosapien could be in LISTEN, REACTION, or SLEEP mode. Press RESET to get his attention.
Robosapien can't "see" the remote signals. Always point the remote control at his head.
Robosapien is too far away. Move closer to him.

Robosapien's head has turned to the right; I have not been able to re-center it.

Do you have any suggestions for repair?

Lower his arms and twist his head all the way to the left, until you hear a "click".

What if Robosapien is not walking well?

Try pressing STEP again for the sure-footed "slow walk" mode, or, if stopped, press STEP-STEP.
Only operate Robosapien on a hard floor or low-pile carpet. He has trouble walking on deep shag, grass, sand, or cloth.
Make sure there are no obstructions, wires, or string limiting Robosapien's motion.
Maybe his batteries need changing.

---

1. FAQ reprinted with permission of WowWee; see http://64.254.158.14/robosapien/more.html.

Why can't Robosapien pick up low objects from the floor?

Robosapien will damage his fingers if he bends down too low. He can only pick up items that are greater than approximately 2" high, such as paper cups, socks in a ball, bent business cards, crumpled paper, etc.

If you put Robosapien in a dimly lit environment, his palm lights will show you where his two pick-up "sweet spots" are located. When you do a pick-up command, he can very reliably pick things up which are placed in these spots located next to his ankles.

Why does Robosapien have two types of hands?

His right hand is for round or bulky things like dolls, cardboard tubes, etc.

His left hand is for thin things like pencils, napkins, dollar bills, business cards, and paper. Use his hands to lift things, hold and carry them, and even put them on steps or in laundry bags, for example.

What if Robosapien doesn't walk while he is carrying something?

If Robosapien is holding something that will flop against his sensor (like a long ruler), the sensor may false trigger and he may stop walking. If that is the case, press SELECT-FORWARD or SELECT-SELECT-FORWARD (bulldozer action) and Robosapien will walk.

Robosapien stops whenever he's stuck against a wall. How do I get him away from it?

Press SELECT-FORWARD or SELECT-BACKWARD to get him away from objects that keep tripping his sensors. You can also press SELECT-SELECT-BULLDOZER to make Robosapien kick his way through things in front of him.

Why can't Robosapien fast walk with his arms all the way up?

On some surfaces your robot cannot walk well while his hands are all the way up or while he's carrying something heavy. However, just press STEP again (or, if stopped, press STEP-STEP) and he'll walk fine.

How do I make Robosapien walk straight when his arms are not balanced?

By pressing the STEP button again, or, if stopped, by pressing STEP-STEP. This puts him into the much more stable "slow-walk" mode. Slow-walk allows Robosapien to push, pull, or kick his way out of many situations. If he continues to stop, use the "SELECT-SELECT-BULLDOZER" mode; he will push through any obstacle he can.

How can I make Robosapien quieter?

Cover the speaker grill on his back with tape.

Is there a way to make Robosapien remember his programming?

No, but in SLEEP mode he will remember his programming for up to 2 hours before he completely turns himself off and forgets everything. In SLEEP mode, he will ignore all touch sensors until you wake him up with your remote control.

Continued

During wake-up, I hear Robosapien making strange humming sounds.

Is this something to worry about?

No, it is part of the normal wake-up protocol.

Why does Robosapien have lights in his palms?

So he can look cool patrolling around at night, of course. Several command functions cause his palm lights to come on.

Can my Robosapien do housework?

Sort of. He can push lightweight boxes, kick toys against a wall, retrieve handkerchiefs and pile them on steps, pick up light laundry and throw it in bags, among other housekeeping chores.

Why didn't Robosapien start after I put in fresh batteries?

Make sure he is not lying down when you power him up or he'll think he's stuck and won't power on. Always power on Robosapien standing upright in a clear, open space.
Make certain that the battery-pull straps inside his feet are not caught between the batteries and contacts.
Check that all batteries are placed in the correct direction in the battery housings.

What happens if I forget to turn off Robosapien?

If you ignore him, Robosapien will stop and go to sleep after 5 minutes. If he gets no remote signal for 2 hours, he will shut off completely (even if the power button is still in the "on" position).

What are the 4 programming modes?

1. Master Program (P) General control programs
2. Right Sensor Program (R>) Triggered by touch to finger, toe or heel sensor on right side
3. Left Sensor Program (L>) Triggered by touch to finger, toe or heel sensor on left side
4. Sonic Sensor Program (S>) Triggered by a sharp sound or tap on his body.

What is the function of the wires that stick out of Robosapien's arms?

The wires carry power and sensor information to and from his hands.
They also act as soft bumpers if Robosapien gets too close to a wall.

Robosapien.tk

The "1st Unofficial Robosapien Hacks and Mods Site" was among the first independent Robosapien webpages on the Internet. Dutch Robosapien enthusiast Bas Pruimboom runs the site and forums purely as a hobby, but has ended up creating the best resource anywhere for Robosapien news, hacks, and questions. I should perhaps say "the best resource anywhere *not including this book*."

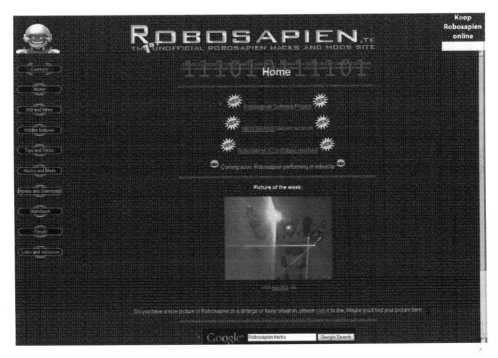

Figure 10-3. *Here's the front page of the Robosapien.tk website.*

Robosapien.tk features regularly updated content (including some directly from Mark Tilden) on tips and tricks, hacks, and even multimedia downloads. But besides all that, the site features very active forums where Robosapien users can come to show off their latest hacks, ask questions, discuss Robosapien news, or just chat with other Robosapien enthusiasts. Some of the ongoing discussions on complicated Robosapien hacking projects and detailed "how-to's" are outstanding.

Figure 10-4. *The Robosapien.tk forum index offers something for everyone!*

I-Cybie and Robotic Pet Forum

The I-Cybie is a robotic dog, sort of a cheap version of the Sony Aibo (see Figure 10-5).

Figure 10-5. *The I-Cybie robotic dog contains over 1,400 parts.*

It was originally released in 2001. Considerably more complicated than Robosapien, the $200 I-Cybie contains over 1,400 parts and more than 90 feet of wire. One thing is for sure, the guys who hack, program, and mod I-Cybies definitely know what they are talking about when it comes to toy hacking and, in most cases, robotics. The Robosapien forum is a bit slow, but some of the regular participants have done some really cool things with Robosapien. It's definitely worth checking out, and be sure to visit the photo album section, where users post pictures of their hacks and mods on I-Cybies, Robosapiens, and a veritable menagerie of other robots.

Therobosapien.com

This website is pretty nice from a navigational standpoint, but you won't find much here that you can't find on either the WowWee or Robosapien.tk website. Although the forums are billed as the "Official Robosapien Forums," I don't think WowWee has any relationship with the website or forums. It offers decent forums, but they aren't very active; however, the programming forum has some ideas for neat routines that I haven't seen anywhere else.

GadgetMadness.com "Ultimate Robosapien Review"

GadgetMadness.com offers reviews and news on lots of different gadgets, but I felt they deserved a mention here for their incredible "Ultimate Robosapien Review" published in August 2004. As in all of their reviews, they tested Robosapien to the limit and in a wide variety of interesting circumstances. They also have a fantastic interview on their site with Mark Tilden that showcases their trademark sense of humor.

Personal Hacker Sites and Blogs

Personal "blogs," or web logs, chronicling Robosapien and people's Robosapien projects spring up on the Web all of the time, and often disappear as quickly as they are created. These are some that have been around for a while and which I expect to stay around for some time. Since we will look at many of these in greater detail in Chapter 15, when I cover advanced Robosapien hacks, here I just provide a list of some of my favorites:

- RobosapienPet's Robosapien page: `http://aibohack.com/robosap/index.html`

- Robosapien 1: `http://www.robosapien1.com/`

- Mirobosapiens (Spanish): `http://www.mirobosapiens.com/pagina/default.asp`

- Mark Craig's Robosapien Pages: `http://homepages.strath.ac.uk/~lau01246/robot/robos.shtml`

- Knitsu's Robosapien Pages: `http://www.geocities.com/chancebrown2003/index.html`

- RoboHackers.com: `http://www.robohackers.com/`

- My own (winning) *Servo* magazine "Hack-a-Sapien" contest entry: `http://home.comcast.net/~robosapien/servomain.htm`

- Olivier Lanvin's Robosapien Pages (French): `http://pageperso.aol.fr/olanvin/`

- Microbi's Robosapien Pages: `http://www.angelfire.com/droid/rsv2/`

Programming Examples from the Web

Although sharing Robosapien programs over the Internet is more cumbersome than it should be, a great many programs are floating around in cyberspace, with new additions all the time. In this section we discuss a few Robosapien programs that have been circulating, some since Robosapien's release. These are all a lot of fun to experiment with and will give you some more examples of how to "link in" the sensor programs to create longer Robosapien programming routines. I have also included some other good tricks that you can use to fill out your Robosapien repertoire, like "glitching" Robosapien's waist tilts and manual turning using the robot's arms. Check them out!

Thanks to "Soulvasq," "Knitsu," "ThrashCC," "Hong," "Robo-maniac," "Hal," "The Stepford Children," "Robby the Robot," "Vellosman," and so many others for contributing to many of these routines. Thanks also to Robosapien.tk and Therobosapien.com for providing areas where Robosapien owners can share and exchange their favorite programming examples.

Saturday Night Fever

In this dance routine, Robosapien does a great impression of John Travolta from *Saturday Night Fever*. Watch Robosapien do the Hustle! Just press the following keys:

1. R>

2. SELECT – Left-Hand Pickup

3. Right Arm Up

4. Right Arm Up

5. SELECT – Lean Backward

6. SELECT – Lean Forward

7. Stop

8. S>

9. SELECT – Lean Backward

10. SELECT – Lean Forward

11. Stop

12. SELECT – Lean Backward

13. SELECT – Lean Forward

14. Stop

15. L>

16. SELECT – Lean Backward

17. SELECT – Lean Forward

18. Stop

19. SELECT – Lean Backward

20. SELECT – Lean Forward

21. Stop

22. P

23. SELECT – R>

24. SELECT – S>

25. SELECT – L>

26. SELECT – Left-Hand Thump

27. SELECT – Lean Backward

28. SELECT – Lean Forward

29. Stop

30. SELECT – Lean Backward

31. SELECT – Lean Forward

32. Stop

33. SELECT – Lean Backward

34. SELECT – Lean Forward

35. SELECT – SELECT – Roar

36. SELECT – Sleep

Figure 10-6. *Robosapien is 1/5 of Mark Tilden. I wonder what a robot that is 1/5 of John Travolta would look like?*

Bruce Lee Moves

Robosapien does a great set of moves that could be right out of *Enter the Dragon*.

1. R>

2. Right Arm In

3. Stop

4. Right Arm Out

5. Stop

6. Right Arm In

7. SELECT – Left-Hand Sweep

8. L>

9. Right Arm In

10. Right Arm Out

11. SELECT – SELECT – Left-Hand Strike 1

12. Right Arm In

13. SELECT – SELECT – Left-Hand Strike 3

14. Left Arm Out

15. S>

16. SELECT – SELECT – Left-Hand Strike 1

17. SELECT – Lean Forward

18. SELECT – Lean Backward

19. SELECT – SELECT – Left-Hand Strike 2

20. SELECT – Right-Hand Thump

21. SELECT – SELECT – Right-Hand Strike 3

22. P

23. SELECT – R>

24. SELECT – Right-Hand Pickup

25. Right Arm Up

26. Right Arm Up

27. SELECT – S>

28. SELECT – R>

29. SELECT – Turn Right

30. SELECT – SELECT – Roar

31. SELECT – Turn Left

32. Right Arm Out

33. SELECT – L>

34. SELECT – S>

35. Right Arm Up

36. SELECT – L>

The Macarena

Hopefully the song doesn't get stuck in your head for the rest of the day!

1. R>

2. Right Arm In

3. Left Arm Down

4. Right Arm Down

5. SELECT – Lean Backward

6. SELECT – Lean Forward

7. SELECT – Lean Backward

8. L>

9. SELECT – Lean Forward

10. Left Arm Out

11. Right Arm Out

12. Left Arm In

13. Right Arm In

14. Left Arm Up

15. S>

16. Right Arm Up

17. SELECT – Lean Backward

18. SELECT – Lean Forward

19. SELECT – Lean Backward

20. Right Arm Down

21. Left Arm In

22. P

23. Left Arm Up

24. Right Arm Up

25. Left Arm Out

26. Right Arm Out

27. Left Arm In

28. Right Arm In

29. Left Arm Up

30. Right Arm Up

31. Left Arm Out

32. Right Arm Out

33. Left Arm In

34. SELECT – R>

35. SELECT – L>

36. SELECT – S>

Chatterbox

Just because Robosapien speaks international caveman speech and has only 12K of memory doesn't mean that it can't have a lot on its mind!

1. R>

2. Stop

3. SELECT – SELECT – Talk Back

4. SELECT – SELECT – Whistle

5. Stop

6. SELECT – SELECT – Talk Back

7. SELECT – SELECT – Burp

8. P

9. SELECT – R> 14 times to fill up the master command program

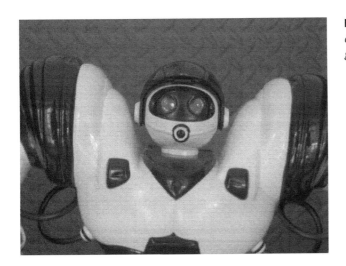

Figure 10-7. *Robosapien can be quite chatty if you give it the opportunity.*

Jackie Chan Moves

Robosapien mimics martial arts great Jackie Chan in this routine:

1. R>
2. Tilt Body Left
3. Tilt Body Right
4. Right Arm Out
5. Left Arm Out
6. SELECT – Left-Hand Thump
7. SELECT – Right-Hand Thump
8. L>
9. SELECT – Lean Backward
10. SELECT – Lean Backward
11. SELECT – Lean Forward
12. SELECT – SELECT – Right-Hand Strike 3
13. SELECT – SELECT – Left-Hand Strike 2
14. SELECT – Reset
15. P
16. Right Arm Up
17. Left Arm Up

18. Right Arm Out

19. Left Arm Out

20. SELECT – Right-Hand Thump

21. SELECT – Left-Hand Thump

22. SELECT – Lean Backward

23. SELECT – Lean Forward

24. SELECT – SELECT – Right-Hand Strike 1

25. SELECT – SELECT – Right-Hand Sweep

26. SELECT – SELECT – Left-Hand Strike 1

27. SELECT – SELECT – Left-Hand Sweep

28. SELECT – R>

29. SELECT – L>

Figure 10-8. *Like martial arts masters Bruce Lee and Jackie Chan, Robosapien's arms and upper body become a blur when performing karate moves.*

"The Robot"

Even though it doesn't come preprogrammed, you can still set up Robosapien to do "the Robot" dance.

1. R>

2. Right Arm Down

3. Tilt Body Right

4. Right Arm Up

5. Right Arm Out

6. Right Arm In

7. Right Arm In

8. L>

9. Left Arm Down

10. Tilt Body Left

11. Left Arm Up

12. Left Arm Out

13. Left Arm In

14. Left Arm In

15. P

16. SELECT – R>

17. SELECT – L>

18. SELECT – R>

19. SELECT – L>

20. SELECT – R>

21. SELECT – L>

22. SELECT – R>

23. SELECT – L>

24. SELECT – R>

25. SELECT – L>

26. SELECT – R>

27. SELECT – L>

28. SELECT – R>

29. SELECT – L>

Rocking Robosapien

Program this routine to one of the sensors and it makes a great "transition move" between dance routines. Or, program it into the master command program 14 times to see Robosapien really "rock."

1. S>

2. SELECT – Lean Forward

3. SELECT – Lean Forward

4. SELECT – Lean Backward

5. SELECT – Lean Backward

6. SELECT – Lean Forward

7. SELECT – Lean Backward

8. P

9. SELECT – S> 14 times to fill up the master command program

Walking Blues

Here are some great tips you can use to experiment with Robosapien's walking mechanics.

Figure 10-9. *Any walking experiments with Robosapien should be done in a large area with a smooth floor. Dogs and other pets are encouraged, but optional.*

Samba Move

While Robosapien is walking forward, press either Turn Left or Turn Right on the remote control. The robot will change into a gait that looks like a samba move (or maybe the gait of a pirate with a peg leg) and walk in a large circle.

Figure 10-10. *The "samba" move makes Robosapien walk in a wide circle.*

Manual Turn

While Robosapien is walking forward, extend the left arm all the way out and the robot will begin turning toward the left. The same goes for the right arm.

Figure 10-11. *Use an outstretched arm to manually turn Robosapien when it is walking. Raise the arm lower or higher to change the severity of the turn.*

Quick Walking

Position both of Robosapien's arms so that both shoulders are all the way down, and both arms are all the way out with both claws open. Robosapien will gain quite a bit of side-to-side swaying motion, which results in the feet moving further forward with each step. The ultimate result is a large increase in walking speed. Note that in some cases the robot will sway so far that it will trigger its finger sensors on the floor.

Monster Bulldozer

Program the Bulldozer (SELECT – SELECT – Walk Forward) into the Sonic programming mode (S>) six times. Then press P and enter SELECT – S> 14 times. Robosapien will "bulldoze" through anything in its path for over 8 minutes—or 1,344 steps!

Voice-Controlled Robosapien

Using this program, you can trick your friends into thinking Robosapien actually listens to you.

1. S>

2. SELECT – Right-Hand Pickup

3. SELECT – Walk Forward

4. SELECT – Walk Forward

5. SELECT – Right-Hand Throw

6. SELECT – Listen

7. SELECT – SELECT – High 5

8. Position Robosapien's cup near his right foot for pickup and put the robot into listen mode (SELECT – Listen).

9. Now, yell "Bring me that cup!" and Robosapien will pick up the cup, walk forward two steps, throw it at you, and go into listen mode. Say "thanks" and Robosapien will reply with a "Heyyy" and look for a high 5.

Figure 10-12. *"Voice-controlled" programs that use the sonic sensor can be a lot of fun.*

Manual Pickup

By pressing either the Tilt Body Left or Tilt Body Right button repeatedly you can "glitch" Robosapien and cause the robot to lock in a sideways leaning position. While still pressing one of the tilt keys repeatedly, you can weave in other arm commands (you'll need to use both hands on the remote) such as shoulder up and down and arm in and out. Using this method you can get Robosapien to pick up items that are in places other than the "sweet spot" near the robot's heel.

Figure 10-13. *Here we are "glitching" Robosapien into a constant sideways tilt.*

Summary

The online Robosapien community is very vibrant, and it is a good place to start looking for ideas if you would like to get the most out of your Robosapien. Have a great idea for a programming routine? Post it online and see if other people have any tips or tricks that can make your idea even better. Although a lot of these are based on the conditional reflex programming we looked at in Chapter 9, the collaborative nature of Internet forums really goes a long way toward fleshing out some pretty neat ideas.

CHAPTER 11

■ ■ ■

Using Your Computer to Control Robosapien

Figure 11-1. *Is Robosapien a "control freak"?*

Controlling Robosapien with a computer has a lot of advantages, but like everything it isn't without its downsides. In this chapter I examine both the plusses and the minuses to using a PC to control your Robosapien. I also provide a step-by-step tutorial on setting up a fully skinnable PC interface to control Robosapien using commercially available software and hardware. Finally, I look at some of the "homebrew" PC control schemes that people have been developing since Robosapien's release.

Advantages and Disadvantages

One of the things that's cool about the mechanism, if you press something like say, the lean forward, lean backward ... there's a point where you can actually press and move the motors faster than the robot does.... Hidden secret #13. <Laughs> You can, through an IR port, move him faster than he can move himself. We put the IR into one of the only direct interrupts that goes into the processor. So if you are feeding that thing precise controlled IR codes, you can give him much more degree and resolution motion than he is capable of on his own.

—Mark Tilden, February 13, 2005

Besides allowing you to send IR commands to Robosapien faster than you can manually by using the remote control, the real advantage of using a PC to control Robosapien is being able to string together macros with as many steps as you would like, and of course being able to save and store them on your computer. No more being limited to the 84 total steps that we learned how to "link in" using the remote and the reactive sensor routines, and no more writing down each and every step. The sky is the limit, or, I guess I should say, Robosapien's motors and motor driver are the limit. Using a PC, the most commands I have put together are about 125 repetitions of Right Arm In, then Right Arm Out (250 commands total). I was worried, as you should be if you go this route, that too many repetitions beyond what Robosapien is designed to handle could strain the robot's motors and/or its motor driver circuitry.

With that warning out of the way, another advantage is that once your computer is controlling Robosapien, you can schedule events and begin to automate the robot at high levels. For example, you can send a "null" command every few minutes to keep Robosapien from going into sleep mode or turning itself off. You can set it up to perform certain events at various times throughout the day, or when certain conditions are met; for instance, when you receive a new email, you can program Robosapien to do its Roar command.

Combined with a wireless camera (see Chapter 14) and some networking know-how, PC control of Robosapien even allows you to operate the robot remotely over a local network or over the Internet.

In a sense, by using a PC to control Robosapien, you are replacing Robosapien's tiny brain with the memory, processing power, and abilities of your computer. Remember, Mark Tilden said that the brain used in Robosapien is the same 70 cent chip "...that sang 'Happy Birthday to You' 20 years ago in Hallmark cards." However, Robosapien still needs to be in infrared range of a computer.

(Photo courtesy of Mark Tilden, WowWee Ltd.)

Figure 11-2. *This early Robosapien prototype's brains were too big to fit on its frame, so they sort of dragged along behind the robot. Imagine Robosapien trying to drag a laptop around with it!*

This loss of portability turns out to be fairly minor, considering you would need to be in range of the remote control anyway. And it is not the biggest hurdle to PC control of Robosapien. We touched on the main problem when we discussed infrared basics in Chapter 6. Most computers do not come with the capability to send and receive infrared signals, and if they do, it is usually based on the IRDA specification. If you will recall, Robosapien uses "consumer IR," which is slower than IRDA but has a much longer range. So before you can even think about using a computer to control Robosapien, you need to buy an infrared transceiver, sometimes known as a "blaster," for your PC. Not only will it need to be capable of sending out the IR commands, like Robosapien's stock remote, but it also must be able to receive them in order to "learn" Robosapien's unique IR codes.

But this problem doesn't end there. It turns out there is no "standard" for infrared that software engineers use when they write infrared remote control software. What I mean is that for the most part, the software has to be written specifically for the infrared device. Or, simply put, just because you have an IR transceiver doesn't mean that any software is going to work with it. Oh, and did I mention that you are probably going to need to buy software too?

So computer control of Robosapien gives you extended programming capabilities, storage, and some automation, but at the expense of portability—and you'll have to buy an infrared transceiver and possibly some software. Still sounds like a pretty good deal to me. Let's look at how to do it.

A Computer Control How-To

Figure 11-3. *Here you see a PC control scheme for Robosapien designed using Cinemar's Main-Lobby 2 software. The central circular control button cluster controls movement and leaning. The identical circular control button clusters in the top corners control each arm (up, down, in, out; macros that perform all the way up, all the way down, all the way in, all the way out; and a macro that resets the arm to the lowest, furthest in position for walking). The three small buttons that run along the inside curve are macro buttons assignable to whatever I have programmed in Girder. Unlike the Robosapien, Girder places no limit on the number of steps you can put in a macro.*

In my living room, if you walk toward my TV and listen carefully you might hear the faint whir of a fan. If you look closely underneath my TV set, mixed in with the surround sound receiver and the various tuners from my satellite and cable providers (and dust!) you will notice that my DVD player is larger than most and that it seems to be the source of the faint fan noise. You might also notice a funny little black box that hooks up via a USB cable. If during your investigations you happen to make too much noise you will trigger Robosapien's sonic sensor and be greeted with a roar as he starts his macro'ed wake-up routine.

Figure 11-4. *Robosapien claims another unsuspecting victim.*

The big DVD player, it turns out, is actually a home theater computer (HTPC for short). It acts as a brain of sorts for my home entertainment center. I use it to do a lot of things: to play and record DVDs and CDs; as a DVR (digital video recorder, like a TiVo) to watch, schedule, and record television; to access my file server to play my digital music and video collection over my TV and stereo system; to access the Internet; to access our collection of digital pictures and display them on my TV; and even to dim the lights. I do all of those things via IR with a single remote control, using a collection of hardware and software well known by most HTPC enthusiasts: the USB-UIRT IR transceiver, and the programs Girder (from Promixis) and MainLobby 2 (from Cinemar). It just so happens that this bundle of hardware and software is also extremely useful for programming, automating, and controlling the Robosapien robot, and it's not too complicated to set up for this purpose at all.

As we have already seen, unfortunately there is no standard application programming interface (API) for sending and receiving IR signals. Almost all of the hardware transceivers do it slightly differently and as such there isn't a whole lot of compatibility. In my opinion as an HTPC and home automation enthusiast, the best and most powerful automation software out there is Girder, so I am basing this tutorial around it. MainLobby 2 has full Girder support built in and is a well-designed piece of software that lets you build custom-skinned interfaces or "front ends."

The good news is that the command files set up in Girder and the skinned interfaces created in MainLobby 2 can be swapped and will work as long as users use the same combination of hardware and software.

Hardware

Here's what you'll need:

- USB-UIRT, $50 (http://www.usbuirt.com)

- Robosapien, ~$100

I used the USB-UIRT as my IR transceiver. I don't think it is the cheapest option, but I had an extra lying around from an HTPC project. The creator, Jon Rhees, hand-makes them and provides excellent support, and the device is pretty much custom-made to work with Girder. As an added bonus, a dynamic link library (DLL) file and associated API are available so that you can work on developing your own software, if you are so inclined.

Figure 11-5. *The USB-UIRT IR tranceiver processes IR data and exchanges it with the host PC via a high-speed USB link.*

The USB-UIRT uses an onboard microcontroller to handle all IR reception and transmission, which reduces the load on your PC. Infrared data is then processed and exchanged with the host PC via a high-speed USB link. Note that two models are offered: if you are just going to use it with Robosapien the base model will do, but if you also want to use it to learn IR from a lot of stereo and home theater components you need to get the version with the additional 56KHz IR sensor. Once you plug in the USB-UIRT for first time, be sure to install the latest drivers from the support section of the website.

Software

Here's what you'll need:

- Girder, free to try, $19.99 to register (http://www.promixis.com/)

- USB-UIRT Girder plug-in, free (http://www.usbuirt.com/support.htm)

- MainLobby 2, free 30-day trial, $59.99 thereafter (http://www.cinemaronline.com/index.html)

- ML Server, free (http://www.cinemaronline.com/mlserver.html)

Girder

Girder is Windows automation software that is very popular with the HTPC crowd. It can be complicated and has a steep learning curve, especially if you get into scripting, but in terms of depth of control and raw power it is the best thing out there by far. We are going to use it primarily to learn, organize, and store the IR commands from the Robosapien remote, and then execute them when called by clicking a button in the MainLobby 2 interface.

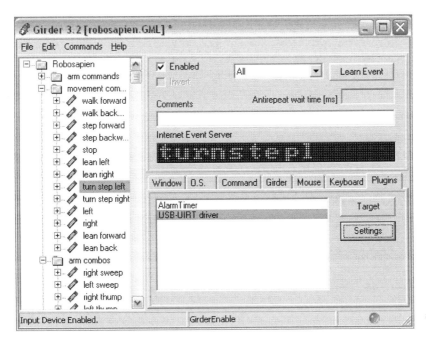

Figure 11-6. *This screenshot shows the main Girder window where you will be doing most of your work.*

Another extremely useful feature of Girder is the ability to program macros (called multi-groups) with an unlimited number of steps. In setting up Girder to work with Robosapien we are using only a fraction of the software's capabilities—you can also use Girder to control your PC via IR remote, to send and receive serial commands, and a million other things.

MainLobby 2

MainLobby 2 is designed to be an HTPC front end. It allows you to create a custom graphical user interface (GUI) with buttons that you can set up to launch programs, execute files, trigger events in Girder to send IR commands, and so on. It is entirely skinnable, so the sky is the limit in terms of graphics, and the design is accomplished via an easy drop-and-drag interface. When I wrote this guide I was using the trial version of MainLobby 2, and for our example (see Figure 11-3) I just used buttons and a background from the included libraries. I'd love to design a custom Robosapien-themed setup.

ML Server is the MainLobby 2 application used to interact with Girder.

Setup

So how do we get all these pieces set up and communicating with each other? First thing, make sure that the USB-UIRT (including drivers), Girder, ML Server, and MainLobby 2 are all installed and running on your PC.

Girder Setup and Configuration

In Girder, select File ➤ Settings and click the Plugins tab. Make sure that the Internet Event Server and USB-UIRT Driver plug-ins are checked (which means they're installed). Also make sure that the Auto Enable Input Device box is checked. Click Apply and then click OK.

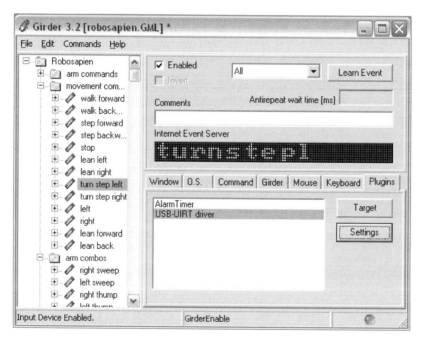

Figure 11-7. *On Girder's Settings screen, select the Plugins tab to see these options.*

You should now be back at the main Girder screen, and the light in the bottom-right corner should be green (see Figure 11-6). The green light means that the plug-ins are enabled and operational. If it is not green, click the File menu and choose Enable Input Device(s), or press F9. Now that the plug-ins are set up, let's start learning the Girder Robosapien commands.

1. Click File ➤ New. In the large white area on the left of the screen, right-click and choose Add Command. A folder named New and a command named New will be created.

2. Select the folder first and right-click to rename it. The folder is what's called a "group" and is used in Girder to organize commands. Let's rename it as "arm commands" and use it to store all of Robosapien's individual arm movements.

3. Now select the command, right-click, and rename it as "R arm up."

4. While the command is still selected, look in the top right of the screen and select Internet Event Server from the drop-down menu. Click the Learn Event button and enter an event string name—for example, "rarmup" (see Figure 11-8). Notice that underneath the command on the left, there is a new item called an EventString. This is the command that MainLobby 2 will send to trigger Girder to send out the appropriate IR command.

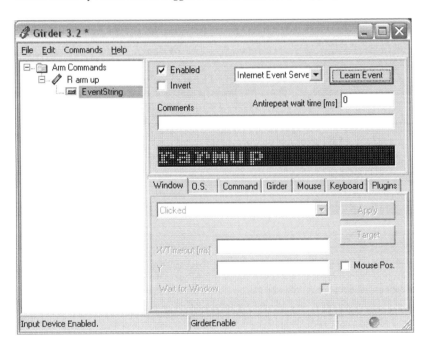

Figure 11-8. *Set up Girder to learn the Robosapien IR commands.*

5. Click OK.

6. Make sure the "R arm up" command is still selected and in the bottom right choose the Plugins tab to the far right.

7. Select USB-UIRT Driver from the list and then click Settings. A USB-UIRT driver window will pop up.

8. Click on the Learn button. Another window will now appear and await the IR signal.

9. Take Robosapien's remote and point it at your USB-UIRT, the closer the better. Continue pressing the right arm up button until Girder learns the command and returns you to the USB-UIRT Driver window.

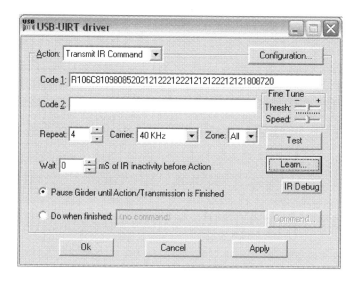

Figure 11-9. *The USB-UIRT Driver window is where Girder "learns" Robosapien's IR commands.*

I know that the instructions in the window say to *hold* the button on the remote, but Robosapien's IR isn't a constant signal; rather, it is a burst, so you might have to click the Accept Burst button if it is having trouble completing the full learning process.

Now that you are back at the USB-UIRT Driver window, point the USB-UIRT at Robosapien and hit the Test button to make sure that the command was learned successfully. Robosapien should raise its right arm. If not, repeat the process and "relearn" it. Also pay attention to the Repeat box. You will want to set this to a value of 1 in most cases, so that Girder only sends the IR command once (unless you want it to send the IR command multiple times—for example, I have commands set up to move the arm all the way up, all the way down, all the way out, and all the way in that utilize the repeat function).

Congratulations! Now you have taught Girder the first Robosapien command. Repeat the above steps for each command on the remote, and organize them in groups as you see fit (see Figure 11-10). By the time you finish entering all of Robosapien's commands, you will be an old pro at using Girder, believe me!

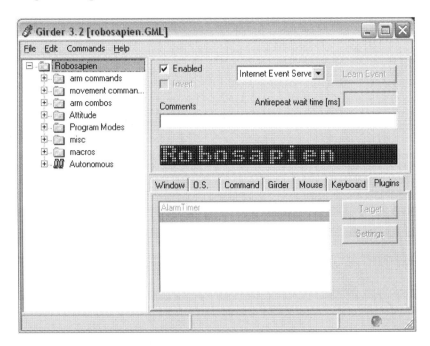

Figure 11-10. *Robosapien's commands are organized in Girder.*

One other thing worth mentioning in Girder, which I touched on earlier in this chapter, is the use of multigroups. These are basically macros—you can take any Girder command you have created, right-click on it and select Copy, and then paste it into a multigroup. String together and arrange unlimited commands, but keep in mind that you might have to mess around with some more advanced settings to get the timing right when using Robosapien's combination or attitude moves. Also, don't forget to add an event string for them so you can call them from MainLobby 2.

Once you have your IR commands learned into Girder, save your file, and then click File ➤ Close Window to send Girder to your system tray.

ML Server Setup and Configuration

To set up ML Server:

1. Open ML Server and make sure that MLGirder is listed in the Plug-Ins section at the bottom.

2. Open Windows Explorer and find the file gireventlib.dll (it should be in the folder C:\Program Files\girder) and copy it to your C:\Windows\system32 folder. Alternatively, you can add the file to your path.

3. Select Options in ML Server and choose Hide to send ML Server to the system tray. Figure 11-11 shows the ML Server window.

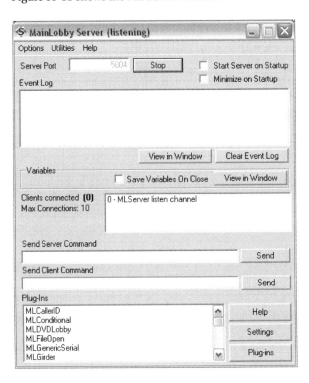

Figure 11-11. *The ML server window, like Girder, will be minimized to your system tray when in use.*

■**Important** Make sure you hit the Start button next to the Server Port window to put ML Server into listening mode (if it is already in listening mode, the button will read Stop), or MainLobby 2 won't know that Girder is trying to send it commands.

MainLobby 2 Setup and Configuration

With MainLobby 2 open, go to the top of the screen to bring up the menu bar. Just hover your mouse pointer there at the top of the window and the menu bar will appear (see Figure 11-12).

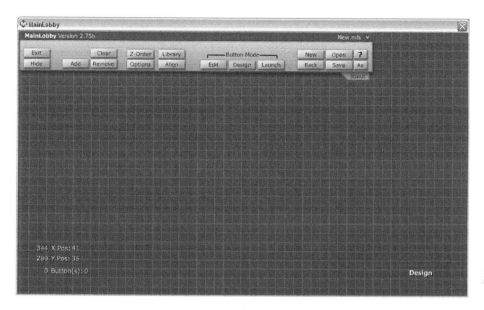

Figure 11-12. *Hover your mouse pointer at the top of the screen to open the MainLobby 2 drop-down configuration menu.*

1. On the menu bar, click the Options button, and you will be presented with the Scene Options Panel.

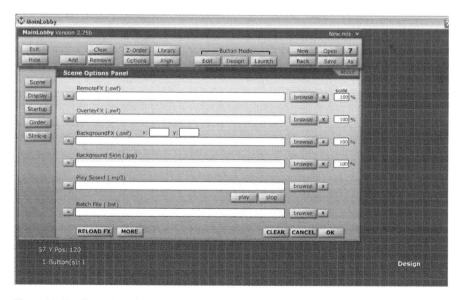

Figure 11-13. *The MainLobby 2 Scene Options Panel is where you will design your interface.*

2. Click the Girder button at the left. Here is where you tell MainLobby the location of both Girder.exe and the Internet Event Server (ieventc.exe) on your hard drive. Both files should be in the main Girder directory on your hard drive.

3. Once you have Girder set up, click the Scene button on the left side of the window. Here is where you choose your background skin, any animated effects, and so on. You can set these up however you choose, or leave them empty and come back to them later. Either way, this is where you will customize the look of your control scheme.

4. When you've finished, click OK to exit the Options screen.

5. Now move your mouse to the top menu bar, and click the Design button under Button Mode.

6. Click Add to add a button; any button shape will do for now. You can load custom buttons of your own or click the Library button to choose from those included with MainLobby 2.

7. Once you see the button appear on your background, you can drag it around and drop it wherever you like. When you have it positioned, click the Edit mode button in the top menu bar and click the button you just created. A screen with tons of options, called the Button Properties Panel, will open (Figure 11-14).

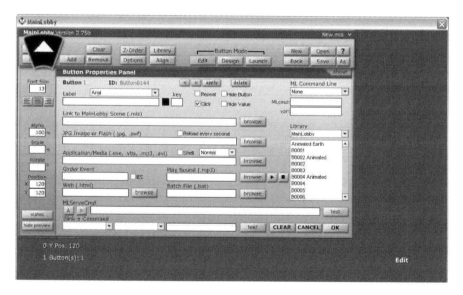

Figure 11-14. *This is the MainLobby 2 Button Properties Panel, where you will set up and design your button.*

This panel lets you customize your button:

1. In the MLServeCmd area at the bottom, click the A button. A new window will pop up.

2. From the drop-down list in the MLServeCmd panel, choose MLGirder. This will populate the following statement in the box: MLServeCmd.MLGirder.

3. Add the event string you created in Girder for a particular Robosapien command to the end of this statement. If we use the command we created earlier for raising Robosapien's right arm, "rarmup", the text inside the box should read "MLServeCmd.MLGirder|rarmup".

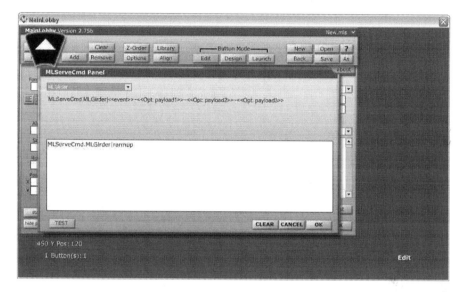

Figure 11-15. *This is MainLobby 2's MLServeCmd Panel, where you set up your buttons to correspond with the event strings you created in Girder for each of Robosapien's IR commands.*

4. You can now test it via the Test button to ensure it works, or click OK and test it from the button's properties panel. Click OK when finished.

5. You should now be able to choose Launch from the top menu bar and click the button you created, and Robosapien should raise its right arm.

Repeat the above steps in MainLobby 2 for each button you want to create; you are well on your way to PC control of Robosapien!

"Homebrew" PC Control Schemes

When I designed and wrote the first version of the "PC Control How-To" in the summer of 2004, shortly after Robosapien's release, I knew it was only a matter of time before programmers began writing their own custom Robosapien control programs that don't use the commercial software that my example uses (see the sidebar "Links to Robosapien Control Schemes on the Web"). I have been surprised at how long it has taken some of these to show up; I think that the lack of a "standard" consumer IR device for PCs is one thing that held back the development. In recent months it seems that the USB-UIRT has emerged as a favorite among programmers designing PC-based programs for Robosapien.

LINKS TO ROBOSAPIEN CONTROL SCHEMES ON THE WEB

- SapBench, by RobosapienPet: `http://www.aibohack.com/robosap/sapbench.htm`

- Robosapien Dance Machine, by roschler: `http://sourceforge.net/projects/robodance`

- Robot Dreams: PC-Based Robosapien Control Project: `http://isobe.typepad.com/robotics/pc_based_robosapien_control_project/index.html`

- Robosapien Controller, by Patrick Dugan: `http://pruim037.proboards23.com/index.cgi?board=programmb&action=display&thread=1112920419`

SapBench

The first entry, which even predated my scheme, was not designed for the PC, but rather for PDAs. SapBench, sometimes called Robosapien Bench, is a program that runs on the Palm OS. The program essentially replaces the Robosapien remote, and gives the user the ability to script, edit, and download programming routines.

But wait, don't Palm Pilots have IRDA? Yes, and that is the beauty, and the curse, of Sap-Bench. It is based on the OrLib library, part of the OmniRemote program, which "tricks" the PDA's IRDA blaster into sending out signals that can be read by consumer IR devices. That is really cool, but unfortunately IRDA's limited range really comes into play. The range depends on the strength of the IR LED in the device, but at most you are going to get maybe a 7-foot range. Using my older Palm III, I get a range of maybe 3 to 4 feet. That is just long enough to control a Robosapien on the floor while sitting in a chair, and just short enough that I constantly have to get up because the robot walks out of range.

Figure 11-16. *SapBench will even run on my ancient Palm III.*

Robosapien Dance Machine

A new entry onto the PC control scheme is the Robosapien Dance Machine, an open source project developed by Robert Oschler and hosted on SourceForge.net. It has gotten quite a bit of attention and even won the May 2005 SourceForge Project of the Month award. It is a very cool little program that is self-contained, meaning that you don't need Girder or any other software installed on your PC to run it—although like all of the "homebrew" PC control programs, you do need a USB-UIRT.

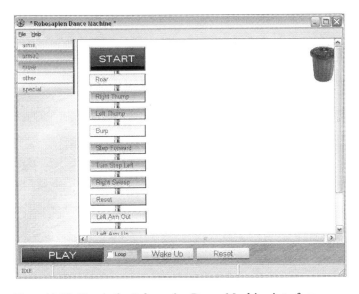

Figure 11-17. *Here is the Robosapien Dance Machine interface.*

Robosapien Dance Machine allows you to easily script and play back complicated routines, and save them to your computer. Only a month after it was released, Version 2, which supports integrated speech recognition, was released. Very cool stuff, and highly recommended! In my opinion this is the "gold standard" that all other PC-based control programs should seek to emulate.

Other PC Programs

There are a number of other Robosapien PC control programs out there and I feel certain that even more will be available by the time this book is published. Almost all of them use the USB-UIRT for infrared transmission and are self-contained. There are some very promising projects waiting to be discovered!

Figure 11-18. *The Robot Dreams: PC-Based Robosapien Control Project has one of the nicer interfaces. I haven't had the opportunity to try it: it was developed on a Japanese version of Windows XP and at this writing has some compatability issues.*

Figure 11-19. *The Robosapien Controller magically appeared one day on the Robosapien.tk forums and was posted by Patrick Dugan for download. It also uses the USB-UIRT and works very well.*

Summary

Using a computer to take over the control of your Robosapien is in many ways the "ultimate" modification that you can make. Think back to Chapter 2, where we discussed BEAM robotics and the "less is more" concept when it comes to robotic brains. By using a PC to control Robosapien you really get the best of both worlds—you maintain the simplicity inherent in the BEAM design, but by using the more advanced capabilities of your computer, you can augment the robot's abilities as you see fit.

PART 4

■ ■ ■

Hacking the Robosapien

CHAPTER 12

■■■

An Introduction to Hacking Robosapien

Figure 12-1. *Having taken iRobot's Roomba the robotic vacuum apart, Robosapien looks for interesting modification opportunities.*

The word "hack" can mean a lot of different things. It is a piece of equipment used in the ice sport of curling. It can be also be used to refer to an unskilled journalist or a particularly partisan politico. In some parts of the world, taxicabs are still sometimes referred to as hacks; a derivative of "hackney carriage," which was the seventeenth-century English term for "vehicle for hire." Tracing it all the way back, the word originally referred to a person who constructed furniture with an axe. Honestly, for a chapter intended as an introduction to modifying Robosapien, you can't get much better foreshadowing than that!

More likely, though, the word "hack" conjures up images of computer nerds, piles of empty Mountain Dew soda cans, and pizza boxes, all lit by the dim glow of computer monitors. Most people today mistakenly think of hackers as programmers and software engineers who use their skills to gain unauthorized access to other computer systems and networks; in fact, this activity is what is known as "cracking" and the people who do it are "crackers."

Today, the term "hacker" has come to define a person who stretches the capabilities of either software or hardware further than the designers of the software or hardware envisioned. Axes are optional. For purposes of our discussion on Robosapien, "hacking" refers to modifying and/or enhancing the robot beyond its out-of-the-box capabilities.

I hated when all of a sudden you realized that planned obsolescence in toys was designed so that when it was taken apart it could not be reverse-engineered or put back together. You look at B.I.O. Bugs, though, you look at Robosapien, and all of a sudden you realize that this thing is not just designed to sort of go back together, it is designed to be improved, modified, and basically transferred on. What I wanted was, I wanted a toy where after I figured out everything that the toy designer had put into it, what else could I put in?

—*Mark Tilden, February 13, 2005*

It is no secret that Robosapien's "hackability" is planned, and as we began to see in Chapter 5 (which covered Robosapien's anatomy), much of the design is based around allowing the robot to be easily modified, augmented, and even repaired.

Figure 12-2. *Compared to the maze of wires and PCBs in the iRobot Roomba "Discovery" robot vacuum cleaner, Robosapien's internal design is simple and straightforward.*

This chapter takes a look at what hacking Robosapien really means, and we begin thinking about some of the ways that Robosapien can be hacked.

Robosapien and Hacking

So what is it that makes Robosapien so hackable?

> *B.I.O. Bugs were pretty cool, but again they were still insects. We've got lots of good stories, but the bottom line is that very few have actually been hacked. Robosapien, on the other hand, people seem to be somehow* obligated *to hack it.*
>
> *—Mark Tilden, February 13, 2005*

For one thing, as we see in Chapter 13, the robot is extremely easy to take apart. Another factor is the amount of space found in Robosapien's chest cavity.

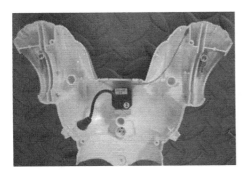 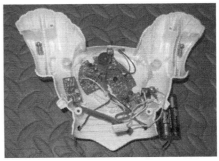

Figures 12-3 and 12-4. *Robosapien's torso shell contains a ton of extra room for additions and modifications.*

Take, for example, Figures 12-3 and 12-4. Figure 12-3 shows a small wireless camera installed in Robosapien's front chest cavity. Even with the camera installed, there is still plenty of room left over in the front for additional components. Figure 12-4 shows Robosapien's back cavity. I removed the speaker and the surrounding plastic in this Robosapien, in order to make space for a wireless RF receiver that receives MP3 and other sound files from my computer. Figure 12-5 shows this particular Robosapien with its own speaker backpack and upgraded sound system, a part of the project for which I won *Servo* magazine's "Hack-a-Sapien" contest. The fact is, there is a bunch of space in Robosapien's chest cavity, by design. Robosapien could have easily been designed with a more streamlined outer shell that didn't give as much interior room for adding extras and upgrades.

Figure 12-5. *This Robosapien has an upgraded speaker system and audio amplifier. It receives audio from a radio transmitter connected to my PC. It also plays back Robosapien's native international caveman speech through the upgraded audio system.*

Another thing to consider is that almost every connection inside Robosapien is labeled and socketed, and hooks up to a connector. There are even gold-plated contact points on the robot's various PCBs to solder on your own devices.

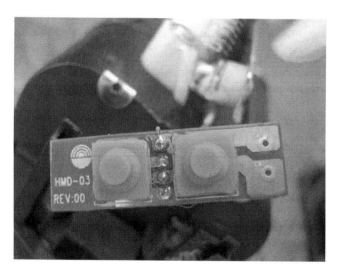

Figure 12-6. *This is a photo of the small PCB that contains one of Robosapien's heel sensors. Note the gold-plated solder points on the right.*

Even within the tight confines of the forearm, the connections from the finger sensor as well as the palm light in the claw connect to a tiny, labeled PCB, complete with sockets (see Figure 12-7). This sort of construction just begs to be taken apart. It's all too easy. No soldering irons to mess around with, and no trying to remember which wire goes where in order to get the thing back together. As my mother would be quick to tell you, as a child I spent many a Christmas morning disassembling all of my new toys, and many a Christmas afternoon in tears because I couldn't get most of them back together.

The gearboxes and the control mechanisms inside, the fact that you actually have sealed gear boxes; they were designed to be hacked. One of the things that I was so pleased about with the B.I.O. Bugs was that it was my first super hackable toy. I remember as a kid, opening up toys and all of a sudden gears would fall out all over the place, and you found out there was nothing you could actually do with the toy, except use it as a toy. Robosapien basically has so many things inside of it, that you can't find them all... and that basically turned out to be the fourth [selling point]. And the big fifth, and this is the hidden fifth, was the fact that not only was [Robosapien] reliable, but it was eminently hackable. How many times have you tried to hack someone else's technology... for instance take a look at this stupid camera. Look at that connector! Yeah right! <Laughs> It's got wire contacts too small to even see. I hate that. I know somewhere on there is a video out, and there's a power in, probably a couple other lines, but I can't access that. I hate that about modern technology. Give me the good old days, when you know, you and a soldering iron, and a screwdriver, and you own that toy. The bottom line is, you take a screwdriver [Robosapien], you open it up, everything's color coded. Everything's labeled. Everything does what it's supposed to do. There's hardly any wires at all. There's always gold-plated contacts, you wouldn't believe how hard I fought to make sure that they were always gold plated. As soon as you opened it up, the possibilities skyrocketed. For anybody who was like me when I was 7 years old...

—*Mark Tilden, February 13, 2005*

Figure 12-7. *Robosapien's forearm, like the rest of the robot, is fully labeled and socketed. This is a tremendous advantage for the hacker.*

Finally, another factor that shouldn't be overlooked is the price. Sure, $100 might seem like an expensive toy to dismantle, or, if we stick with the historical definition of a hacker, to take an axe to. But consider the price of other robots, like the Sony Aibo, which is not designed to be hacked and taken apart.

Sorry that the sockets are so cheap, but hey, at least they are there. For the cost of one Aibo, you can buy 20 Robosapiens. Having that number of interchangeable, exchangeable parts...when you make a mistake; there are standard replaceable parts from the next robot over.

—Mark Tilden, February 13, 2005

The iRobot Roomba vacuum cleaner (see Figure 12-2), which costs almost triple what you'll pay for Robosapien, provides another good example. Figure 12-2 notwithstanding, the Roomba is in no way, shape, or form designed to be dismantled, improved, or "user serviced." The Roomba pictured in this chapter lost a fight with a throw rug and burnt out one of its motors. It ended up being replaced under warranty, and they let me keep the old one, which meant I had a guinea pig to experiment on.

But the Roomba and the Aibo aren't really toys. The Roomba is a service robot (and a very nice one, especially for cleaning crumbs and dust off hardwood floors… just watch the throw rugs!), and the Aibo… well I am not sure exactly what the Aibo is. The Sony website lists the latest model, the ERS-7M2, at $1,999. So I guess it is expensive if it is anything!

Ever play with an Aibo? Four-minute boot time. It sits there and beeps at you, and I mean no disrespect, but any toy that spends a fifth of its battery life... booting.... <Shakes head> Any toy that consumes more power standing up than it does basically even walking... you gotta wonder about that.

—Mark Tilden, February 13, 2005

Our comparison wouldn't be complete without looking at our friend Ramon the Robot.

Figure 12-8. *Ramon the Robot is not programmable.*

Ramon is a bipedal robot like Robosapien, but it came in at a lower price point, around $60. Ramon is not programmable, it has a lot fewer features than Robosapien does, and it is nowhere near as smooth and refined. But it is a good example to look at since (at least as of this writing) it is the only other battery-powered bipedal walking robot on the market. Like most toys, Ramon is absolutely not made to be hacked. I think I could get it apart, but not without damaging it fairly badly, maybe irreparably. For one thing, there are no connectors; everything is soldered. Figure 12-9 shows how far I was able to get the main processor's PCB out of the robot until I got worried that I was going to break one of the connections or solder joints. To get it completely out, and continue disassembling the robot, you would either have to cut or unsolder the majority of the connections.

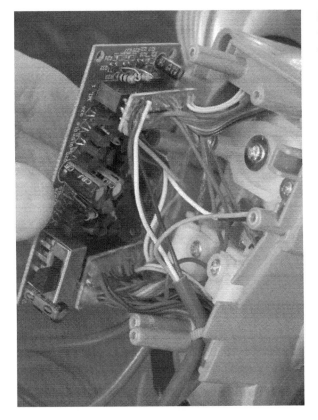

Figure 12-9. *This is about as far as I was able to get Ramon apart, without using substantial force.*

So while you might have some trepidation about taking apart your $100 "toy," fear not. The Robosapien is absolutely designed to be taken apart, modified, and hacked. A great example of this came in one of my discussions with Mark Tilden while I was doing research for this book. He was showing me a slide show presentation about the development of Robosapien, much of which ended up becoming Chapter 3 of this book. All of a sudden, a large group of kids playing with Robosapien pops up on the screen. The next slide showed a bunch of nerdy guys in white laboratory jackets; how you might imagine a group of research scientists would look like. Mark explained each slide as follows:

The real cool thing is we've always kept our eye on the two major customers. One: the kids. Kids want something basically as a pure toy. One of the things, for example, which I fought like hell for with the Robosapien... you have to look really close to get an actual label on it. When you see a Microsoft product it's always labeled. Think "Intel Inside." When you see a Sony Aibo it's always "Sony." You look at Robosapien, no. It's pure toy. It has nothing that basically tells you, or reminds you, that you are basically doing something fictitious. [Cut to second slide] This is also the primary market: my science buddies. The people I have been talking to for 10 years, who keep on saying, "Oh, as soon as we get a good body, then I can put my computer brains into it, and therefore it'll go." But the cheapest robot body you can buy is Sarcos, the million-dollar robot that runs on hydraulics, pneumatics, and things like that. And they don't sell enough to make it worthwhile. Plus why risk it?

—Mark Tilden, February 13, 2005

The bottom line is that there is very little risk to taking Robosapien apart; the robot is designed to be unassembled, poked, prodded, and then put back together. The Robosapien that I use for hacking and modifications, the one that I do most of my projects on, has been taken completely apart literally hundreds of times over the past year with no ill effects. This isn't to say that you shouldn't take your time and use care because you should. But we will discuss that in greater detail in Chapter 13.

Starting the Hack

While it is all well and good to discuss the philosophy behind Robosapien's hacker-friendly construction and design, the real fun comes in rolling up your sleeves and testing out Robosapien's "hackability" for yourself.

Robosapien Hacking Theories

I think Robosapien hacks can be divided into five broad categories, listed here in their approximate order of complexity.

Cosmetic Hacks

These are projects that change Robosapien's appearance either permanently or temporarily. This can be something as simple as adding accessories (parts and accessories from 1/60th-scale Gundam kits are just the right size) or even leftover water-slide decals from plastic model kits (see Figure 12-10). Some people have even "dressed" Robosapien (see Figure 12-11) and added things like backpacks and wigs. More complicated hacks in this category include new paint jobs, or even completely recasting Robosapien's shell. That last one would probably be extremely complicated!

Apparently, early in Robosapien's design phase, WowWee envisioned a complete line of accessories and accoutrements. These never saw the light of day (return to Chapter 3 and see Figure 3-35 and the accompanying sidebar "What Didn't Make the Cut" for some examples).

One cosmetic hack that I am anxious to do is to install flashing blue and red LEDs into the shoulders and chest of my metallic blue Sharper Image Robosapien. It would be the Robosapien Robocop Edition...

Figure 12-10. *Water-slide decals from scale model kits make a great, easy, and reversable mod.*

Figure 12-11. *The guys at GadgetMadness.com are at it again!*

Robosapien Repairs

This isn't really a hack per se, but regardless, it may be something you end up needing to do as a result of a hacking project! For most common problems, Robosapien is relatively easy to troubleshoot and repair. Unless you are doing some pretty complicated electronics, like tapping into Robosapien's power supply to run peripherals or attempting to change the motors or their driver circuitry, most problems with the robot are the result of a loose connector or a wire that has been inadvertently cut or crimped, or you've put the robot back together incorrectly, things along these lines. In Chapter 13 we will look more closely at some methods for troubleshooting common Robosapien problems.

The "Bolt-On" Approach

This is my favorite type of Robosapien hack, and in some ways the easiest, particularly from a technical standpoint. The "bolt-on" approach is just that: bolting on or adding self-contained objects that enhance Robosapien's capabilities. These hacks usually involve adding standalone electronic components or peripherals, as well as their power supplies. The trick is integrating the peripheral and the battery pack into Robosapien.

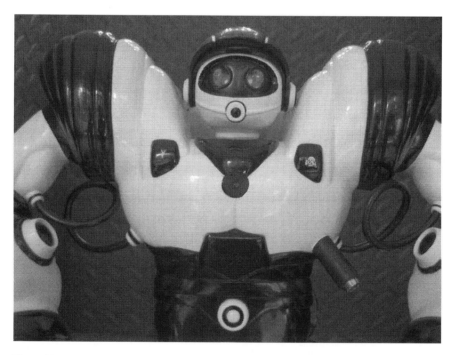

Figure 12-12. *Seamless integration of the peripheral is one of the challenges of the bolt-on approach to hacking Robosapien. If you weren't looking for it, you probably wouldn't even notice the camera in this Robosapien's chest. Alternatively, the integration doesn't always need to be hidden. Note the power connector protruding from Robosapien's chest in the lower-right corner—this hooks up to the battery for the camera. The battery would have easily fit into the chest cavity, but I thought that this was better looking and would save the hassle of having to take the shell completely off to access the battery. Also note the decorative water-slide decals.*

The bolt-on approach is nice because it allows you to add some pretty cool enhancements to your robot, but since you are not really fooling with Robosapien's electronics, the chances of you doing permanent damage to the robot's circuitry are slim. The best part about this type of hack is that you are limited only by your own creativity. You have to be creative in not only coming up with cool ideas of things that would enhance Robosapien, but also in your methods of integrating whatever it is into Robosapien.

Examples of this type of hack include installing a wireless camera (discussed in Chapter 14) and adding a radio frequency audio receiver and amplifier (discussed in Chapter15). One hacker has even gone so far as to outfit his Robosapien with finger and head lasers!

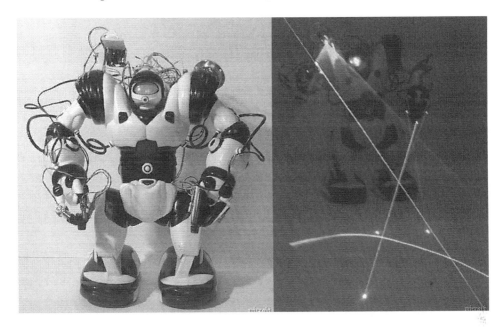

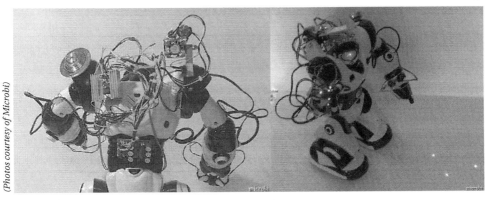

(Photos courtesy of Microbi)

Figures 12-13 and 12-14. *Microbi, a German Robosapien hacker, has outfitted his Robosapien with lasers for a spectacular effect.*

Another area that is fun with this sort of hack is that once you do a couple of them, you will never look at consumer electronic devices (like a set of wireless headphones or a laser pointer) the same way again. You will look at them in terms of "How can I modify that to fit onto Robosapien?"

Enhancement Hacks

This is where technical knowledge of electronics becomes just as important as creativity. Mark Tilden has given a few examples of these types of hacks, such as swapping out the palm LEDs with infrared "ultrabrights" so Robosapien can use them as visual flashlights, replacing the motors and H-Bridge drivers to increase speed and strength, or patching into the robot's existing sensor array with a laser-guided pan-and-tilt camera targeting system. These types of hacks involve a whole different level of dedication and knowledge and are well beyond the scope of this book. But they are neat things to think about and aspire to.

Brain Replacement Hacks

Brain replacement guys. These guys are nuts! But the fact is, some people have the ego to make it happen. The people that are trying to replace his brains, there are some sophisticated ways of doing that, but there are also some nonsophisticated ways that you can try that don't sacrifice the brain of your robot.

—*Mark Tilden, February 13, 2005*

Brain replacement is the pinnacle of Robosapien hacking, and there are very few people actually doing it at this point. This involves augmenting Robosapien with upgraded processor chips and entirely new circuitry. Some of the chips that are being used include the BASIC Stamp, the Atmel AT90S8535 chip, the Atmel AVR90S2313, and the BasicX-24. These types of hacks usually involve adding more sensors to Robosapien, and/or limited vision capabilities, and the capability to process the information and integrate it with Robosapien's own native feedback routines. Some people are even adding new processors to tailor the robot's movements to their whims. Complicated stuff, but well worth looking into if it is an area you are interested in. The Robosapien makes an excellent platform for this type of experimentation.

Of course, the second type of brain replacement that Mark alludes to in the quote above as "nonsophisticated ways that you can try that doesn't sacrifice the brain of your robot" was covered in Chapter 11 on PC interfacing.

The Hacking Process

As I have said before, the two most important tools you need with regard to Robosapien— whether you are playing with it, programming it, hacking it, or some combination of the three—are your own curiosity and creativity. It's one thing to work through the hacks in this book, or to reproduce projects that people have done and posted on the Internet, but it is really rewarding when you come up with something on your own and then see it all the way through. I'm going to share my process, but remember; everyone's brain works a little bit differently, so do what works best for you.

I think that you should start off by applying your creativity. Take out your Robosapien and put it through the paces. What do you like about it? What could be better? Do you have a specific task that you want the robot to be able to complete? Do you want to improve an existing capability, or add an entirely new capability? Is something not working the way you think it should, and might need to be fixed? Write all of these things down.

Once you have your list, it is time to begin applying your curiosity. Do some Internet searches on some of the things you have written down so that you at least have an idea of what you might be getting into. Be creative in your searches; for example, if you want to paint Robosapien, you probably aren't going to find very much information out there. But there is a wealth of information on painting plastic models, and you can apply this knowledge to your project. If some of your ideas involve internal improvements or modifications, take Robosapien apart and familiarize yourself with the part of the robot that you want to deal with. How does it work? Where are the connectors? What tools will you need? Remember that it is difficult to break anything in Robosapien just by taking the robot apart, so go for it!

These are all things you will need to think about before you begin your hack. Another interesting guideline comes from Dan Danknick, while he was judging the *Servo* magazine "Hack-a-Sapien" contest. "Ultimately," he writes, "the winners were the ones who submitted complete hacks that took the Robosapien out of the realm of 'toy' and into that of 'tool.'"[1] This is interesting, and while it is a great guideline for judging a contest, I am not so sure it is great advice for the beginning hacker. I think it is more important to have fun and learn something, and as you gain experience worry more about distinctions such as this.

What's Next?

The best way to get started hacking your Robosapien is to work through Chapter 13 a few times, taking the robot apart and putting it back together, and trying some of the easier hacks I have outlined not just in this chapter, but throughout the book.

Another good idea is to get is a soldering practice kit (or two). Most electronics stores (online or otherwise) carry them and they are an excellent introduction to how to use a soldering iron. They will usually include a soldering iron, some solder, a practice PCB, a bunch of electronic components, and some instructions. Soldering is definitely something that takes practice. While you might not be interested in doing some of the more complicated types of hacks, soldering is still a good skill to have for some of the easier hacks, too. It will expand your options for integrating bolt-on hacks, it will help you to mount LEDs, hook up battery packs... all in all it is a valuable lesson.

I think the future of hacking the Robosapien is bright. From what I have heard, the new version of Robosapien, dubbed "V2" by WowWee and due out in late 2005, will be nowhere near as hackable as the first version, probably in large part because it abandons much of the simplicity of Robosapien version 1.

---

1. *Servo*, vol. 3, no. 1, January 2005, page 29.

Summary

As time goes on I think we will begin to see more and more hacks and projects involving Robosapien.

> *It's still too early for the science. You won't probably see anything until summertime [2005], because right now, a lot of kids are working on Robosapiens for their final school project. But this June, this July, we're going to see a number of hacks, as part of degrees.... It's all basically happening right now. It's January, and they are saying, ok what can I do with my Robosapien that will get me a grade. Imagine this, you're taking a standard robot course at any college throughout North America. And you know what they have there, usually the Rhino arms or some sort of pathetic Meccano-looking carts, or Lego Mindstorms.... Imagine, there you are and everyone is working with these boring robots and you walk in with a Robosapien, with a new brain. Come on! That is Joe Franken- stein. <in a bad German accent> I have rebuilt him! He is mad!*
>
> —Mark Tilden, February 13, 2005

I think these hacks will come not only from the educational arena, but also from people who have had their Robosapiens for a while and are saying "OK, what's next?" Stay tuned; it should be interesting!

CHAPTER 13

■■■

Hacking Basics

Figure 13-1. *"Hurry up and find that screw, it's FREEZING in here!"*

The purpose of this chapter is to provide you with some more basic information on hacking your Robosapien. Originally, I had intended to fill all of Part 4, Chapters 12 through 15, with step-by-step hacking projects, ranging from simple hacks to more complicated modifications. So why didn't I? For one thing, that proved to be very tedious to read. The majority of hacks are easily found on the Internet anyway; just do a search for "Robosapien hacks." I'm not saying they don't have value—and we look at a few in subsequent chapters—but I just didn't want to make that the primary focus. For another thing, I felt as if it really limited the book. I could provide what *I* think are the coolest projects ever, but if they are not interesting to you, the reader, then I have wasted pages. Finally, new projects and ideas are springing up all the time.

My decision also has a lot to do with the scope and purpose of this book. Throughout all my schooling, there have always been two general types of teachers. There were some who just wanted their students to memorize facts and dates, formulas and concepts, and then spit them back from memory for a grade. This type of instructor gave you everything you needed, up front, and then it was up to you to memorize those facts. While exploring further than that was never discouraged, it wasn't exactly encouraged either.

I much preferred the second type of teacher. These instructors showed you the basics on the topic and got you to the point where you could start applying the concepts on your own. Then they cut you free and graded you based on how you applied the basics and what you came up with.

I found that I always learned much more from the second type of teacher. For one thing it gives you a lot more freedom to focus on the aspects of the subject at hand that you are really interested in. For another, it makes learning a journey of discovery, and for me anyway, I was always more motivated to learn when I was given the basics and allowed to explore the intricacies of the subject on my own.

I want this book to whet your intellectual appetite for coming up with your own hacks, and not just lay out the hacks that others and I have done. My goal is to get you thinking about your own hacks, and to stimulate your creativity and curiosity with regard to Robosapien projects. So toward that end I plan on following the second approach that I outlined above.

In this chapter, we start by looking at some general guidelines and Robosapien hacking "best practices." These are some suggestions that will help keep you organized and efficient while working on your Robosapien.

After this, I will provide you with a step-by-step pictorial covering how to take the robot's shell off so that you can gain easier access to the components inside. Becoming comfortable with taking Robosapien apart and putting it back together is probably the most useful skill in hacking the Robosapien—you will end up doing it a lot! You can't get much more basic than this; disassembly of the shell is in integral part of almost every hacking project, with the exception of some cosmetic hacking projects that I discussed in Chapter 12.

Not to get too far ahead of myself, but in Chapters 14 and 15 I look at troubleshooting and some really easy hacks: adding a volume control and adding a wireless camera. These uncomplicated projects will familiarize you with the basic hacking process, you will "get your feet wet," and then (I hope!) you will be ready to start applying your own talents, creativity, and curiosity.

Robosapien Hacking "Best Practices"

Figure 13-2. *Try to avoid this scenario!*

In this section I set out some suggestions that will keep you organized, and allow you to focus your full attention on your hack. These are mostly things that I have learned by trial and error, and almost all of these will not only apply to hacking Robosapien, but also to almost any other project that you undertake.

One of the most important overall aspects to hacking the Robosapien is to keep a level head. Rudyard Kipling wrote in his poem *If*: "If you can meet with Triumph and Disaster, and treat those two imposters just the same;…Yours is the Earth and everything that's in it…" What he is saying is to keep a positive outlook and don't let setbacks discourage you. Treat your failures the same way that you treat your successes and keep an "even keel." If something doesn't work out the way you expected, try to figure out why, and use your mistakes as a positive learning experience. This is great advice for a beginning hacker, because you *will* make mistakes.

Another piece of good advice is to go slowly. Take your time and don't try to force anything apart that doesn't feel as if it wants to be taken apart. This stuff is common sense, but take it from me, it is all too easy to be excited and in a hurry and screw something up because you are rushing or impatient. By going slowly and paying attention to even the smallest details, you will do a much better job. You will also discover things that you weren't even looking for, and possibly find inspiration for future hacks and projects.

Above all, *have fun*. If you find that you are getting frustrated or that you have reached a dead end, take a break and step away for a while. When you return you will invariably find that you are refreshed and have a new perspective, and that the problems you faced earlier might not seem so insurmountable after all.

Preparation

This section could also be titled "Know What You Are Getting Into, and Don't Bite Off More Than You Can Chew," but that was entirely too long for a subheading! The basic gist is to enter into each and every project thoroughly prepared. Have a clear idea of what you want to accomplish. Do any research that you need to do in advance; don't wait to figure out how to do something in the middle of the project once Robosapien is in a million pieces. Make sure that you have handy all the tools that your project requires. It can be an incredible distraction to have to stop what you are doing and step away from the project to track down a tool or a part that you need.

Keep Track of Time

Maybe it's just me. When I start a project I have an amazing tendency to get so engrossed in what I am doing that I completely lose track of time. There is nothing worse than being at your work area, thoroughly involved in a hack, only to realize that it is getting light outside and you need to be at work in two hours.

The obvious solution to this problem is to outfit your work area with a clock (or outfit Robosapien with some way of keeping track of time!). But even if you are keeping track of the time, stopping your work in the middle of a project because you ran out of time can be a bad distraction, and it can take quite a while to get back on track.

The best way to deal with this problem is to include it in your preparation. If you are undertaking a complicated project, break it up into smaller pieces. Estimate how long you think something is going to take you, and plan accordingly.

Keep a Hacking Journal

What else do you expect from a writer? Keep a Robosapien hacking journal! (It will look great on the bookshelf next to your Robosapien programming journal.) Be sure to include a section for jotting down spontaneous hacking ideas that come to you but that might require more research—this way you won't forget them. Use the journal to organize and outline your research and preparation. Also use it to keep track of tools and components that you need to purchase the next time you are at the electronics store. I find that a binder with loose-leaf paper works best so that you can shuffle things around and add printed pages from Internet research to your handwritten notes.

But where a journal really comes in handy is *during* the actual hack. Use it to keep track of what you are doing step by step. Not only will it make putting everything back together easier (since you can just backtrack), but it will also make it easy to compile and share tutorials on how you accomplished your project. If you want to be especially thorough, you can even include digital photographs of each step in your journal; just remember to make a note of the pictures' filenames.

Stay Organized

As easy as it is to take Robosapien apart, you will still end up with a lot of loose pieces and screws. And not all of the screws or pieces are the same size. Not knowing which screw goes where will not only make reassembly a nightmare, but in some cases, the robot will not go back together properly or some of its functionality may suffer.

Here's an easy way to keep track of things: after you have removed a piece of Robosapien's shell, use that piece of shell as a container to hold all of the screws (see Figure 13-3). Another suggestion that works great, especially for larger pieces, is to use Robosapien's own accessory cup (see Figure 13-4). Those weekly pill boxes that have seven compartments and that are designed to keep track of which pills you are supposed to take on a particular day also work reasonably well, and have the advantage of having a lid for each compartment.

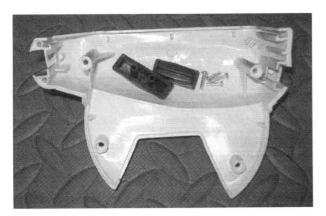

Figure 13-3. *You can use pieces of Robosapien's shell to hold the smaller pieces and screws for that particular component. This shot shows part of Robosapien's foot assembly holding the screws and the touch-sensor pieces.*

Figure 13-4. *Robosapien's accessory cup makes a good container to hold larger pieces and screws. These are the pieces to the Robosapien head I destroyed in Chapter 5.*

While using pieces of the shell and the accessory cup works well in keeping you organized, I find that using paper cups works best, since the cups have sides and you can write on them (see Figure 13-5). I originally used index cards, but found that the screws tended to roll places that I didn't want them to. Next I tried folding the cards into little boxes to hold the screws and components, which was way more work than it was worth. Finally my wife suggested that I cut down some paper cups and use them. It works great!

Figure 13-5. *You can cut down paper cups for easily labeled containers to hold screws and components.*

Other ideas for keeping you organized include sectioned trays designed for fishing gear and trays for holding action figures. You probably have the perfect container lying around somewhere in your garage, attic, or basement.

Reassembly Tips

Pretty much everything I have told you up to this point can also apply to reassembling Robosapien. However, here are a few things that should help you as well.

The first tip is to take apart only one side at a time, at least until you have done it a few times and know what to expect. For instance, if you take apart the left-arm assembly, leave the right arm intact. This way you can reference the right arm to see how to put the left arm back together if you get stuck.

Also, when reinserting a screw, slowly turn it counterclockwise until you hear a slight "click" and feel it drop into place. This will ensure that you reuse the original threads, and the screw will go in much easier. It also saves the screw hole from unnecessary wear and tear, since otherwise you will probably make new threads every time you screw it back in. If you do this enough times the screw will no longer hold at all.

Another really useful tip is to run the diagnostic routines after you have finished putting Robosapien back together and have completed your project. I laid these out in detail at the end of Chapter 4. By doing this you can ensure that you didn't inadvertently damage a wire or some other part of Robosapien while you were doing your hack.

Disassembling the Robosapien

Taking the Robosapien apart is something that any hacker worth his or her salt will do literally hundreds of times while working on various Robosapien projects. You may even find that certain projects work just fine with the robot in a disassembled state, but run into problems when Robosapien is fully assembled.

The goal of any hack is, of course, to modify Robosapien, but if the robot doesn't work once it is put back together then the hack really isn't very successful, is it? So the final goal of any

Robosapien hack should not be to just successfully complete your hack, but rather to successfully complete your hack and integrate it into the robot without compromising any functionality. Of course, the exception to this rule is if you are adding new functionality to Robosapien, or modifying existing functionality to work differently than it does in a stock robot.

Disassembling the Robosapien's shell can be divided into four distinct categories: 1) tools and setup, 2) chest plate and torso, 3) arms and claws, and finally 4) legs and feet. I am not going to discuss disassembling the robot's head. As we saw in Chapter 5, Robosapien's head is glued together and is extremely difficult to take apart without permanently damaging the plastic. It *can* be taken apart, and if this is something that you want to try, by all means go for it. But I want to avoid providing tips that will most likely cause significant damage to your robot.

Likewise, I am primarily going to discuss removing Robosapien's shell, and not really get into motor removal or disassembling the basic structural components. Once you get the shell off, it is fairly obvious how to do these things, but I suggest that you wait to try them until you have some more basic experience under your belt. As with most things, taking Robosapien's shell apart isn't difficult, but getting everything back together and functional can be tricky.

Tools and Setup

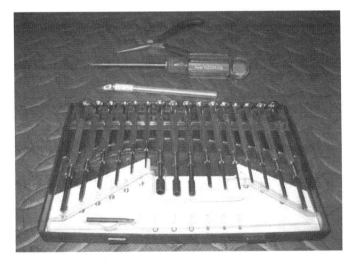

Figure 13-6. *You need only a few simple tools to completely remove Robosapien's shell.*

You only need one tool to completely remove Robosapien's shell. You can do it with just a Phillips head screwdriver, but having a few extras like needle-nose pliers, a hobby knife, and some different-sized precision screw drivers will make the task a lot easier.

Make sure your work area is well lit and free of clutter, and also have a plan in place to organize the parts and screws as you remove them. It also helps if you have a soft surface to work on; this will help keep Robosapien free of scratches, and it will also stop screws from bouncing away if (or when) they fall out. I have a high-density foam pad that I use in my work area, but a folded towel will work just as well. Just remember to remove the soft surface if and when you plug in your soldering iron or use any other electric tools.

Removing the Chest Plate and Torso

All right, with the prep work out of the way, let's get busy!

Chest Plate Removal

The chest plate should always be the first part you take off. Start by making sure Robosapien is turned off at the switch on the back plate. Arrange Robosapien's arms in the all-the-way-in, all-the-way-down position and place the robot face down on your work surface (see Figure 13-7).

Figure 13-7. *Place Robosapien face down in order to begin removing the chest shell.*

Four Phillips head screws hold Robosapien's chest plate together, one at each shoulder, and one on each side of the robot's waist area. Unscrew all these screws until they spin freely in their sockets.

Gently lift the back plate away from Robosapien's body, and disconnect the black cables that go to the robot's arms from the small niches that they snap into (see Figure 13-8).

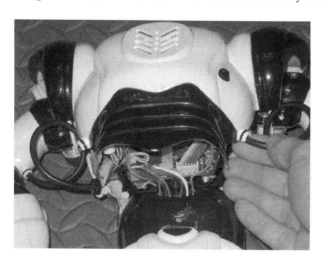

Figure 13-8. *Gently unhook the wires that connect Robosapien's arms to the main processor board.*

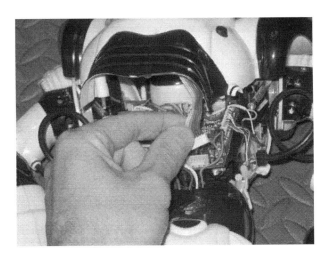

Figure 13-9. *Disconnect the connector that leads from Robosapien's back shell piece to the motherboard. This connection carries the on/off switch connection and the speaker cables. You can use a small flat-head screwdriver or a small pair of needle-nose pliers to help you get it out.*

Once you have unhooked the arm cables and disconnected the connector, you can lift away the back shell. At this stage you can also stand Robosapien up and remove the chest shell.

Tip It is important to make sure that Robosapien is turned off before you begin taking it apart. If the switch is in the ON position, as it is when Robosapien turns itself off automatically, when you reconnect the back plate connector the robot will spring to life, which will definitely scare the bejesus out of you, and possibly damage the robot.

Figure 13-10. *You can access the speaker by removing the three Phillips head screws that hold the cover in place on Robosapien's inside back plate.*

Lower Torso Shell Removal

The next step is to remove the shell from Robosapien's lower torso. Again, place your robot face down on your work area. For some reason, WowWee decided to put screw covers on the top two of the three screw holes that hold these pieces together. Depending on the individual robot, these could be simply set in or glued in. Either way, you can carefully pry them out with a small flat-head screwdriver or a hobby knife (see Figure 13-11). You may end up scratching the black paint a bit trying to get these out, but don't worry—this area is mostly covered by the chest plate when Robosapien is fully assembled. You can also touch up any scratches with some gloss enamel paint designed for plastic models.

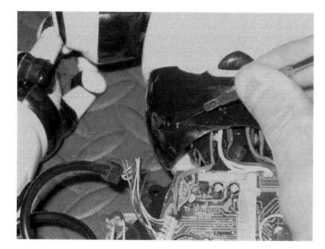

Figure 13-11. *Carefully pry away the screw covers on Robosapien's lower torso.*

Once you have removed the screw covers, unscrew the three Phillips head screws that hold Robosapien's lower torso shell together. When you have unscrewed the three screws, the lower torso plates should fall away easily.

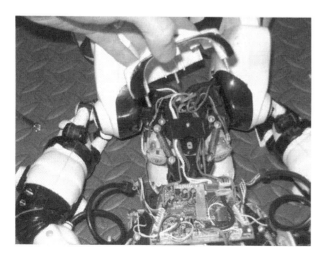

Figure 13-12. *Remove the lower torso shell.*

Removing the Arms

The next step is to have a look at Robosapien's arms. Note that you can remove the plate that covers the robot's forearm (and the claws) without removing the chest shell, but if you want to completely remove the arm at the shoulder, you need to remove the chest shell.

Lower Arm Disassembly

Start by removing the six Phillips head screws located on the underside of Robosapien's forearm. Note that in the earliest Robosapien models, the forearm shell is glued together and has only four screws. If your Robosapien has only four screws and is glued, it might take some force on your part to pry the top part of the shell away once you have removed the screws.

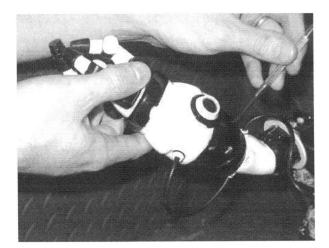

Figure 13-13. *Remove the six screws that hold Robosapien's forearm shell in place.*

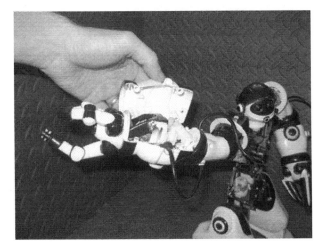

Figure 13-14. *With the six screws removed, you should be able to pull away the top of the forearm shell, giving you access to the interior. The forearm motor is attached to the lower part of the forearm shell. Note all of the grease in there— you might want to keep a rag handy to wipe the excess away and to clean it off your fingers.*

To remove the claw once the top part of the forearm shell is removed, grasp it and gently turn it clockwise. This should disengage it from the forearm and allow you to pull it away. You will also need to disconnect the tiny connectors for the palm LED and the finger-touch sensor to fully remove it (see Figure 13-15).

Tip Robosapien's claws are fully interchangeable. Switch the left claw with the right claw, or, if you have two Robosapiens, give one of them a set of the rounded-fingered claws, and the other a set of the straight-fingered claws.

Figure 13-15. *Once Robosapien's claw is free of the forearm, disconnect the LED and sensor connectors from the tiny PCB in the forearm.*

Upper Arm Disassembly

Our next step is to open up and remove Robosapien's upper arm. Note that you can have the forearm and/or claw apart or together for this step; it doesn't matter.

Start by removing the four Phillips head screws, three are located up at the shoulder, and the fourth is located down at the elbow.

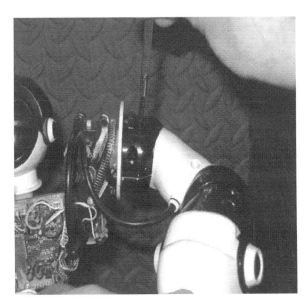

Figure 13-16. *Removing the screws in Robosapien's upper arm shell.*

Once the screws are removed, you will need to start at the shoulder and gently pry the two pieces that make up the upper arm shell apart. There will probably be a lot of extra grease here, so have your rag handy. The lower part of the shell will eventually come free, along with the entire forearm assembly.

Figure 13-17. *Take apart Robosapien's upper arm.*

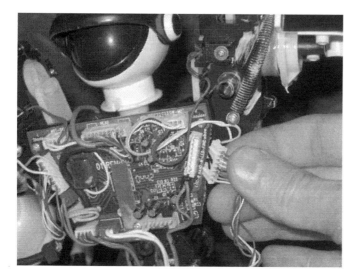

Figure 13-18. *You can disconnect the arm cable at the motherboard and completely free the lower-arm assembly from the robot.*

Pay attention to the loop connected to the wire leading to the forearm; it fits on a peg inside the top upper-arm shell, which feeds it through the slots in the bicep correctly (see Figure 13-19). Also note, as we discussed in Chapter 5, that the entire upper arm is hollow.

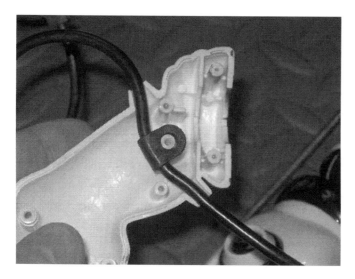

Figure 13-19. *Note how the arm cable is attached in the top part of the upper-arm shell.*

The top half of the upper-arm shell connects to a hole in the shoulder mechanism. To detach it, simply lift it off (see Figures 13-20 and 13-21).

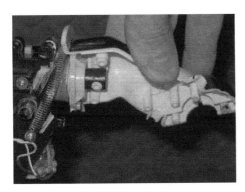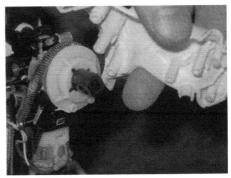

Figures 13-20 and 13-21. *Completely remove the upper-arm shell.*

Removing the Leg Shells

The final stage of our disassembly covers Robosapien's leg-shell pieces. These are slightly more difficult to remove due to the fact that some of the screws are tricky to reach, but it can definitely be done. This is where having a smaller-sized precision style screwdriver really comes in handy. You will need to have Robosapien's lower-torso shell removed to access these screws.

Upper Leg

The inner part of Robosapien's upper-leg shell is attached to the underlying frame, as we saw in Chapter 5 (see Figures 5-26 through 5-28). In order to remove the inner shell you need to take off the entire leg mechanism, which is relatively self-explanatory, once you get the outer shell off.

To remove the outer shell covering Robosapien's upper leg, there are four screws: two in the white plastic at the bottom, near the "knee," and two in the black plastic at the top where the hip joint is. The back screw at the hip is very tricky to reach, but you should be able to bend Robosapien's hip joint to gain access to it.

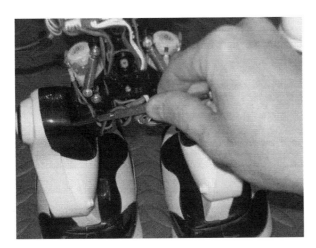

Figure 13-22. *The screw at the rear of Robosapien's hip joint can be difficult to access.*

Figure 13-23. *Once you have removed all four screws, you can pull off the outer shell, which exposes the inside of Robosapien's hip joint. Note the three screws that attach the inner part of the leg to the robot's hip motor.*

Lower Leg and Foot

Removing Robosapien's lower leg and foot shell is fairly straightforward. The shells are connected with four screws on the inside of the robot's leg: two in the black plastic near the bottom of the foot, and two in the white plastic just below the knee joint.

Start by removing the four screws. You will need to manually bend Robosapien at the knee in order to access them—the inner-thigh shell can block them. Once the screws are removed, pull it apart at the bottom of the foot (see Figure 13-24), paying attention to how the heel and toe sensor pads align with the exterior shell and the rubber sensor pads inside the foot assembly.

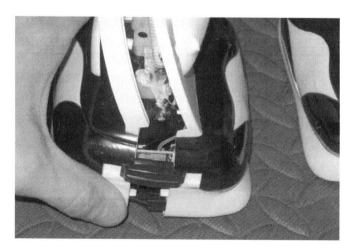

Figure 13-24. *Remove the outer portion of Robosapien's lower leg and foot.*

You can either slip off the inside part of the lower leg and foot shell, or remove the entire leg by unscrewing the three screws on the outside of the hip joint (see Figure 13-23), and the single screw on the inside of Robosapien's upper leg (see Figure 13-25).

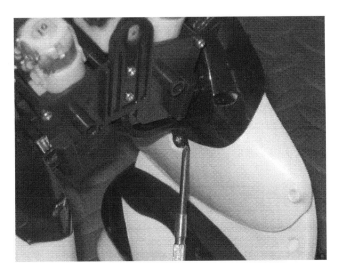

Figure 13-25. *After removing the three screws that attach Robosapien's leg mechanism to the robot's hip, remove this screw to completely remove the leg.*

Summary

So there you have it: a complete guide to disassembling your Robosapien, the cornerstone of any Robosapien hacking project. Just make sure when you put it all back together to run the diagnostic routines to make sure that you didn't inadvertently disconnect a wire when you were poking around inside.

CHAPTER 14

■■■

Troubleshooting Your Robosapien

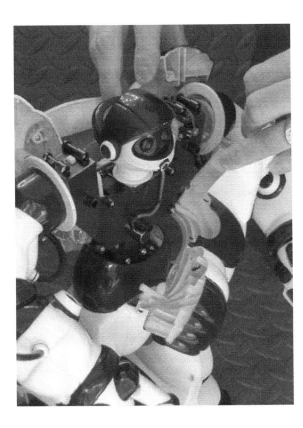

Figure 14-1. *Open up and say "ahh."*

So are you beginning to feel like a real robot hacker? Up to this point, you should have a basic understanding of the principles and history behind Robosapien, and you have completed a few simple hacks if you have worked your way through the book. In Chapter 13 you began learning how to take your Robosapien apart and put it back together. You are well on your way, and I hope you are starting to have some ideas floating around in your head about some potential Robosapien modifications you'd like to begin working on.

The next step to pulling together everything that you've learned is to start working through some basic hacks. By doing this and applying some of your own ideas and techniques, the possibilities you see when you look at Robosapien should begin to skyrocket. Later in this chapter I show you how to add a volume control and an on/off switch to Robosapien's speaker. This is a great exercise because not only is it a cool hack, but it also gets you thinking about ways to integrate components into Robosapien.

But before we start, it is worth looking at something every hacker has to do at one point or another: troubleshooting.

Troubleshooting Robosapien

I can tell you one of the things I learned from the toy industry is that you can't sell broken toys.

—Mark Tilden, February 13, 2005

One of the remarkable things about Robosapien is really just how durable it is. Remember first that Robosapien is a *toy*, something designed to be played with (it's easy to lose sight of that, isn't it?). Then consider that Robosapien is designed to be taken apart and modified... and one would think that these little robots would have an extremely limited lifespan, right?

It's just not so. Robosapien is amazingly durable. I have put a couple of my Robosapiens through the ringer, and for months at a time—not only through hacking the living daylights out of a couple, but also by doing all of the photography for this book. Through all of that I have yet to break a Robosapien beyond repair; in fact, with the exception of the head that I destroyed in Chapter 5, I have yet to even *slightly damage* a Robosapien, unless I was really trying to.

[You can put Robosapien through the paces] like you wouldn't believe. It's one of its hidden features that it actually has the ability... I mean you can kick the crap out of that thing, it can take a tumble down the stairs. The fifth major sell feature was this: for a seven-motor toy we have had less than a 0.03 percent return rate. That means one in every 340 robots sold actually had some sort of mechanical defect.... That's astonishing! In [the] toy industry, normally there is always a 3 percent [return rate]—every standard radio-controlled toy that you see sold has an average of 3 percent to 50 percent return. Furby was a 33 percent return. You've got to remember, any toy that is returned, you have to sell two toys to recover the costs. Because a toy that is returned is not refunded from the money from the retailer, it is refunded by the money from the actual distributor— that is the person who actually owns the toy. The retailer just basically leases us the space to move our product. We own it. So the Robosapien was a big risk this year. And the reason that Hasbro got rid of [WowWee, formerly owned by Hasbro] was because of the Robosapien. Because they'd seen the problem that they'd had just with the Furby, with one motor, and this thing has seven? And you expect it's going to be reliable? We've got some statistics for you...

—Mark Tilden, February 13, 2005

Figures 14-2 and 14-3. *Despite mangling the shell pretty badly and reducing it to a pile of plastic, I found that Robosapien's head will go together nicely with a little glue. It could probably be reassembled perfectly with a little modeler's putty and white touch-up paint.*

Even given Robosapien's remarkable durability, accidents can still happen, mistakes can be made, and sometimes, although certainly extremely rarely in Robosapien's case, quality control can be shoddy. This brings us to troubleshooting.

The first question you need to ask yourself is "Do I want to troubleshoot this?" I think if the problem is minor enough the answer should always be "yes." However, depending on where you purchased your Robosapien and what that retailer's return policy is, simply returning it for a refund or a replacement can also be an easy option, and get you back up and running quickly. But if the problem is the result of something you have done, or if you have modified your Robosapien extensively, you probably aren't going to be able to return it, and you probably won't want to anyway. Of course, another option is to utilize WowWee's customer support (see the accompanying sidebar).

Troubleshooting techniques are important not only to diagnose problems with your Robosapien, but you can also apply the same principles when you are testing your hacks and modifications and trying to make sure that they work as intended.

WOWWEE CUSTOMER SUPPORT

From all indications, WowWee's customer support of Robosapien has been outstanding. While I have never personally had to use it, every account I have heard about it seems to have ended with a favorable resolution. Additionally, since Robosapien's release, several people have shared the letters and emails that they have received from WowWee, and these have always been informative and helpful. In a few cases, WowWee has even sent out replacement parts, but I am sure that this is rare and is done on a case-by-case basis.

Check out `http://www.robosapienonline.com` for WowWee customer support contact information.

With this in mind I begin by looking at a few basic troubleshooting concepts and then move on to some Robosapien-specific ideas.

Figure 14-4. *Don't you hate calling customer support lines and getting stuck talking to a machine?*

Troubleshooting Fundamentals

It almost goes without saying that the number one rule in troubleshooting *anything* is to not make the problem worse through your actions. As long as you keep this most basic rule in mind, applying the following four commonsense troubleshooting recommendations should be a snap.

Write Down Your Steps

By now you are probably wondering if I own stock in a company that manufactures note-books. I promise I don't! But because I have always saved so much time and subsequent effort by writing things down, it is a point I want to hammer home. By writing down your trouble-shooting steps you won't repeat something you've already tried, and you can easily take a step back and look at what you've already done. If you hit a dead end, going back and reviewing your steps can jump-start the process and get you back on track.

Don't Rush

Writing down your steps also helps with this suggestion. It naturally slows you down, and the process of writing gives you time to fully consider alternative strategies. Just as you don't want to rush when doing your hacks, rushing while troubleshooting is a bad thing. Not only does it increase your chances of missing something, but it also increases your chances of making the problem worse.

Believe me, when something isn't working the way that it should, I am the worst offender in this category. I want to know *right now* why something isn't working so that I can get busy figuring out how to fix it. Slowing down and taking your time can be a real challenge, but I think you will find that writing down your troubleshooting steps will help you to slow down and consider the problem from as many angles as possible.

Check Simple Things First and Don't Assume Anything

If you are challenging yourself, and getting into something that you don't know a lot about, it is easy to overlook the simplest solutions. For example, before you shatter Robosapien's helmet to look inside the robot's head, make sure the cable leading from the head to the main controller board is plugged in. Before you even take Robosapien's chest shell off to investigate a problem, be sure the robot has fresh batteries and that it is turned on.

Use your head, don't always assume the worst, and don't get so caught up trying to figure out complex problems and solutions that you overlook the obvious.

Use a Systematic Approach

If Robosapien is having a problem with one of its arms, then don't worry about the robot's legs. Try one thing at a time, write it down, and if it doesn't help you pinpoint the problem then try something else. Just keep a cool head, observe everything, and go slowly, and chances are you will figure out what is wrong. Now whether or not you will be able to fix it is another thing altogether…

Robosapien-Specific Troubleshooting

One of the things that the people who are interested in artificial life don't realize is that the real world is filled with artificial death.

—Mark Tilden, February 13, 2005

In this section I apply some of the basic commonsense troubleshooting techniques we looked at specifically to Robosapien.

Batteries

The first thing you should do if your robot has a problem that isn't immediately obvious (i.e., it's been run over by a car, it's missing its legs, etc.) is to try fresh batteries. Don't use "new" batteries that have been in your desk drawer for who knows how long, but go to the store and buy new batteries for both the robot and the remote.

People have put some of the worst, crappiest batteries in the feet that you could possible imagine. Carbon cell batteries… you'd be amazed at how much of the world still uses 1970s battery technology. <Laughs>

We went up to Tibet and we got the crappiest, cheapest, the worst god-awful batteries you could possibly imagine. And we still got two hours of play out of the Robosapien. So we realized, no matter where this goes, you're going to get two hours of play, that's a good amount of time.

—Mark Tilden, February 13, 2005

I don't know how many times over the past year people have come to the Robosapien.tk forums to ask for help with a problem, only to report back with "Well, I tried new batteries and my robot is now working great!"

You should try fresh batteries for pretty much any problem you face with Robosapien: from the robot not powering on, to a lack of movement in one or more limbs, to static and changes in Robosapien's "voice."

Figure 14-5. *When installing fresh batteries in Robosapien, make sure that the cloth strip designed to help "pop" the batteries out does not cover any of the battery contact points.*

Applying the Systematic Approach

If new batteries don't solve your problem, it is time to think about it a bit more critically. Using a systematic approach, first attempt to localize the problem. Is it an arm or a leg? Run Robosapien through all of the possible arm movements and walking gaits and see if you can identify a repeatable example of the problem. For instance, "The left arm works fine, unless it is all the way up, and then Robosapien will not open its claw." By isolating the problem, you narrow down your options of where to look.

Physical Examination

The next step is to do a physical examination. Take off any applicable pieces of Robosapien's shell surrounding the affected area and look for obvious problems such as broken wires or burnt components on the PCB—things that you can find just by using your powers of observation. Remember, even if you don't know how to fix the problem yourself, being able to accurately and completely describe it can be a great aid to someone trying to assist you—whether you call WowWee customer support, post your problem on a Robosapien message board, or have a friend or a relative come and help you.

Swapping Components

If you have narrowed down the problem with your Robosapien to one of the robot's arms or legs, an easy way to continue your diagnosis is to swap the appendages. Now, I don't mean take it completely off, but rather, swap the connectors on the robot's main processor board (see Figure 14-6).

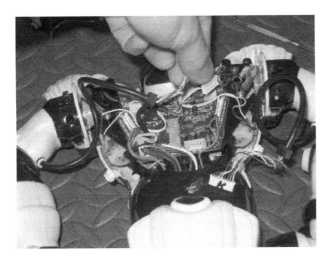

Figure 14-6. *Swapping the connectors for Robosapien's appendages is a great trouble-shooting tool. In this photo I am attaching Robosapien's lower-left arm to the right-arm connector on the main processor board.*

For example, if your Robosapien's right-side palm LED isn't working properly, hook up the robot's right-arm connector to the left-arm connector on the processor board, and vice versa. Run both arms through all of their possible permutations and carefully note the results for both arms. If the LED now works, then you know you probably have a problem somewhere on the main controller board. If the LED still doesn't work even when plugged into the left arm's connector, then you can assume that your problem lies somewhere in the right arm, either in the wiring or the LED itself.

Specific Issues

I wouldn't necessarily say all of the following are "common" Robosapien problems, but they are ones that I have seen crop up more often than any others over the past year.

Walking Problems

This is a big thing they found with all the girls doing our tests. The robot had to sort of operate within certain performance parameters. And many robots were doing things like "Oh it walks off, it's obviously defective" and then they'd test it again and be like "No, it walks straight..." I'm sorry, but the robot is based upon a law of indeterminism, which is not wholly measurable in all possible instances.
—*Mark Tilden, February 13, 2005*

We covered Robosapien's walking mechanics in detail in Chapter 6. The bottom line, as we saw, is that all Robosapiens have problems walking straight. If you fear that there is a problem with one of the robot's legs, pick it up while it is walking and observe both legs. If you see a problem with one of the legs, try swapping the right and left leg connectors on the main controller board and note the results.

Body Tilts

The earliest Robosapiens had significant problems with their waist springs; essentially the springs were not strong enough to provide the level of suspension that the robot needs to balance itself and its walking. The telltale sign of this problem is a robot that permanently leans more to one side than the other, even when powered off.

If your Robosapien has this problem there are a few things you can try. One piece of advice is to attach a small piece of lead, like a fishing weight, to one side to try to balance Robosapien this way. Another approach is to put in new springs or to strengthen the weak spring with rubber bands.

Pay close attention to this problem. If your Robosapien doesn't lean all the time but only when walking, it could be indicative of a problem with Robosapien's feedback system. This is far beyond my level of expertise, but this sort of thing might have something to do with an uneven drain on the batteries. Try fresh batteries!

Something else worth mentioning is that as you begin to add peripherals and components to Robosapien, eventually the weight can add up and throw Robosapien off balance. Keep this in mind as you are planning your hacks.

Arm Wiring Problems

Arm wiring problems seem to be one of the more common difficulties with Robosapien as well. Symptoms include irregular sensor reactions, failure of the palm LED to work properly (or at all), or an incomplete range of motion with the arm (i.e., it does everything but open the claw, won't go all the way up, etc.).

This sort of problem is almost always related to the arm wiring. Start by swapping the right and left arm connectors on the main processor board and see if you can pinpoint it that way. Next, try jiggling the black-sleeved wire harnesses to see if you can restore the connection, even momentarily. The black sleeves, or casing, for all of the arm wiring looks very cool, but it impedes your ability to check for physical imperfections or breaks in the wires. If you have a multimeter, you can always check the continuity of the individual wires that way.

■**Tip** Robosapien's arm cables contain eight individual wires. If you have narrowed your problem down to a broken or damaged wire, standard Cat-5 networking cable also contains eight individual wires and would make for a nice replacement.

If the problem is confined to one of the palm LEDs, place a 3-volt current (from a separate battery pack or power supply) across the two pins for that LED on the main controller board. If the LED lights, then you can be sure that it is not the LED or the wiring.

The final thing to pay attention to with regard to Robosapien arm problems is the way the arm wiring sleeves are coiled (see Figures 14-7 and 14-8). It is very easy, when you are putting Robosapien's chest shell back together, to get these out of alignment. These not only house the wiring that passes the signals to the lower arm and claw, but they also provide tension to the upper part of the arm. If they are coiled improperly, they can cause that arm to act somewhat strangely or appear to be "weak."

Figure 14-7. *This photo shows Robosapien's arm wiring sleeves properly coiled.*

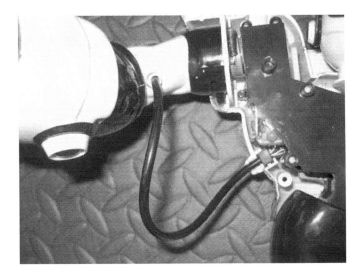

Figure 14-8. *This is an improperly coiled arm wiring sleeve.*

Add Volume Control and an On/Off Switch to Your Robosapien

When I added a wireless sound system to my Robosapien, I completely cut out the robot's internal speaker to make room for the RF receiver. At this point in time I had been working on Robosapien for a while, and had begun to tire of the international caveman speech, and in particular the loud volume. I figured that I would never miss Robosapien's noisy chatter.

I quickly discovered that even though I had given Robosapien the ability to play sounds and music from my computer, meaning that the robot was far from mute, I still missed Robosapien's trademark grunts and groans. What I realized is that Robosapien does have a "personality." Mark Tilden told me that one of Robosapien's main selling points is that it "…has a vitality and an aliveness that is beyond the sum of its parts." Take away the robot's international caveman speech and you will quickly see just how large a role the robot's personality plays in its overall appeal.

But this doesn't change the fact that it can eventually get annoying, and that the volume can sometimes seem a bit too loud. Sure, I had put clear tape over the speaker grille to reduce the volume, as WowWee suggests on its website, and this worked to a degree, but I felt that a more permanent and *adjustable* solution was in order.

Toward this end, I will show you how to install a volume control and an on/off switch for complete control of the loudness of your Robosapien. Just for kicks, I also installed an LED that will flash whenever Robosapien makes a sound, but this is optional. This is an easy hack: it is reversible and you need to cut only one wire to complete it. You will, however, have to do some soldering, and if you want to integrate the volume control and the on/off switch into your Robosapien's shell, you will have to do some drilling too.

Tools and Materials

Here's a brief rundown of what you will need to complete this hack:

- A Phillips head screwdriver for disassembly.

- A soldering iron, solder, and heat shrink sleeving.

- Wire cutter/stripper.

- A drill, rotary tool, and hot-glue gun if you plan on integrating the new controls into Robosapien's shell.

- A SPST (single-pole, single-throw) sub-mini toggle switch, or you can use a sub-mini slide switch; it's your choice (optional).

- An LED (optional).

- A small length of hookup wire roughly the same gauge as Robosapien's yellow speaker wire.

- A variable resistor (sometimes called a potentiometer). You will want to use one in the 1K ohm to 2K ohm range; anything much higher than 5K ohm will be too sensitive to be of much use.

For purposes of this tutorial, I used off-the-shelf parts from Radio Shack (see Figure 14-9). If you want to stay true to BEAM philosophy, you can use salvaged parts from other devices. The small slider volume control usually found on cheap headphones should work great. Using parts other than those I have used in this tutorial gives you a lot more options in terms of integrating the controls into Robosapien's shell.

Figure 14-9. *I used standard Radio Shack parts for this project. The toggle switch is part #275-612. You could also use a slide switch if you would like (part #275-406). The only suitable potentiometer that Radio Shack had came in a 12-pack assortment (part #271-1605).*

Step-by-Step Instructions

Let's roll up our sleeves and get to work!

Step One

Start by removing Robosapien's back shell (see Figure 14-10), and completely remove the speaker cover, speaker, and the small PCB that houses Robosapien's on/off switch (see Figure 14-11). You can set your Robosapien to the side, as everything that you will need to modify for this hack is part of Robosapien's back shell. Don't put Robosapien too far out of reach, though, as you will want to periodically plug things in for testing purposes.

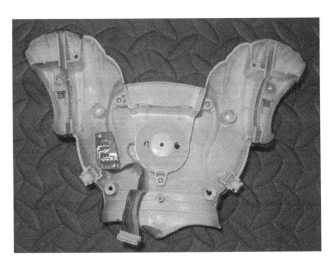

Figure 14-10. *The first step is to take off Robosapien's back shell.*

Figure 14-11. *Next, disassemble the back shell and remove the speaker and its wiring harness.*

You don't need to completely remove the wiring harness from Robosapien, but doing so will make things a lot easier for you, especially later when we are testing and integrating the mod.

Step Two

Pick up the wiring harness and separate the two yellow speaker wires from the rest of the wires. Then, separate the two yellow speaker wires from each other (see Figure 14-12).

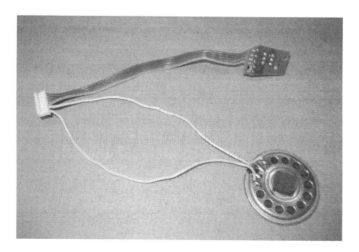

Figure 14-12. *Separate the speaker wires from the rest of the wiring and from each other.*

Once you have prepared the wires, cut one of the yellow speaker wires about halfway through, and strip the resulting ends about 1/8 inch (see Figure 14-13).

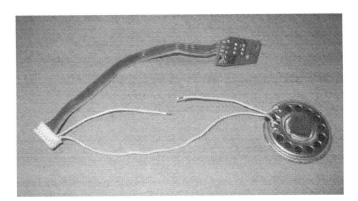

Figure 14-13. *Cut one of the speaker wires and strip the ends.*

Step Three

Now it is time to add in the components with your soldering iron. Your basic configuration, when done, should look like Figure 14-14. Setting this up is fairly straightforward, but it is worth pointing out that the potentiometer has three pins: two rails that will be on the same side, and one pin by itself (called the wiper). You will want to hook up to one of the pins (it doesn't matter) and the wiper. Your final configuration should be as follows:

- The original yellow wire coming from the speaker connects to the rail of the potentiometer.

- The wire from the potentiometer's wiper is attached to the LED.

- The wire from the other side of the LED is hooked up to one of the terminals on the on/off switch.

- The wire from the other terminal on the on/off switch is attached to the original yellow wire leading to the connector.

Of course, you can do this hack any way that you like—you can only add the on/off switch, or only add the volume control. As you are making your solder connections, use your heat shrink sleeving liberally to cover soldering joints. This not only protects against short circuits, but also protects and strengthens the solder joints. Just remember to cut your sleeving and slide it onto the wire *before* you solder the connection.

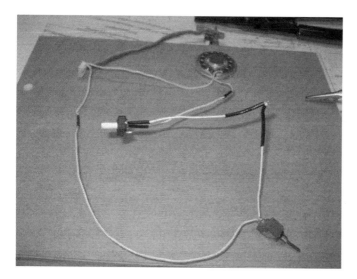

Figure 14-14. *This is what the final setup should look like.*

Once you have everything soldered and hooked up, go ahead and plug the wiring harness into Robosapien's main processor board, power up the robot, and make sure everything works. If it doesn't, you probably mixed up the polarity of the LED or have a broken solder joint. Note that when you power up Robosapien without its chest shell, the robot will spin its arms all the way around behind its back. Pay attention to the springs at Robosapien's shoulders and make sure you get the arms situated correctly before you put the robot back together.

Step Four

Now that we have completed the wiring, it is time to prepare Robosapien's shell to hold all of the new additions. If you are not sure you want this to be a permanent mod, or don't want to modify the robot's shell for whatever reason, you can always set up the wiring for the mod to be "exterior" and leave the volume control dangling outside the robot's shell.

My favorite spot to add things like these are on the small ledge behind Robosapien's head, but you can put them anywhere. Before you drill or do anything permanent to your Robosapien, *make sure* that you have tried and tested the hack and that you are happy with how it works.

The first thing you need to do to integrate the components into Robosapien's shell is to drill the holes (see Figure 14-15). But before you even pick up your drill, make sure that the components will fit where you want them when Robosapien is put back together. Measure the spots for your holes and use a pen to mark where you plan on drilling. As soon as the drill bit hits the plastic there is no turning back, so spend a little extra time making sure that everything is lined up properly. Believe me, a clean hack looks so much better than a hurried, sloppy one.

For the parts that I used, I needed a 1/4-inch drill bit for the on/off switch, a 1/8-inch drill bit for the LED, and a 5/32-inch drill bit for the volume control. You may need different sizes depending on the components that you use.

Figure 14-15. *Robosapien's shell has been drilled to accept the new components.*

Once the holes are drilled, smooth them out with a hobby knife. You will find that drilling through the Robosapien's plastic is a messy job, and there will be a lot of little bits of leftover plastic that need to be cleaned up.

Before you put your drill away, make sure everything fits.

Step Five

The final step is to situate the components and wiring, and put your Robosapien back together. I like to use a hot-glue gun to attach components like this, because it is easy to remove and "undo." I found that hot glue was not strong enough to hold the volume control knob in place, so I ended up using a stronger glue. Once you have situated all of your components and arranged the wiring so that it is out of the way (see Figure 14-16) go ahead and put the robot's on/off assembly back together, replace the speaker cover, and put Robosapien back together. Power up the robot and enjoy your adjustable volume!

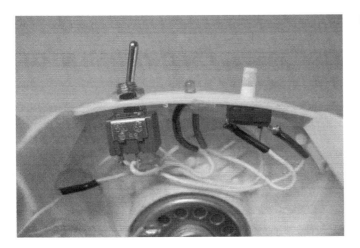

Figure 14-16. *Arrange the wiring so that it isn't in the way of any parts.*

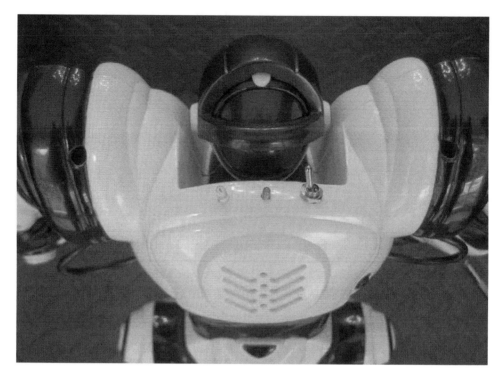

Figure 14-17. *The completed hack looks like this.*

Summary

Troubleshooting techniques are no mystery, and they involve the same type of critical thinking and creativity that go into dreaming up great hacks. Fortunately, Robosapien is so sturdy that I have found I am able to spend much more time hacking than troubleshooting. As far as easy hacks are concerned, adding an on/off switch and a volume control is one of the most useful hacks that I have ever performed on Robosapien.

CHAPTER 15

■■■

Advanced Hack: Wireless Camera Installation

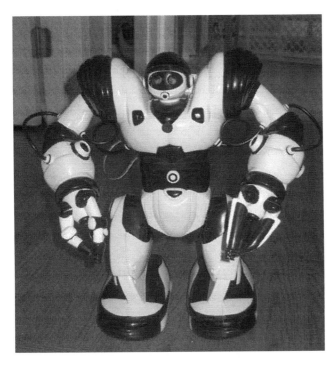

Figure 15-1. *Can you find the camera on this robot?*

In this chapter, I present a step-by-step guide on how to add a wireless RF (radio frequency) camera to your Robosapien. This is not a difficult hack to complete and requires minimal electronics skill. More important, it requires no electronic modifications to Robosapien, so if you make a mistake, your Robosapien will still operate correctly. To complete this hack, the only modifications you need to make to Robosapien are to drill a couple of holes in his shell for camera placement and to run the wires from the camera out to the battery. Of course, should you choose, you can locate the camera on the outside of Robosapien, in which case you don't even need to modify its shell.

Why Bother Adding a Camera?

Why not? Not only is it interesting to see the world from Robosapien's perspective, but with a little imagination, quite a few interesting possibilities open up once you give your Robosapien vision capabilities. Some of these include hooking the video output up to a PC for recording, combining it with a PC control scheme for true remote control of Robosapien over a network (or the Internet), and of course, spying on people. Who would ever suspect that the small, lumbering robot following them was actually filming them? Although to be perfectly honest, if I found myself being followed by a small, bipedal robot I would be worried about more than whether or not it was filming me!

What Type of Camera Should I Use?

For this project I used a small "ZT-802"-type RF mini camera (see Figure 15-2). You can find them easily on eBay; I paid about $40 (including shipping from Hong Kong) for mine. It will transmit both audio and video. The actual camera is about the size of a sugar cube, which gives you a lot of options in terms of where to mount the camera.

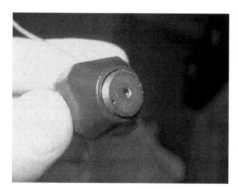

Figure 15-2. *You can find the ZT-802 miniature camera easily on eBay.*

The separate receiver (see Figure 15-3) has composite (RCA-style) outputs that you can plug into a TV, a VCR, a TV tuner card in your computer, or pretty much anything that will accept a video signal.

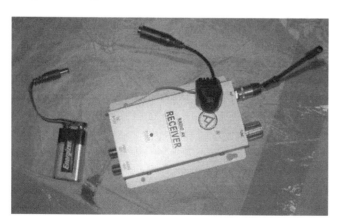

Figure 15-3. *The complete ZT-802 kit includes the camera, the receiver, and the battery connector.*

Note If you plan on outputting the video signal from the wireless Robosapien camera into a computer, you will need something called a "TV tuner card." This device allows your PC to receive, play, and record video signals. It can either be a separate USB device, a card that fits into a PCI expansion slot on your computer's motherboard, or some graphics cards, most notably the ATI "All in Wonder" line, including video inputs. I highly recommend the products made by a company called Hauppauge, in particular the PVR-250. Find out more at http://www.hauppauge.com.

I am sure that by the time this is published—no, by the time I finish writing this paragraph—there will probably be better, more advanced cameras on the market. The technology changes that quickly. Try doing an Internet search for "spy camera," "wireless camera," "miniature camera," and the like. This will give you a good idea of what is out there. You can base your decision on form factor, quality, and price.

I like the ZT-802-type mini camera because it is cheap and light, and it has a nice, small size. I also like that it is capable of receiving and transmitting both audio and video, and has a snapshot feature for taking still images.

Preparing for Installation

OK, so you have your camera, and you're ready to get started. Not so fast! Before you begin it is a good idea to test the camera, not only to make sure it works, but to make sure you are happy with the quality of the images and with the setup (i.e., plugging it into a TV or VCR probably isn't as much fun as plugging it into a PC that can control Robosapien and record the images).

Also, now is a good time to consider where you want to place the camera on your Robosapien. This hack will show you how to place the camera in Robosapien's chest cavity. I feel that this arrangement has some significant advantages. Obviously, it allows for a nice clean—and dare I say stealthy—placement. As you can see from the photo at the beginning of this chapter, the average person probably will not notice that there is a camera installed in the robot. Another advantage to placing the camera in Robosapien's chest cavity is that, since it is close to the center of the robot's body, it minimizes the swaying inherent in Robosapien's walking. It doesn't do away with it entirely, but it is a significant difference compared to say, installing the camera in or on Robosapien's head. Finally, it is the point furthest away from Robosapien's motors; this helps to cut down on the motors interfering with the RF signal that the camera transmits.

There are, however, some advantages to installing the camera outside of Robosapien's body. The most obvious, of course, is that you will not have to drill through Robosapien's shell. This is a big help if you don't have a drill or very steady hands! Along similar lines, another advantage is that it makes the hack 100 percent reversible. Finally, installing the camera on Robosapien's head has a few interesting advantages. It can be easily placed there and you only need some tape or a square of Velcro to secure it (be careful not to use too much tape or you may block the IR signals from Robosapien's remote control). The most interesting advantage is that, since Robosapien's head turns when you raise and lower its arms, you can in effect pan the camera side to side.

Drilling the Hole

The camera lens on the ZT-802 is 1/2 inch, so that's what size hole we need to drill in Robosapien's chest (see Figure 15-4). I think Robosapien will probably have nightmares of this drill for a long time to come!

Figure 15-4. *If your Robosapien had eyes, this picture would scare it to death!*

I tried using smaller holes and placing the camera up against the inside of the shell, but the result wasn't as good as letting the entire lens come through the Robosapien shell. It also looks nicest to put the camera lens flush with the robot's chest.

Figure 15-5 shows what it looks like after I drilled the hole.

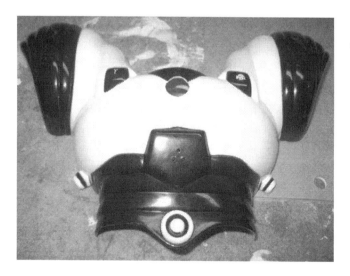

Figure 15-5. *Here is the front view of Robosapien's shell after I drilled the appropriate hole for the camera.*

As I mentioned earlier, I chose the center location in Robosapien's chest for several reasons. For one, it was the spot where the chest cavity is the deepest. Also, it is the furthest point away from the robot's arm and waist motors, so interference is kept to a minimum. I didn't even need to shield Robosapien's motors.

▓**Note** If you find you are getting interference from Robosapien's motors, you can use regular aluminum foil to shield them from the camera.

This center spot is also one of the more stable points on Robosapien, and because it is dead center, it shouldn't affect the robot's balance. Finally, I felt it was the most aesthetically pleasing place for the camera.

A few notes on drilling the hole. *Make sure you take your time and go slowly, since once the hole is there, you can't easily fix it.* I started with a 1/8-inch drill bit, and drilled in the center point there on the chest, right where the robot's "cleavage" meets the black "throat piece" (or as I refer to it, the ascot). Once I made this hole and cleaned it up with a hobby knife, I moved to a 1/4-inch drill bit and enlarged the hole and again smoothed the edges with a hobby knife. Finally, it was time for the "big daddy" 1/2-inch drill bit. This made a mess because the plastic is so thin (comparatively) and required a lot of the old in-and-out with the drill to smooth the hole. It also required quite a bit of sculpting with the hobby knife to get the edges nice and smooth.

As you can see in the photo of the inside of the hole (see Figure 15-6), I used a Dremel tool and ground down the molded lines from Robosapien's ascot on the inside of the chest cavity near the hole.

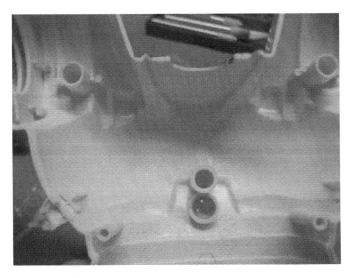

Figure 15-6. *Here's the view from inside Robosapien's shell after I drilled the hole. Note how the interior has been slightly ground down to accommodate the flat front of the camera.*

This helps the flat front of the camera sit flush with the inside of Robosapien's shell. Be careful doing this; it is easy to go too far and grind right through the shell. As with drilling the hole, if you take your time and go slowly you will be fine.

Mounting the Camera

Once the hole is made, you need to start fitting the camera in it and making any adjustments to the hole (see Figure 15-7).

Figure 15-7. *Once your hole is drilled, make sure the lens will fit through the hole.*

As you can see in Figure 15-7, there is really no place to attach the camera—I don't really think it would be a smart idea to hot-glue it onto the inside of the chest shell where the lens goes through. Although you probably could, the threaded lens screws in and out of the camera body in order to focus, and the glue would eliminate its ability to do this. I guess you could try to make the hole for the camera higher, so you could glue it to the top part of the chest shell, or lower, so you could attach it to the bottom support peg there. I think either of these options would make drilling the hole much more difficult, however.

I used a small piece of wood to attach the camera to the robot's chest shell (see Figure 15-8). I used a spongy sanding block to make the piece of wood nice and smooth, and more important to get it exactly the right size and shape.

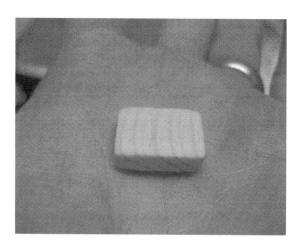

Figure 15-8. *A small piece of sanded wood makes a nice mounting block for the camera.*

Note that unless you want Robosapien to film people's shoes only, you have to angle the camera upward slightly. A nice sandable piece of wood is perfect in this regard. Make sure you fit it exactly how you want it before you even plug in your hot-glue gun (see Figure 15-9).

Figure 15-9. *Before you glue it in place, spend some time fitting the camera and the mounting block in the robot's chest cavity. Make sure the angle and fit are exactly as you want them.*

Apply the hot glue to the piece of wood, and press the camera into place (see Figure 15-10). This makes the camera much easier to install.

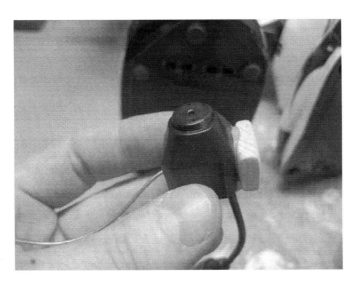

Figure 15-10. *Using a hot-glue gun, attach the bottom of the camera to the wooden mounting block.*

I used the center support peg there to glue the apparatus to (see Figure 15-11).

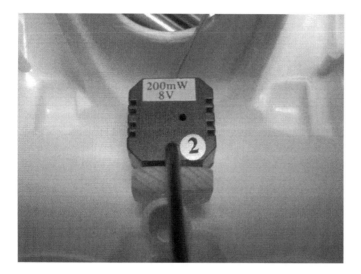

Figure 15-11. *Spread the glue on the mounting block and then secure it inside the chest cavity, gluing it to the center support peg.*

I left the antenna for the camera inside the chest cavity. Now that the camera is attached to Robosapien's shell, hook everything up and make sure the camera still works, and that the position, angle, and so on are to your liking (see Figure 15-12).

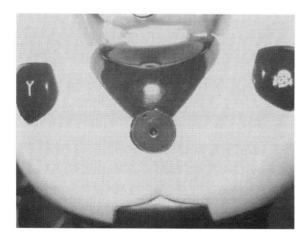

Figure 15-12. *This is a close-up of the camera mounted in the hole we made.*

Hooking Up the Power Supply

The ZT-802 camera I used in this hack uses a 9-volt battery and a rather bulky connector. If you have room in the chest cavity (and you should, unless you have done other hacks to your Robosapien), you can leave this connector inside Robosapien's chest and run the wires for the batteries out to a 9-volt battery, which you can Velcro to Robosapien's back. To do this you can elongate the battery cables (see Figure 15-13) and drill a hole in Robosapien's back for the cables to run through (see Figure 15-14). If you choose to elongate the battery cables and feed them through a hole in Robosapien's shell, make sure you run the wires through the shell before connecting the battery snap!

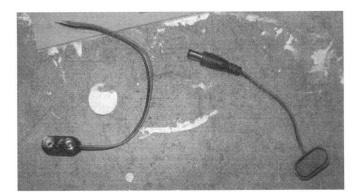

Figure 15-13. *To elongate the battery wires, simply cut the connector included with the ZT-802, and splice in a new 9-volt battery snap.*

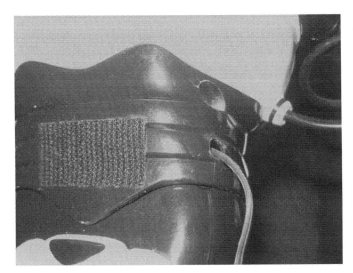

Figure 15-14. *Here's where you'd place the Velcro for attaching the camera's 9-volt battery. To the right you can see the hole for running the battery wires, if you choose to leave the connector inside the chest cavity.*

Alternatively, you can drill a hole in Robosapien's shell large enough for the connector to sit in firmly (see Figure 15-15). If you go this route, make certain that the protruding connector won't interfere with Robosapien's arm movements.

Figure 15-15. *In the lower-right corner, notice the battery connector protruding from Robosapien's chest cavity. This allows for easy hook-up.*

You need to keep the camera unplugged when not in use or you'll find that the battery will be dead every time you turn it on. For this reason, I feel that the second method of hooking up the power supply is the best. You probably won't have to elongate the battery cables, and also the connector protruding out of Robosapien's chest gives the robot even more of a futuristic look.

Putting It All Back Together

All you need to do now is replace the shell and turn on the camera. Voilà! Your Robosapien should now have vision capabilities. Here are some photos taken with Robosapien's internal camera as I spied on my dogs.

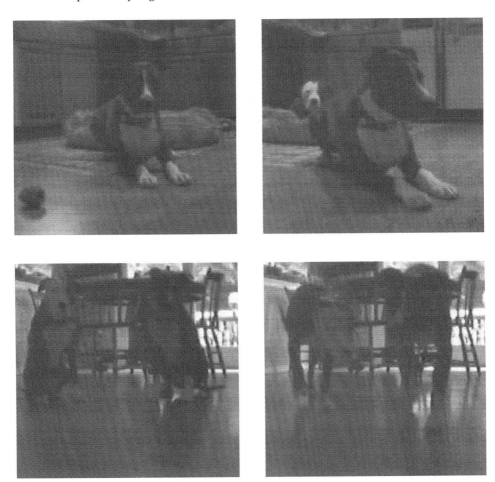

Figures 15-16 through 15-19. *These photos were taken using Robosapien's new camera. Judging from that last shot, I believe the robot may be in trouble!*

Depending on the camera you used, you may have to add additional lighting capabilities. I found that the ZT-802 needed a lot of light to give an adequate picture. I experimented by hot-gluing an inexpensive headlamp to Robosapien's lower torso (see Figure 15-20). This aided the light levels in darkness, and even in daylight it helped to clear up the images.

Figure 15-20. *I used an inexpensive headlamp to help boost light levels for the camera.*

Figure 15-21. *Robosapien is on nighttime patrol.*

Summary

Adding a wireless camera to your Robosapien isn't exactly a complicated procedure, but the results are outstanding. Not only is it a cool modification on its own, but it also opens up many possibilities in terms of future projects. Things like PC-based control and network capabilities become viable options once you have installed a camera in your Robosapien.

PART 5

A Look Ahead

CHAPTER 16

■■■

A New Line of Robots

(Photo courtesy of WowWee Ltd.)

Figure 16-1. *Roboraptor (left), Robosapien V2 (center), and Robopet (right) are all set for release in 2005.*

Coming up in 2005 is an exciting new line of robots from WowWee (scheduled for release after press time). Now wait just a minute. You're saying that after you've spent $100 on a Robosapien less than a year ago, you've bought this book, and you're finally beginning to understand how the robot works and how you can make improvements to it, that WowWee is coming out with a whole *new* line of robots? Well, the answer to that question is yes *and* no.

It is true that WowWee has an ambitious new line of robots and other gadgets scheduled to be released throughout the second half of 2005. But what is also true, according to multiple sources within WowWee, is that there are no plans to stop producing the original Robosapien either. In a "b-roll" video from the New York Toy Fair that I was given by WowWee, in one of the shots the camera pans over the entire new line of robots. I was happy to see the original Robosapien prominently included in the line for 2005–2006.

It is my impression (from speaking with both Mark Tilden and WowWee executives) that the company still views the original Robosapien as very much a core part of its product family and will continue producing the robot as long as people are buying it.

Another factor is hackability. I have a feeling, given the added features and complexity of all the new robots, that they will lack the original Robosapien's simplicity. If I had to guess, I would say that the original Robosapien will remain the robot of choice for the hackers. If anything, maybe the introduction of new robots will encourage some people to finally open up their original Robosapiens and we will see some interesting new hacks.

Take that as you will, but for now, let's see what WowWee has in store for 2005 and beyond.

Unveiling the New Line

So all of this year's generations basically combine what we learned from the B.I.O. Bugs with what we learned from Robosapien. That is, he is a minion at your command, but now what happens is he has his own personality and he is interactive on a one-to-one basis.

—Mark Tilden, February 13, 2005

WowWee unveiled its new lineup of robots at the Consumer Electronics Show (CES) in January 2005. On tap are Robosapien V2, Roboraptor, Robopet, a Speak2Click computer peripheral, and an animatronics-style chimpanzee head, known as Facetronics Chimpanzee. In addition to these, "mini" versions are set to be produced for the V2, Roboraptor, and Robopet.

Also of note is a reorganization within WowWee Ltd. The company is now divided into four divisions: WowWee Robotics, WowWee Tech, WowWee Alive, and WowWee RC.

After CES, the next showing of these robots was at the New York Toy Fair in February 2005. After the Toy Fair was over, Mark Tilden went back to Hong Kong to finish the development and tooling of the entire new line, and WowWee has been very quiet about what is going on with its new line of robots. Think back to Chapter 3, and how long it took to develop the original Robosapien. And that was just one robot. This year we're expecting three new robots, far more advanced and complicated than the original Robosapien, plus two other products. I have a feeling it has been a busy year!

The information in this chapter is based primarily on what was exhibited and made available during the New York Toy Fair. There is a good chance that by the time you read this the robots will already be on store shelves and you can try them out for yourself. If anything, this chapter may prove interesting to see what, if any, functions or abilities that were promised at the Toy Fair got cut from the final product. Just keep in mind as you read this that it is all subject to change!

WowWee Robotics Robosapien V2

Robosapien V2 is an extremely ambitious and exciting upgrade to the original bipedal Robosapien. Standing almost 10 inches taller than the original, and featuring an advanced vision system and finely tuned, precision hands, by all accounts it looks to be a fantastic robot.

> *The new generation robot, Robosapien V2.… It can get itself up, roll itself over... it's actually pretty adept. It's exactly one centimeter taller than the Sony QRIO. But it's like 1/1,000th of the cost. The Japanese come out with these new and beautiful things....*
>
> —*Mark Tilden, February 13, 2005*

Figure 16-2. *WowWee displayed Robosapien V2 at the New York Toy Fair.*

(Photo courtesy of WowWee Ltd.)

(Photo courtesy of WowWee Ltd.)

Figure 16-3. *This photo, also from the display at the Toy Fair, features Robosapien V2's packaging.*

One notable change in Robosapien V2 is that it has abandoned the international caveman speech and now speaks English. Once you power up the robot, it gives a stretch reminiscent of the original Robosapien's wake-up routine and says in a metallic, very robotic-sounding voice, "Self-diagnostic initiated. I am WowWee Robotics model RS-2."

But even without international caveman speech, V2 is loaded with personality. From an updated Dance Demo, to a cautionary "Calm down and nobody will get hurt," this robot has got as much, if not more, personality as the original. An example is the new Oops! command—the robot still farts, but it now advises anyone within earshot to "Run for your life!" It also appears that the original's trademark wolf whistle has been replaced with an oh-so-smooth "Hey baby!" Mark Tilden says that even though the robot speaks English, almost all the phrases are from "bad science fiction movies," meaning that they will be fairly recognizable to everyone.

(Photo courtesy of WowWee Ltd.)

Figure 16-4. *The Robosapien V2 features a new remote control modeled after a video game controller.*

Based on what I've seen, the robot, from a physical standpoint, is amazing. Early estimates are a 10-hour battery life on six D-cell batteries. It has 12 motors, and many of them can run simultaneously, giving the robot incredibly fluid movement ability. From a standing position, it can actually lay itself down, sit up, and even stand up from both a face-up or face-down position. The hands have also received a major upgrade. They look to be much more capable than the original Robosapien's claws, and are much stronger, too. The demo robot at the New York Toy Fair was capable of picking up and carrying a 12-ounce can of soda.

But for all the personality and physical improvements, where V2 is really groundbreaking is in its new vision system. Mark Tilden has said, "What Robosapien V1 did for walking, V2 will do for vision." Using infrared distance sensors, the robot is capable of "seeing" its surroundings; it can detect obstacles, track movements, and reach out and take objects that you hand it. That's pretty amazing, but the vision system doesn't stop there. Additionally, V2 is equipped with a secondary vision sensory system that is able to detect and discern colors. This helps the robot recognize objects, and as WowWee claims, even skin tones. The robot is also equipped with a stereo sound system, and of course the sonic sensor capabilities of the original Robosapien.

In terms of programming, one interesting thing is that you can actually use your hands to program the robot with "up to hundreds of moves." This means that, by manually moving the robot's appendages, you show it what you want it to do, and then it will play back those same steps. Want the robot to raise its left arm all the way up? Take ahold of its arm and move it there. For walking, you touch sensors on its toes to walk forward and its heels to walk backward. The programmability is also linked to its vision system, at least in the prototype; you can show it a colored ball, and then send it off to find the ball up to two meters away, pick it up, and return it to you. WowWee promises that V2 will also have a lot more options in terms of autonomous operation than the original Robosapien. Just the ability to avoid obstacles with a vision system, as opposed to the touch sensors the current Robosapien uses, is a major upgrade in terms of autonomy.

(Photo courtesy of WowWee Ltd.)

Figure 16-5. *The rings on V2's hands not only protect the delicate fingers, but do double duty as touch sensors and handles to aid in programming the robot.*

Another change in V2 is the remote control. It is now shaped more like a wireless video game controller with two thumb sticks. The remote is also equipped with what WowWee calls "laser tracking." Press a button on the remote, and trace a "laser" path on the ground and the robot will follow it. Robosapien V2 is also supposed to be able to control the other new robots: Roboraptor and Robopet.

So, as cool as all of this sounds, it is still anyone's guess how many of these features will make it into the final product. Robosapien V2 is expected to cost around $250, and is scheduled to be available starting in December 2005.

(Photo courtesy of WowWee Ltd.)

Figure 16-6. *This photo shows Mark Tilden and V2 at the WowWee booth at the New York Toy Fair.*

WowWee Robotics Roboraptor

Roboraptor is another new robot scheduled for release in 2005.

What it is, is a combination of the Robosapien walking structure with the sinuous sort of locomotion mechanism. Um, it's actually a bit of an interesting problem, because we had to overcome, basically, second-order resonance dynamics. So the Robosapien is pretty cool because it's just an upwards walking pendulum. But with this thing you've got the neck and the head which is actually extremely fluid, OK? And those act as a major damping source, so you can't use the same walking gaits in the dinosaur as you did with the Robosapien, even though internally, they are based upon exactly the same mechanism.

—Mark Tilden, February 13, 2005

(Photo courtesy of WowWee Ltd.)

Figure 16-7. *The WowWee Robotics Roboraptor features three walking gaits.*

Expected to retail for about $120 and be available in summer 2005, the 32-inch-long Roboraptor is a combination of Robosapien and an eel-like BEAM robot that Mark Tilden built in the late 1990s known as "Lamprey."

It features three distinct walking gaits—predatory, walking, and running—and has "multisensor environmental awareness." What this means is that Roboraptor has vision, sound, and touch sensors.

Roboraptor seems to have quite a bit of built-in autonomy, and even its own moods. For example, if you approach its face while it is in hunting mode it will react aggressively, but it also has a playful side and will nuzzle your hand. The prototype I saw uses the video game controller-style remote control, and also includes the laser tracking ability available on V2.

For example the T Rex... it's a beautiful thing. Your own pet dinosaur. Robosapien V1 can annoy your dogs, this one can hunt them. It's great. It's got a lot of built-in autonomy, it's got a lot of B.I.O. Bug–like features. So it's got the whole Robosapien-style control, but it also has its own complete interactive play.

—Mark Tilden, February 13, 2005

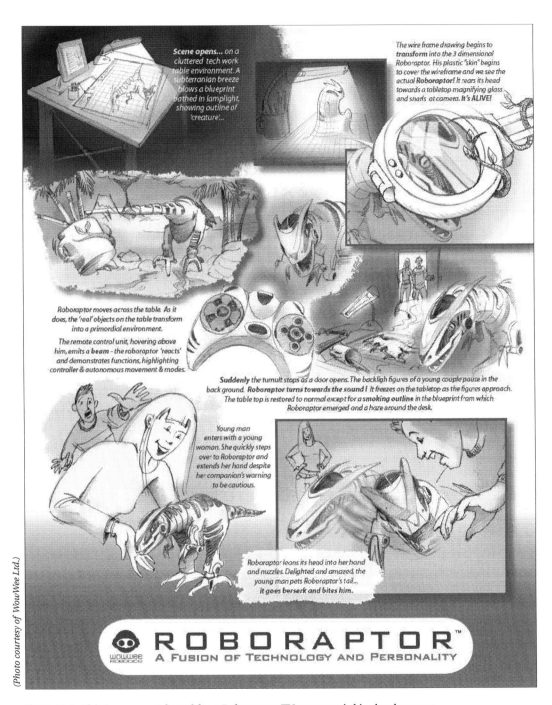

(Photo courtesy of WowWee Ltd.)

Figure 16-8. *This is a concept board for a Roboraptor TV commercial in development.*

WowWee Robotics Robopet

The final new robotic offering from WowWee Robotics is "Robosapien's best friend," Robopet. Sort of a cross between a dog and an insect, the $90 Robopet is expected to be available in fall 2005.

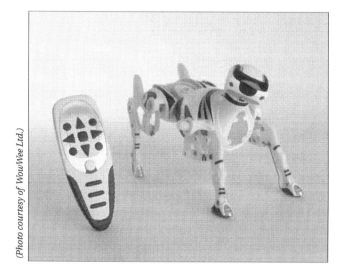

Figure 16-9. *This appears to be a prototype model of the WowWee Robotics Robopet.*

(Photo courtesy of WowWee Ltd.)

The first thing I noticed about Robopet is its chirps and noises; it immediately reminded me of a slightly less annoying B.I.O. Bug. But what really impressed me is its extreme mobility. From a standing position it can completely roll itself over; it can run, jump, beg, and even howl. It also has "multiple sensors" as well as the remote control–based laser-tracking ability found in V2 and Roboraptor. Robopet is able to avoid obstacles, which means it has some sort of vision system, and of course it also has a sonic sensor. I am not sure whether or not the final version will have touch sensors.

Robopet is also "trainable" and will react to positive and negative reinforcement—after all, what else would you expect from a pet! All in all, it looks like a neat little robot. I can't wait to see how it interacts with Robosapien V2.

WowWee Tech Speak2Click

WowWee Tech's innovative Speak2Click is really an interesting product. It's definitely a little bit creepy, but interesting all the same. What does it do? In a nutshell, it uses voice recognition to replace the mouse on your PC.

The futuristic female android head is maybe one half scale and connects to your PC or laptop via USB. The female head is named "Jesse," and her eyes light up and move in response to your commands. For example, in the demonstration I saw, Mark Tilden says "Jessie: Webpage. Robosapien." The android's eyes light up and it launches a web browser on the attached laptop, and then points the browser to the Robosapien webpage. "Jessie: Email Peter" launches a new email message addressed to Peter. During this she says things like "activating" or "opening" in a pleasant, slightly android-sounding female voice.

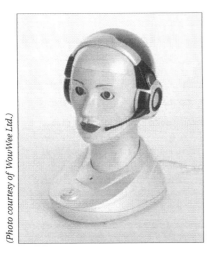

Figure 16-10. *Here's WowWee Tech's Speak2Click; the android is named "Jessie."*

(Photo courtesy of WowWee Ltd.)

Seems like this sort of thing would take a lot of work and effort to set up, but it really doesn't. The first time you plug the Speak2Click into your computer, it searches your system for files and applications, and generates a list with simple words assigned to each one. You can either use the default phrases or customize the list with your own. Easy!

It wasn't operating at the Toy Fair, but there is also a planned version with a male voice. Instead of a humanoid head, it is in the form of a Robosapien V2 head. I have a feeling that one might be a better seller; "Jessie" is just a bit too unnerving!

Speak2Click should end up retailing for about $80 and be available in fall 2005.

WowWee Alive Facetronics Chimpanzee

OK, if you agree that the android head is slightly disturbing, wait until you see the Facetronics Chimpanzee from the WowWee Alive division. The Facetronic was developed by Greg York, a Hollywood special effects wizard who has over 16 years of experience creating animatronics and prosthetics in the entertainment industry.

Figure 16-11. *The WowWee Alive Facetronic Chimpanzee is meticulously crafted.*

(Photo courtesy of WowWee Ltd.)

Unlike Speak2Click, which isn't life size, the Facetronics chimp is so realistic it will scare you. Not only is it life size, but it is also meticulously crafted, right down to the tiny hairs on its upper lip. But it does far more than just look real; it acts real too. Its eyes, eyelids, and brow move; its lips are incredibly lifelike; and its jaws are fully articulated, as is its neck. When it curls back its lips, furrows its brow, and gives a fearsome scream like only a chimpanzee can, you might find yourself wondering what you have gotten yourself into. Even Mark Tilden said, "Let's face it; this is freaky!"

It can be controlled via remote, or it also has an autonomous mode. It has sound and touch sensors, as well as IR-based vision. Based on interaction, when it is in autonomous mode it shifts between several moods. It can be happy, curious, playful, fearful, and even aggressive.

WowWee Alive has really accomplished something with this first Facetronics, and I do hope they continue adding to the line with new animals. The level of realism is simply unparalleled. The best part is that it should retail for only about $130. It is scheduled to be available in late 2005.

Summary

Based on the early looks I have had of all of these new products, WowWee seems to have an exciting lineup in place for release. It is important to note, however, that while these new robots definitely have some great features and interesting capabilities, they are set to complement our old friend Robosapien and not replace it.

APPENDIX

■■■

Interview with Mark Tilden

(Photo courtesy of WowWee Ltd.)

Figure A-1. *Here's Mark Tilden at the 2005 New York Toy Fair.*

I have used excerpts from this interview throughout the book where applicable, but I also wanted to print it in its entirety. Some things, like Mark's wonderful commentary on Hong Kong cuisine and his off-the-cuff comments on everything and anything, just didn't fit into the structure of *The Robosapien Companion*, but they will be of interest to anyone who is curious about or admires the man behind the robots.

This interview was conducted on February 13, 2005, at Wolfgang's Steakhouse in the Murray Hill neighborhood of midtown Manhattan, in New York City. I recorded it with an Olympus DM-10 voice recorder. The dining room at Wolfgang's is known for its historic tiled ceilings designed by Raphael Guastavino. They are beautiful, but they are an acoustic nightmare! Fortunately, my trusty DM-10 was up to the task.

I have edited this only very lightly, mainly breaks where we spoke to waiters and so on. Also note that during a portion of this interview, Mark is showing me a slideshow on a little portable LCD screen. Most of the pictures from the slideshow ended up in Chapter 3. But if during the interview he seems to be making a reference, chances are it is to something on the screen.

Without further ado, here is the full text of the interview.

▓ ▓ ▓

SAMANS: *Tell me about your work at Los Alamos...*

TILDEN: When I went to Los Alamos National Labs, basically I was brought in literally under the genius clause, which is kind of nice. I didn't have a PhD at the time. So what happened is that I get down there and I basically say two things: I don't have the credentials, so I could have said "Hi, you *have* to believe me." *<Laughs>* So I promised that I would only ever say things if I had something that actually worked. Boy did that do me both good and bad. Good: I was able to build things successfully that are now still working in museums and various places across the country. Bad, because there are an awful lot of people, primarily roboticists, who have their entire reputation based entirely upon virtual presence. "Oh one day the robots will basically take over. Do you have any evidence? Well no, but my toaster is hostile!"

SAMANS: *Two quotes of yours really stood out to me. One, you said they have all these great robots that work great in the computers and they are all based on sort of virtual, weightless rope...*

TILDEN: That was a beautiful detail of my original history in America. I worked for approximately 30 agencies (DARPA, NASA, etc.) and there's a great book called Virtual—something like Virtual Minds or something like that—which has a beautiful chronology. Basically what happened when I moved down to New Mexico, I was thinking that I would be able to get in tight with the artificial life guys. Because obviously that's what I was doing: I was building self-evolving mechanisms that are capable of doing real work in the real world. But I wasn't playing by their rules. That's just it. As soon as you start measuring against their stuff, they suddenly realized: "OK, well, we can't support you, because unfortunately you are invalidating all of our theory."

SAMANS: *Which brings me to the second funny quote I remembered. You described a robot you built out of like three broken Walkmans, that beat a robot at a sumo competition that someone had spent something like 10 years working on.*

TILDEN: The stories just went on. They would show up, and there would be the MIT team: 20 kids and one robot. And then there was the JPL [Jet Propulsion Laboratories, the leading U.S. center for robotic exploration of the solar system] team, and there was oh, University of

Wisconsin, Washington, Delaware, Carnegie Mellon, and there is uh, Los Alamos National labs—hi!

For example, there was a big thing JPL put on back in 1998. We were at this major JPL conference, and it was exactly like that. Everyone else shows up with like 20 people and one robot. I always showed up with one roboticist and 20 robots. Literally I would come out with this nonstop flea circus. Some of these things people still remember: "I remember when you put a robot on an overhead projector and it kept moving the entire time when you were talking and you never had to worry about it falling off!" Yeah, of course! Doesn't your robot work completely autonomously and independently regardless of whether or not you are around to look at it? No?

SAMANS: *<Laughing> Right, they start looking to all their buddies on their team...*

TILDEN: *<Laughing>* That's right, how many grad students do YOU have working on your machine?

One of the things I talked about earlier on in my career: Wizard of Oz demonstrations. Stand back, don't touch, and pay no attention to that cable leading behind the curtain. I am the great powerful roboticist of Oz. And there are an awful lot of great and powerful roboticists of Oz. Asimo, for example. You never see the whole picture, you see only the robot. You don't see the guy over in the corner who is getting paid $23,000 a day. Asimo also comes with two guys who look after it, and I actually saw this happen in Tokyo. When Asimo starts to fall over, it is their job to throw themselves under the robot, because you've got $15 million worth of robot hitting the ground. So it's gonna be either squishy Japanese people, or a broken robot toy.

I can tell you one of the things I learned from the toy industry is that you can't sell broken toys.

SAMANS: *Which is one of the coolest things about the Robosapien. You can really put that thing through the paces.*

TILDEN: Like you wouldn't believe. It's one of its hidden features that it actually has the ability... I mean you can kick the crap out of that thing, it can take a tumble down the stairs. The fifth major sell feature was this: for a seven-motor toy we have had less than a 0.03 percent return rate. That means one in every 340 robots sold actually had some sort of mechanical defect.

SAMANS: *Excellent.*

TILDEN: That's astonishing! In [the] toy industry, normally there is always a 3 percent [return rate]—every standard radio-controlled toy that you see sold has an average of 3 percent to 50 percent return. Furby was a 33 percent return. You've got to remember, any toy that is returned, you have to sell two toys to recover the costs. Because a toy that is returned is not refunded from the money from the retailer, it is refunded by the money from the actual distributor—that is the person who actually owns the toy. The retailer just basically leases us the space to move our product. We own it. So the Robosapien was a big risk this year. And the reason that Hasbro got rid of [WowWee, formerly owned by Hasbro] was because of the Robosapien. Because they'd seen the problem that they'd had just with the Furby, with one motor, and this thing has seven? And you expect it's going to be reliable? We've got some statistics for you...

The thing was, that they didn't know, they'd only ever seen conventional robots go out. The Robosapien is, and it's really cool to look at the awards—and we just got our stats and data in and it's fantastic.

▓ ▓ ▓

TILDEN: Unfortunately, living in Hong Kong has taught me to basically be very scared. They eat things that you don't even see on the Discovery Channel. There are some fish that are obviously a lot happier at the bottom of the ocean. I'm talking about some pretty ugly-looking things. The thing is, they don't eat the part you'd think they would. I was actually in Japan when they served me the head of a 600-pound tuna. So we're talking about an eye the same size of one of these buns here. And you're basically saying "Oh, wow, that's... wonderful!" Because you know it's some sort of honor, but I'm sorry, I just don't know what part of the fish head to eat! You're supposed to eat the cheeks, suck the retinas—thank you—I mean these are the sort of things they don't put in the tour guides.

Some sushi I like in China, but again you have to watch out what you are eating. You get a little bit of rice, and all of a sudden there's this octopus tentacle right on top of it, and it's a foot long! You can see the suckers. All I can think of, if I stuck a battery in it, would it come to life? The temptation is very high to give it a try.

There are a couple restaurants in Hong Kong, what they do is they bring you out steamed fish, they bring you out this thing and there's the head. And the entire body is steamed, but the head is raw and still going "gloop gloop gloop gloop," and I am basically saying "thank you." I don't want my fish, my animal sick or wounded, I want it dead. I don't want it suffering; I don't want it still watching TV. I don't want any expression on its little eyes saying "What?!?"

I can understand that it is a different culture and stuff like that. Little things like sea cucumber. Whoever ate this for the first time must have been starving. Obviously there are some things that became tradition because some people were like this close to death and they were eating anything that would basically give them protein without getting bitten. Chinese cuisine: Whatever you can get down your throat best two times out of three is obviously good for you.

SAMANS: *Tell me about your move to Hong Kong.*

TILDEN: It was part of a long and very drawn-out sort of process. Transferring my stuff into industry has been something I wanted to do for a long, long time. One of the cool things about all my technology is that it allows one person to do a hell of a lot, and demonstrate something with an incredible facility, in a very short period of time. Anyone who's ever tried to build a robot realizes that you have a week's worth of fun with the mechanics, and then a year's worth of hell basically trying to, you know, port Windows to your portable toaster. My stuff allowed me to build things in record time, basically building a complete working robot from two broken Walkmen and a calculator in less than 20 minutes. What was it—"Robots Rising"—a 1997 a Discovery Channel documentary. They have a time lapse of me, parts, brrrr, finished, and then robot moving. Without plans, or anything like that.

I'm amazed how far and how fast this has sort of secured a reputation, because robots have always been very slow things to build. And now what happens is you have the ability to crank something out in record time. And WowWee has taken advantage of this.

Have you seen our latest line?

SAMANS: *I have seen only the coverage from CES [the 2005 International Consumer Electronics Show].*

TILDEN: It's massive. The dinosaur, for example, is something I have wanted to work on for five years. I gave the original principles to Peter ages ago...

SAMANS: *The first thing I thought of when I saw it, and I saw a video of it sort of moving, I thought "It's the eel!"*

TILDEN: Exactly right. What it is, is a combination of the Robosapien walking structure with the sinuous sort of locomotion mechanism. Um, it's actually a bit of an interesting problem, because we had to overcome, basically, second-order resonance dynamics. So the Robosapien is pretty cool because it's just an upwards-walking pendulum. But with this thing you've got the neck and the head, which is actually extremely fluid, OK? And those act as a major damping source, so you can't use the same walking gaits in the dinosaur as you did with the Robosapien, even though internally, they are based upon exactly the same mechanism. That was actually a real problem, in China...

There is nothing worse than having a technology that everyone wants, but no one can understand. I build these prototypes and I show it to these guys, and I say those wonderful Chinese words *<says something in Chinese>* which means "Do it like this." And then they come back to me with all kinds of questions like "How does it work?" And that's when I basically resort to my second Chinese words, which is *<says the same Chinese phrase, with one added word>* which means "*<expletive>* do it like this." Don't ask any questions, you don't want to know!

One of my favorite stories: When I first went off to China it was for the B.I.O. Bugs. The B.I.O. Bugs were basically my first major introduction to mass-marketed toys.

SAMANS: *I've got one; I've got the green one.*

TILDEN: We did OK... they've got a lot of play depth. The problem was they were released 9/8/2001. Three days later it was hard to make sales. What's one to do? The gearboxes and the control mechanisms inside, the fact that you actually have sealed gearboxes; they were designed to be hacked. One of the things that I was so pleased about with the B.I.O. Bugs was that it was my first super hackable toy. I remember as a kid, opening up toys and all of a sudden gears would fall out all over the place, and you found out there was nothing you could actually do with the toy, except use it as a toy. Robosapien basically has so many things inside of it, that you can't find them all... and that basically turned out to be the fourth [selling point]. And the big fifth, and this is the hidden fifth, was the fact that not only was [Robosapien] reliable, but it was eminently hackable. How many times have you tried to hack someone else's technology... for instance take a look at this stupid camera. Look at that connector! Yeah right! *<Laughs>* It's got wire contacts too small to even see. I hate that. I know somewhere on there is a video out, and there's a power in, probably a couple other lines, but I can't access that. I hate that about modern technology. Give me the good old days, when you know, you and a soldering iron, and a screwdriver, and you own that toy. The bottom line is, you take a screwdriver [to Robosapien], you open it up, everything's color coded. Everything's labeled. Everything does what it's supposed to do. There's hardly any wires at all. There's always gold-plated contacts, you wouldn't believe how hard I fought to make sure that they were always gold plated. As soon as you opened it up, the possibilities skyrocketed. For anybody who was like me when I was 7 years old.

SAMANS: *My mother often tells the stories from Christmas mornings as a kid... by 1 P.M. I would have all my new toys taken completely apart, and I would be crying because I couldn't get them back together....*

TILDEN: Exactly right. I hated when all of a sudden you realized that planned obsolescence in toys was designed so that when it was taken apart it could not be reverse-engineered or put back together. You look at B.I.O. Bugs, though, you look at Robosapien, and all of a sudden you realize that this thing is not just designed to sort of go back together, it is designed to be improved, modified, and basically transferred on. What I wanted was, I wanted a toy where after I figured out everything that the toy designer had put into it, what else could I put in?

What's amazing is typing in the words Robosapien hacks. B.I.O. Bugs were pretty cool, but again they were still insects. We've got lots of good stories, but the bottom line is that very few have actually been hacked. Robosapien, on the other hand, people seem to be somehow *obligated* to hack it. I mean the emails I get, people do occasionally find my email, I don't put it out for very obvious reasons. I get an awful lot of people saying "Yes, hi, Mr. Tilden. This is what you should have done, and here's what I want in the next one." Yeah, well, can you see figure 1? *<Gives middle finger, laughing>*

The thing is that they don't realize, the hidden secret to Robosapien is that, it can take a tumble down the stairs, and its seven-motor design it can get up and still keep dancing. The current version that we just put out, has 28 hours continuous operation battery life.

SAMANS: *Now is that version 1 or version 2?*

TILDEN: Version 1.

SAMANS: *One of the things I noticed, I bought my first Robosapien last spring, then I bought a Sharper Image one over the summer, then recently I bought another, I needed a clean one that wasn't hacked all to hell. There are improvements in every single one.*

TILDEN: Every single one. The systematic improvements that we basically did. Once they finally understood what the principles were... and they had a real problem with it... you gotta understand. For example... I have to give you this slideshow, showing the history of Robosapien.

This is the first computer render model. Don't forget, my stuff was originally based upon what is called thermodynamic conduit engines, so in other words, transferring energy from one form to another. I used to build these little solar engines that were single fire neurons that you could use to optimize both energy and efficiency. What these things allowed me to do though, and I built literally thousands and thousands and thousands of these things... not just this, but this gives you an idea. You take the single mechanisms, and you basically expand their characteristics. The nervous network, right, is to the body as the neural network is to the brain. The body is all about rhythms and patterns, whereas the brain is all about memorizing trends. So we're all about rhythms down here and we're all about memorizing patterns up there. And that's exactly what a nervous net neuron does. Basically my principle was: everybody keeps working on better and better brains, but nobody is working on better and better bodies. If you've got a really good body but a very small brain you can still run for governor of California, in fact that works pretty well. *<Laughs>*

Now the thing that I found out and this is the most important thing. If you take these little rhythms and you basically put them into certain larger patterns... have you ever seen those desk things with steel balls and they go "whack whack whack"? Imagine that was in a ring, so you hit one and it goes around. So what's to stop you from having two clacks going around? And they would—they would pass right through each other and have all sorts of characteristics. It's called two-ary necklace functions, and this is a true digital approximation to what is in fact a very analog thing. But what it does is it optimizes the number of possible patterns for the smallest number of transistors. Now what that does, in less than 12 transistors, you can get up to six different patterns. Now this is the big secret I found after ten years. Take a pattern of six, fold it into a figure eight, put it into a symmetric mechanical body and what happens is it falls into all these interesting little patterns. And these patterns exactly mimic walking, running, jumping, sitting, slithering, hopping, everything that basically people have been putting a lot of stuff into... it does it completely automatically, and allows you to basically mess around with the smallest number of components, and it's noise resistant, noise tolerant, extremely minimal, battery efficient, and dah dah dah. The secret to BEAM technology is performance-to-silicon ratio. If you had to basically restart the entire computer robotics industry on a desert island, this would be the technology you would use. This is the secret that [John] Von Neumann, and [Michael] Brady, and [Alan] Turing, and everyone else was looking for. Asynchronous real-world control in the smallest number of possible transistors to the maximum possible effect.

For example, this right here is exactly 12 transistors. It is a prototype for a complete walking praying mantis. In 12 transistors this thing could hop on its back legs, it can run, walk, turn in place, it is extremely adept. And this sort of thing is the precursor to the B.I.O. Bugs.

So anyway, B.I.O. Bugs was my first major experiment trying to look at mass marketing. We've done things like Solarbotics since 1991, but that's a limited market. We've actually got a big educational base right now, and that's cool, it's a million-dollar-a-year industry. You still have to do it yourself and the skill necessary for doing that sort of thing is long gone. So building sort of a personality in something like this, and then making it so that essentially it is inherently hackable, we tried to promote it as much as possible, but 9/11 got in the way. Anyway, that was 2001.

We were bought by Hasbro, and I did a large number, I did over 20 toys for Hasbro. So the whole idea was to try and make something that essentially has that sort of ability, but the problem was it was totally lost in the worst tragedy in 20 years.

The cool thing was I actually did have some fun. One of the great things about selling 3 million robots is you can put them in situations of extreme duress. I have these great shots—we took one hundred B.I.O. Bugs to White Sands, New Mexico, and basically watched them walk around and get around. And that was fascinating. One of the things I wanted to do under NASA for years, you know, "Hi, let's study some swarm robots." I mean that's the sort of thing that you only get the chance to do in computers. Well, guess what, now I have a huge number of disposable swarm robots that I can essentially put into harm's way. And I could, I could basically just let them go, and they were covered in sand, falling down dunes, and they would fight each other, they get stepped on and broken and who cares?

SAMANS: *Which is one of the cool things about BEAM, getting back to the biological aspect, in that, you can kick it, push it down the stairs, whatever—you kick a traditional robot and it shatters into a million pieces.*

TILDEN: That's just it. One of the things most people don't recognize is that the most prominent thing that a robot needs is in fact the ability for self-grooming. It also has to have the basic fundamentals of self-preservation. One of the things that the people who are interested in artificial life don't realize is that the real world is filled with artificial death. *<Laughing>*

So the cool thing is... you can't put million-dollar NASA robots into peril, but these things cost us less than 4 bucks each to build, so it was very nice to actually finally have an opportunity to do something nasty with them and see how far we can go.

After we did B.I.O. Bugs we did all these other robots for Hasbro, including some pretty cool ones, like "Constructo-Bots," which was a modular form of my robots that you just put together. But unfortunately most of these things never really made it to market, because, well they are there, you can buy them but they are not prominent. What happened is that you have to remove an awful lot of the abilities that would otherwise make them fun, just to hit your price point.

In Asia, right now, you have to understand, robots are huge. In Japan, walking down the street with a really expensive Gundam model in a box, will actually pull girls, girls come up and say "Oooh Master Grade...." and you're like "yeah!" Where else in the world can you walk around with a robot model and pull chicks!

SAMANS: *That is pretty cool...*

TILDEN: The thing is, this is sort of the standard thing they have, and you can see exactly what it is based upon: high power, action, and sort of a very video game attitude towards it. The whole trick was that this is a virtual reality, right? Like the [Honda] P1—take a look at the complexity and the involvement, more motors than you could ever dream of, basically hooked up to a power source that lasts 15 minutes...

SAMANS: *More things that can break...*

TILDEN: Exactly, but it's not just that, the amount of manpower necessary to put something like this together, is just prohibitive. And of course, like, you've got people like my boss Peter, who essentially wants things as complex as this, you know, but instead of $10 billion spent on development and 15 years, he wants it in nine months and he basically wants it for $80. So he looks at me and I say "OK, let me think," and that's exactly what I did.

One of the cool things about the B.I.O. Bugs is that they allowed me to do something that I'd wanted to do through DARPA for a long time, which was to make my own custom gearboxes. If you want to know what the biggest advantage to modern robotics is, it's not the computers, it's not the drivers, it's just the fact that now you can go out and buy high-quality, 66-pound holding force servo motors from Japan. These have more than enough power to basically lift you up by their own power. The thing was is that there was no toy grade equivalent. And when there was it was all sort of in-line things, they were never the right shape for what I really wanted. These things were designed to be the right shape, that is, angular, 90 degrees. Ninety-degree shapes and shells. The other thing that was basically very important was, and this is something I learned from all my years of biomorphic building, is that you don't build things square. Things that are square basically fall down on two axes. And what happens is that Robosapien is basically built entirely upon biological angles. Not the way that you look when you stand, but the way that you basically fall into, the way when you sort of go limp, in something like a Jacuzzi. Your arms don't fall down to your sides, they float right in front of you. And your knees go up as well. And that's exactly what the shape of the Robosapien is based on. All the motor axes, as you can see here, all rotate around a very nice hexagonal frame, all based on very different angles—they're all 30's and 15's and 60's.

So anyway, the evolution of the Robosapien. I spent an entire month thinking about it, and then at the Telluride Workshop in the summer of 2002, I basically built this thing. This is actually the table I built it on. There's the very first one showing the angles of the forearms and various other things. Right, put together the body, what happens is there is a nervous network biomorphic motor controller/driver for every single motor, mount them right on the motor itself, so that the motor itself is its own measure, then you add the head, you mount the body and basically build the rest of the creature, then you mount the torso and the walking measurement, then put on the first legs, then you organize the brain system to something that is a little more understandable, in this case a 28-transistor nervous network system. Four bi-three transistor systems with a couple of motor drivers just to basically help the head and things like that. And all of a sudden now you have a fully functional biomorphic robot. Powered it on the very first time, and he figured his way out in a matter of seconds. And that was actually something that really impressed all of the scientists who saw it for the first time. It's still alive today; of all of the 20 or so prototypes that were built of the Robosapien, it's the only prototype that is still in operation even today.

SAMANS: *Really!*

TILDEN: All the other ones, and I'll show you the prototypes...

The shape of the thing is based upon things which are based upon reverse kinematics and dynamics, so suspension is one of its biggest friends. For example, how is it that a six-pound robot, like Robosapien, moves as efficiently as it does on motors that are too small to be useful? Well, it's the suspension. It also helped it move in a certain sort of way, so that was cool, it made it so it was able to move and react, its visual apparatus allowed it to see and respond, the original one was able to get itself up when it fell over...

SAMANS: *I saw that is one of the features of the V2...*

TILDEN: V1 was able to do it as well, but these things wound up on the cutting room floor—primarily just because our Chinese designers could just never get their head around it.

Then the actual prototype was sent off to China where all of a sudden things got interesting. I was still doing work here at my science institution in the United States, and I'd ship these things off to China because they had basically said "Oh yeah, just give us a working prototype, we'll have no problem."

SAMANS: *Famous last words, eh?*

TILDEN: <*Laughing.*> So next thing you know I am back in China.

What was happening at the same time, though, is that there is a way something actually works, and then there is the way something actually looks. And the original design that I came up with looked something like this. Sort of a Bruce Lee meets some sort of Terminator thing. His left hand was supposed to be a sort of universal tool, the right hand was supposed to be a large sort of builder thing. You can see it's very, very close to the original structure and physical mechanism. Which I thought would be OK. Well, that's no good for my designers, was it? They were after things that were a lot more sci-fi, or very utilitarian android like, or militaristic Gundam like... Robocop...

SAMANS: *The role of science fiction...*

TILDEN: Exactly right. These things were just what they call "looks likes"—they were just crudely based on the physics of the design...

SAMANS: *Which is such a key element of BEAM and this robot—they still didn't understand...*

TILDEN: That's just it. The fact is, the shape of something basically defines how it works. You have to have form and then function. Thing is, with toys, it's always the other way around. This was bottom-up design versus top-down design engineering. You have to remember with a toy, there are three things: there is the package, there is the appearance of the product, and then and only then is there the function. So how it works is pretty much small bananas in terms of selling.

Anyway, you can see all the different designs that the designers went through, this one is actually quite exotic, but there was no way to ever actually make it. Beautiful-looking thing.

But the entire problem was basically trying to come up with the mechanics that would fit inside something. This was the first Chinese prototype that they put together. And even from the start you can see that there were problems. The problem was that when you talked to any engineer, ANY ENGINEER, and say "Hi, I want you to build a brain for a robot," their idea is to design something that looks like this, and then basically put it in something that looks like that. So the first prototype for the Robosapien built in China, couldn't even carry its own processor. Look at this thing! Even separate binary systems. You could only carry these things around on a pallet, which was really quite embarrassing.

SAMANS: *You could make a centaur robot!*

TILDEN: Yeah, it could have come with its own little red wagon to carry its brain...

SAMANS: *Well, that's an accessory!*

TILDEN: *<Laughing>* Exactly right....

And we kept on saying, you know, OK, no, no, you idiots, it's got to be stand-alone, and like this and this... and this is something I literally whipped up in like a day, while they were watching. I threw a couple of bi-cores on the feet, and then it worked like a charm. So they tried again, and it didn't work.

SAMANS: *Are you fluent in Chinese?*

TILDEN: No, no...

SAMANS: *This must be extremely difficult then.*

TILDEN: The stories are really quite amazing. I went over there, I was a lecturer for a number of years, so I am thinking "OK, no problem," and they are asking me, "OK, how does it work?" So I am basically saying "OK, here's how we do it. How many of you remember your second-order nonlinear dynamics?... OK..." and it wasn't until years later one of them came back to me and said, "OK, remember you were talking about street sign robotics?" Street sign... Sine waves! *<Laughter>*

They didn't understand a word. How many hours did I spend lecturing and basically I suddenly realized <*says something in Chinese*> which means "Do it like this." And that's unfortunately what I had to do. I had to go to China, and basically build these things right in front of them using my stuff. Disposable nervous network controllers. Entire robots built with just a handful of mechanisms, worked like a charm, took massive steps, worked super efficiently, and they just had to try and duplicate it at the appropriate speed. So back and forth and back and forth and finally they built their very first one that combined their engineering with our design and shape, and my internal physics. And this is the first simian-looking Robosapien that we actually got working.

It's actually pretty good, although it no longer works, but it worked at the time, which was amazing. I knew that the thing was scale invariant. Which means it could be two inches high or three feet high, it wouldn't have mattered. They didn't quite understand that. So we had to build special arms, could we get a robot to bring us a beer? How do you make a fully functional arm and only two motors? Ask anyone and they will say it has to have at least three.

SAMANS: *Well, he's got the shoulder, one in the forearm, and then his hand is basically a cam setup...*

TILDEN: It's a combination of different degrees and angles. He has the ability to move his hands to one of 12 different positions.

Anyway, we built that very first one, and we found out is doesn't matter how heavy they really were, they still were able to work. We kept on building these prototypes, this one was basically working really good, it had fantastic amounts of brains, but at least it was able to carry them, but then we had a problem when this factory that was building the things went belly up. All of a sudden they are in Chapter 11. They went completely bankrupt.

One of the things that was really a shame was that originally, Robosapien's head was supposed to carry a complete vision mechanism. It took a long time, but they were finally able to understand it.

SAMANS: *How does this relate to the LEDs in the hands?*

TILDEN: If you take a look at the way his hands are set up, the LEDs in his palms perfectly illuminate any environment that he basically points around. You take away the cam, there are all kinds of things you can do, and I'll give you exact details, like interesting things, that you can hack on Robosapien. For example, the head is designed so that they can track into it. When he raises one arm and this hand is down, the angle of the head is always looking exactly at the ends of the fingers. It's a feature, not a bug, right? These are the little things, basically, that are already built right into the structure of the mechanism, and they are just leftovers from things that wound up on the cutting-room floor.

So this robot was looking pretty good, and then all of a sudden they went bankrupt. And we had to go up to China, and jump through dumpsters to get our prototypes.

SAMANS: *I imagine the industrial espionage in the toy industry is pretty bad.*

TILDEN: Ah, it's amazing. You'd be astonished. There are secrets I signed off on when I worked for the U.S. government that I can't talk about for another 20 years. Believe me, they are boring compared to the secrets about what's happening with next year's line.

It's very interesting in our particular case, because our bosses are basically saying someone is going to knock us off, and I say look, no one is going to knock us off.

SAMANS: *There is the one, Roboactor...*

TILDEN: That was an exact copy.

SAMANS: *It isn't programmable, it doesn't have some of the features, but in terms of the physical characteristics, it is an exact copy.*

TILDEN: They're pretty bad.

SAMANS: *A few people have come by the board and sort of been like "Eww, I got this thing called a Roboactor... I thought it was going to be the same..."*

TILDEN: No, no, no... it's actually pretty amazing what they are doing. You take a Robosapien completely apart, completely reverse... They didn't try and engineer it, they just copied it, our beta. Even the gearboxes. What they did, though, is find out that it will work even if the motors are running at less than 50 percent speed. So the Roboactor, I'll tell you right now, it resamples everything at 6 bits, very slow. But it still works, but it doesn't have any of the major features. It certainly isn't very much fun, but it's half the price.

We did something almost unheard of in the toy industry. We defended ourselves. And that is just astonishing to me. The toy industry is based upon this rather interesting idea. Nine months to put something on the shelves, protect it like hell until Christmas, then after that, who cares. The thing was with this, for some reason we had such a feel of potential. We knew it was seminal. We knew also that these people were smart enough to build one from a sample they picked up last spring, now; you wouldn't believe the amount of people trying to build their own robot. And let's face it; Robosapien is a $200 million toy. The entire radio control market for the entire world is only half a billion dollars.

SAMANS: *That is unbelievable.*

TILDEN: You have to remember, only a year ago, Robosapien was basically being reintroduced to all of our major buyers. And all of them were saying things like "Oh, robot toys... we've seen robots." There are certain people, who worked in certain companies, who looked at the robot and said, "Oh I wouldn't give you $5 for it. We've seen robots and we can't sell them." And that's why one of the funniest things you could ever do, especially last Christmas, is go to a Radio Shack and ask if they have a Robosapien.

SAMANS: *I went to Radio Shack a lot to buy parts to hack my Robosapien. And they were like "What are you working on?" and I said, "Oh, I am hacking my Robosapien" and they were like "Well, we have this $200 robot that runs off a BX-24 chip..." and I was like "Yeah, but can it walk on two legs?" <Laughter>*

TILDEN: That's one thing the toy industry really taught me... for years when I was developing my stuff, I was trying to come up with something that would look like how you would expect a robot... and the thing was, you have to remember about the Robosapien, he is not a devolved human but rather an evolved robot. He started out as a singular cellular mechanism back in 1988, and then it moved up through bugs, and snakes, and lizards, I built so many variations on a theme that it's not funny. But the Robosapien finally happened and he was based upon the neat-o design which essentially I'd been working on since about 1995. And that was just theoretical. What I was doing at the time, was when you work for the U.S. government, you basically run around and try to beg people to give you money to develop something that they need. Which is basically sort of a gun-for-hire type thing. And I was able to solve all those problems, but nothing really ever went anywhere. What I found was really awful, was some of the things I built for Quantico, for the American military, I built 50 robots for them for mine-field location and detonation and they sat for seven years inside a government warehouse, and I only just found out that they had been thrown away and destroyed. They paid a lot of money for those robots, you know, you could have used them, or I'd take them back! As it is, I have a few in my garage, but that's about it. So it's just really weird how these sorts of things happen.

SAMANS: *Which is I guess influenced your decision to head over to the toy industry...*

TILDEN: Scientists hate the people in the industry, because they always want product first, and then there is only a chance you might make the market. Whereas science people, they work for the government, they give you all the money up front, and so you are secure for quite a while. And you might get sick and tired of working on something that you came up with an idea on three or four years ago, but the fact is, at least your money is guaranteed.

SAMANS: *Especially for someone like you, who applies these theories and can build things very, very quickly....*

TILDEN: Well, that was in fact one of my major advantages at Los Alamos. I was the robotics department at Los Alamos National Lab. It was funny, for a long time people were saying "Oh, wow, the lab there at Los Alamos must be huuuge!"

SAMANS: *Right... vast underground caverns and so on...*

TILDEN: <*Laughing*> It was funny, when you basically have access to U.S. government junk piles... Wooo-wee! How much platinum can you spare me? Titanium... don't you have some-thing in a nicer color? <*Laughs*> I was picking up sheets of throwaway titanium.... I'm just wondering about this stuff... hmm, I can't cut it... it's as thin as tinfoil but I can't cut it with scissors. And when I try and burn it I get these beautiful rainbow colors... wait a minute...
   Building robots out of gold and titanium and space qualified 300 rad space hard motors... you are building a robot that will last forever. It's true! The museums where my robots are on exhibit, the robots are still working, on display, after ten years.

SAMANS: *Yeah, I read that some of them had to actually be glued down so they wouldn't walk away...*

TILDEN: Yeah, that's right! They're still alive for chrissakes! It's one thing to build a robot, it's another thing to build a robot that lasts, that has its own life force.

One of my favorite things, I saw someone actually quote me on this, which I thought was pretty cool: "When you can build a robot that can find its own way out of a mud puddle in a blinding nighttime rainstorm, and still know which way it has to go, you're damn close to actually building something that has its own autonomous life force." And it's true. Giving something its own sense of vitality, and basically one of the first things you do is remove the off switch. Give it the ability to find, recognize, and manage its own power source.

SAMANS: *Which is one of the things I thought was really cool about the B.I.O. Bugs. You just set it loose in the room...*

TILDEN: And there it goes...

SAMANS: *And it annoys the hell out of my wife... <Laughter>*

TILDEN: B.I.O. Bugs were an astonishing lesson to me. The feedback from Hasbro was really quite amazing. Things like "I hate this toy, my child took it everywhere for a month." Take a look at that statement. As a designer, I'm thinking "OK, my key demographic, children, loved the toy." But as a businessperson, "My chief buyer, the parents, hated the toy." That was my first lesson in real-world robotics. Making something that can survive by itself in the forest is EASY compared to making something that can survive on the shelves at Toys"R"Us.

And that's where all of a sudden, everything is. The first thing that sells the Robosapien is boy, is it cool. It has a vitality and an aliveness that is beyond the sum of its parts. One of the things we did with the Robosapien—and this is something that right now we are in the middle of we have no idea where we are going—we set a performance-to-price specification that is 15 times cheaper than our nearest competition. You go out and pick out any other robot that's out there; it will do one or two things. Oh, this one records sound, this one moves forwards and backwards, oh, look this one can sort of walk around and pick things up. Standard Radio Shack stuff.

This thing has 67 functions!

Thing was we've been releasing them slowly, for the past little while. There are certain little secrets, for example, just knock your Robosapien on his back and you'll see that he goes to sleep in less than two minutes. And he has a double sensor, so that his hand sensors are holding onto two things at the same time, and then he basically starts a secondary counter. Little things like that that are important, so that when he falls over and is trapped, he goes to sleep faster than otherwise.

You've got to remember, there are certain secrets to Robosapien that allow you to trigger his uber dance routine, which keeps him dancing for up to 24 hours. That's a problem, you see, the thing is, he's got two motions—there's reactive ones, where he will essentially time out, and then there are other ones which are basically just blindly placed functions. Well, if he is caught underneath a couch or a chair, he can cause himself damage by overloading his motor drivers. There are ways around that, but what we are interested in now... we overdesigned for exactly those sort of things. So far we have seen no sign or evidence of them.

Christmas Day, 2004. 740,000 Robosapiens were opened on Christmas morning. I burped around the world! <Laughter>And that was just North America. We had an equal number in Europe, in Afghanistan, there's a Robosapien at the South Pole... Robosapien is literally on every continent now.

We did a variety of press and presentation things. We faced a very big obstacle. Robots are not new. You just have to see this thing dance once to realize that this is something different from your dad's pet robot.

SAMANS: *One thing I noticed is the robot's interaction with my dogs. Initially, they hated them, and then they started ignoring them. Finally, we noticed that they were exhibiting pack behaviors towards the robots.*

TILDEN: Fascinating. One of the things we originally saw, we saw this with the B.I.O. Bugs. When you put a Robosapien down, and there are people in the room, the dogs are jealous of the attention that the robot gets, and so the dogs start paying more attention to the human beings.

Some people have actually put cameras on top of the robot, and there is a secret reason why, his shoulders are here and his head mounts there. If you put a piece of paper over top of the robot's head, you can put a pinhole camera right on top, and it is exactly where his head would be if he was exactly proportional all the way around. That's something I thought a lot of people would have discovered by now, but it seems very few have. In Hong Kong, for example, you can get these sugar cube–size cameras for less than $20.

I saw some, I was actually really impressed with some of the counterbalance mechanisms, but I didn't really realize the problem until I started doing the project myself. And I suddenly realized, boy that robot bounces a lot. And it's true.

He is exactly 1/5 me, exactly 1/5 of my dimensions. With the exception of the legs. So he's not just my personality, not just my programming, not just my physics, he's actually a little mini me in a lot of ways. I suddenly realized at 1/5 size, he also runs five times faster than the equivalent human. So if I were to put a camera right here and walk down the street, you'd be able to see what was going on. But for a camera, it's like you are slowing that camera down to sort of like, well, six frames a second.

I was amazed when people started putting it in the chest, then they were getting interference so they used tinfoil to shield it.

What I was really pleased about with the Robosapien, once we finally got that thing down, when we finally realized that the chest was mostly empty space, then we did calculations and found out that the payload capacity is almost a pound.

SAMANS: *I've put way more than a pound on it, and it walks a bit slower, which for my purposes, actually makes his camera a little bit steadier. One guy put a camera in the head, which I thought was interesting since he could then use the arms to pan it. But that proved amazingly difficult because the head is glued together.*

TILDEN: We had to do that. The worst condition in toys is called the drop test. One-meter drop test. All toys have to be able to take a fall, from a height like this table, onto a solid concrete surface, and pop back up with less than one chance in nine of breaking. We doubled that, we made him so that he could take a two-meter drop test, but the problem with that is that to make that work, we found that the head had to be glued together, it was too fragile, even protected by the shoulders, the head would just crack into pieces. The other thing with the fingers, which had to be ultrasonically welded together, and of course the forearm, which also had to be Superglued down... you can actually find now you can just crack them open, just like a lobster.

SAMANS: *I've noticed that later models of the Robosapien actually have more screws in the arms, allowing for easier access.*

TILDEN: Exactly right. We found out that some were getting a break in the upper arm.... The thing is, the robot has actually been a fantastic study in materials assessment and analysis. We want to use less and less plastic, because plastic is expensive now, thank you, Mr. Bush. That's the reason why this year's Robosapien is actually not cheaper than last year's Robosapien. Because, while the cost of our production has gone down, the cost of plastic has almost doubled, and that's a real problem for us.

It's a real problem especially for our new generation of robots. For example the T Rex, the T Rex... it's a beautiful thing. Your own pet dinosaur. Robosapien V1 can annoy your dogs, this one can hunt them. It's great. It's got a lot of built-in autonomy, it's got a lot of B.I.O. Bug–like features. So it's got the whole Robosapien-style control, but it also has its own complete interactive play.

The biggest problem with the Robosapien, as I said, on Christmas Day, we got 500 calls from our 1-800 international phone line. And they were all for the remote control. Because if the remote control gets chewed on, or stepped on, or lost, or drooled on, or for some reason just doesn't work, all of a sudden the robot just goes to sleep, and you're basically out of luck.

So all of this year's generations basically combine what we learned from the B.I.O. Bugs with what we learned from Robosapien. That is, he is a minion at your command, but now what happens is he has his own personality and he is interactive on a one-to-one basis.

SAMANS: *This brings me to another point, which is with Robosapien version 1. Once the average user, the person who is NOT going to hack it, once they go through all the stuff, they sort of say "Eh, what now?" Which is the question that my book will hope to answer. But it sounds like the V2 is going to take care of that problem.*

TILDEN: No, the V2 is a rush job. V2 is not going to be as hackable as V1. For example, you wouldn't believe how I fought like hell to keep the six LEDs in the eyes. Because the eyes are the window to that thing's soul. What I mean by that, you pattern match those, and you know exactly what is going on. A beautiful 6-bit interface that tells you exactly what the robot is doing, how he is going on, and what you're doing. It's an 8-wire interface that fits on a 12-wire PIC, if you wanted to do such a thing. And so we made the thing to be hacked in such a beautiful way. And the LEDs of course, you don't have to actually remove them, you can just parasite on to them. When I finally gave them the final layout for the PCB, I said, "OK, we need gold-plated testing contacts... yeah..." *<Laughs>* "We NEED them!" For production they basically set a standard, which is quite neat. So the board itself actually has the two processors, it has the H3 motor driver based on the nervous network controller, and then of course the actual processor itself. Which is basically just a super grown-up sound module.

SAMANS: *It's hard to see because it's under that blob of...*

TILDEN: The chip itself, even if you got to it, you'll find out that it's mostly RAM and ROM, it's a very small processor on there, but everything is encrypted. So even if you did extract the code, you can't reverse-engineer it. What happens is that in the toy industry, you're always this many days away from death. If somebody else comes out with the same toy, that you have as a hit toy, then you are diluting your potential sales market. And if they are a penny cheaper, then they are going to take a lion's share of the sales. So the robot had to be protected in a lot of different ways.

Interestingly enough, all toys are based upon modified sound processors. In other words, things that sang "Happy Birthday to You" 20 years ago in Hallmark cards are still very much the same basic source. Turns out, if you actually called them processors, then Microsoft would insist that they basically be Windows compatible or something like that. Windows has really changed an awful lot of things, to the point where they go around and lobby things such as people who write and are doing new processors for phones. And you have to take a look at the disparity. You've got processors in your laptop, or you've got these modified sound things at the other end, which are just barely able to run a calculator. Where's all the cool stuff in the middle that should be operating cell phones? Unfortunately, it's basically being split legally 25 ways from Sunday.

And so what happened was, when we did the B.I.O. Bugs, with the B.I.O. Bugs we pushed the technology to the absolute limits. We squeezed the silicone until it screamed.

SAMANS: *Well, that's one of the fundamentals of BEAM, isn't it? To take the fewest amount of transistors and get the most out of them.*

TILDEN: Exactly right. That's exactly what I can do. Some might say that oh I am this digital luddite, but that is the last thing! I was trained and I am actually quite a competent expert in advanced modern digital technology architecture and design. I still dream in Zen 80 assembler sometimes. That tells you how much. I've actually had situations where I am programming in Zen 80 assembler on a robot, and I've fallen asleep in my chair, wake up four hours later and I'd still be coding. That basically was the early '80s to me. *<Laughing>* It's a bad scene!

One of the things we did with the biomorphic mechanisms is that we were able to make a proof of concept. Because what I found out in China, and this is very different form the North American attitude, is that there is nothing more worthless than a patent. But there is nothing more valuable than a working prototype.

We get this all the time. We get guys who come and say, "Hi, here is a beautiful patent for my new novel vision algorithm. Make it, and send me the check!" And I basically say, "Oh this is very nice." *<Mark pretends to blow his nose on said patent>* "Here, I have reviewed it…"

■ ■ ■

TILDEN: So we built the first Robosapien, and sent it off, it was ready to go. It was the fall of 2002, then all of a sudden they went Chapter 11. We had to go out and find another vendor, and we found this vendor called Wah Shing. They'd never done this stuff before, and again, I was back to the drawing board.

Robosapien, you wouldn't believe how close he came to absolute death. All of a sudden we got the phone call saying "Hi, you know that company you were working with? This is their bank. How much will you pay us for your prototypes which are now essentially in dumpsters?" They won't even let you crawl through dumpsters without paying them some sort of pittance. Those were some interesting times then.

This thing had basically gone around the world and had been demonstrated so many times it wasn't funny.

SAMANS: *So you were out demo'ing this even at this early stage?*

TILDEN: No, we were trying to convince Hasbro, please don't kill this! Hasbro basically saw it as a high-risk initiative, and the fact is they were completely right.

This is cool, and this is the one thing that saved its ass. All of these other prototypes stopped working literally minutes after we would do the demos. This thing was still working two years later. It had broken its leg... here's something interesting for the Robosapien. You can destroy half of its motors and it will still walk. Either hip can go and he'll still walk. The arms can go and he'll still walk.

SAMANS: *I would have thought that the arms could go but not the hip!*

TILDEN: No, no, it can take either hip and he'll still walk. You can even reduce his waist down to half its power and he'll still keep on going.

So this prototype kept on going. So I said we have to start looking at building something like this. This is my idea of an engineering shell. And this went to our guys, and they did this. This is the first computer render of the final version of Robosapien, based not upon a crazy thing but on what the physics needed. Now you can see the shell, and the lower head to protect things.... Something else, the robot has no pinch points. No matter what you do you could never trap a finger or a pinky. And this is great because the Robosapien has actually been declared safe for all children, all ages, 8 months to 80.

SAMANS: *That's huge...*

TILDEN: That's HUGE from a toy point of view and a liability point of view.... You've got to remember, robots are basically "crush, kill, destroy"—you gotta remember that legally, there's one major problem. The smartest robot in the world can't defend itself legally against the world's dumbest human. The closest we ever came was a great article from a magazine called the *London Star*, which was "Woman Raped by Robosapien, Gives Birth to Flashlight." *<Laughter>* I have that on my wall, I love it! But so far we haven't had any, you know, palimony claims, so that's all right...

So the robot actually looked pretty good. We had all the major features, and stuff like that. Finally what happened was the crush was on, we had to come out, we'd just been kicked out by Hasbro, we'd bought ourselves back. We were running on fumes, so I had to live at the Wah Shing factory in Shenzhen province.

This was my design team, and I went up there and literally lived with these guys. They knew we were under a crunch. We built our first tool prototype, based upon a four-bar linkage system, tested the limits of how it actually winds up going. This is the mathematics and theory based upon resonance.... There was one guy there who had actually gone to a western university and had actually heard the word "resonance" before. So I said, "OK, you don't have to trust me now, but in a little while, this is going to be very, very efficient."

Because they were coming back to me and "Hi, yeah, small motor like this cannot move 2-kilogram robot!"

And I said, "Yes it can, but you gotta know how." So I explained it to this one guy, and he believed, and the rest basically went on.

That's the very first working Robosapien, and this is the design team. Great guy by the name of Edward Chan, probably the biggest ego in all of China, but he knows his stuff. And better yet he was able to act as an interpreter. So while I basically danced like a stupid idiot, like what they call *<says phrase in Chinese>* "crazy white guy"—he would translate it into

Chinese. And it was the funniest thing in the world, because we were sitting in a lunchroom, we have for ten days nonstop, I am basically wearing the same clothes by like day eight. I'd be like "No, no you idiot, the roar doesn't go 'uh uh uh' it goes 'ROAAWWRR!!!!' and then Edward would turn to a programmer and go "wa." *<Laughter>*

And type, type, type, and the next thing you know, the Robosapien was actually doing it, lock it down, lock it down… one after the other… 11 days later, and all this assembler code, we were 4 bytes short of the 12K programming. We squeezed that silicon like you would not believe.

And we finally basically had this thing put together, and all of a sudden there it was. Unit 0. The first working Robosapien. Then came production. I don't know if you can see this very well but that's a solid acre of girls: 508 girls building one Robosapien every five seconds.

SAMANS: *It's like a dream…*

TILDEN: <Laughs> It was really strange! You get the girls who were building, then they test every robot, it was not based on anything predictable, then he is packaged, then kissed, then of course tested to absolute destruction, and it keeps going and going and going. Two million robots! The world's largest private robot humanoid army. And of course it walks, it moves, it's pretty cool!

I bought a Roomba, and this is one of the chrome Robosapiens riding on top of it. Roomba is done by my colleagues at MIT, good luck to them, they think the future is utility robots, I think it's basically things that people can understand…

SAMANS: *I've got a Roomba, I really like it! It was really exciting for the first day… and then great, it does its thing, it goes back to its charger, and I barely notice it anymore.*

TILDEN: <Laughing>

▪ ▪ ▪

TILDEN: The real cool thing is we've always kept our eye on the two major customers. One: the kids. Kids want something basically as a pure toy. One of the things, for example, which I fought like hell for with the Robosapien… you have to look really close to get an actual label on it. When you see a Microsoft product it's always labeled. Think "Intel Inside." When you see a Sony Aibo it's always "Sony." You look at Robosapien, no. It's pure toy. It has nothing that basically tells you, or reminds you, that you are basically doing something fictitious.

SAMANS: *I think if you look very closely, it says WowWee on the back, in tiny letters. It doesn't say Robosapien anywhere.*

TILDEN: That's right. It doesn't have to. The robot basically stood by itself, in more ways than one. That was the primary market. This is also the primary market: my science buddies. The people I have been talking to for ten years, who keep on saying, "Oh, as soon as we get a good body, then I can put my computer brains into it, and therefore it'll go." But the cheapest robot body you can buy is Sarcos, the million-dollar robot that runs on hydraulics, pneumatics, and things like that. And they don't sell enough to make it worthwhile. Plus why risk it?

Then of course there was the long-lost girlfriend. She lives in a box. Well, she existed, and she was beautiful and blonde, but there was one major problem, and that was girls don't play with robots.

When the robot was designed, and this is really neat, is the first Robosapien [prototype] still works. The 28-transistor controller, which you can draw on the back of a napkin, you can put that back into the Robosapien as it is, on all the universal translatable connectors which I had to fight like hell to keep in. And all of a sudden the thing basically goes back to its old analog ways, and rather than having a 28-hour battery life, it now has a 50-hour battery life.

The thing is, you take the Robosapien, and run it with the current efficiency, and you suddenly realize—that thing could go solar, it would be so easy to basically make it.

A lot of people kept on saying, "Why didn't you make it rechargeable? You're that cheap?" *<Laughs>*

The robot is operating so close to its current limits, because by the time the motors, the drivers get through with it, the losses in the wires, between the batteries and the drivers and stuff like that, you're traveling your current along almost two feet of wire. So of course you are going to get a voltage drop. NiCads are already running lower, at 1.2 volts.

For example, putting a solar engine inside a Robosapien. Then basically bypassing the off switch, so it comes alive every now and again and takes two steps forward. Running on a couple 10-farad caps. No problem at all. You can take his arms off; he can walk, even if he doesn't have any batteries in his feet. And that makes him pretty light. So you could in fact, even if you decided to replace his arms...

Some people started to do this, but nobody ever took it to its natural limits. The fact is, you can completely take off the entire shell of the robot, and then get that frame to work. And now you have something which basically runs, literally you are facing the efficiency of the motors which is 48 percent. Take it to the next possible limit. Put on your own arms. The arms come off, now you've reduced him down to a five-motor mechanism. You have all the mechanisms for mounting things in the chest. You don't need the shell, the thing is now you'll be able to run him at a much higher resonance, and he can take much deeper steps. Right now his feet only lap each other by 50 percent. Without the shell they can lap each other by 100 percent.

Here's something interesting. Take the high-quality 130 motors that you normally get for something like electric race cars. Put in high-quality pre-buffers, of the type, again, that you get for electric racecars, and you can make a Robosapien travel up to four times faster. Granted, his battery life is now reduced down to say, 25 percent. Right now he has a nice little speed of say, two inches per second. At eight inches a second, he's fast enough to play real soccer. Or for a real race. Maybe we'll see things like Robosapien racing competitions. It's just a matter of now he is traveling so quick, how do you keep him traveling straight. The footpads, which are removable and replaceable, all of a sudden no longer work.

Here's an interesting trick. Remove all the footpads, and race him only on a carpet surface. What'll happen is he'll automatically re-stabilize, you can put the footpads back in, basically re-find his center of balance, based upon that mechanism.

SAMANS: *I noticed that the most recent Robosapien I bought, the footpads were different from earlier models. I also noticed the motors were different too. The new ones are sort of a greenish color.*

TILDEN: The latest ones are black. You've got to remember, we went through 14 million motors. We have various factories dedicated to just producing Robosapien motors. And they've improved performance. One of the things we were so pleased about, the lifetime of a standard toy grade 130 motor is, maximum, about 144 hours. About a week or so. We've never had a failure on a Robosapien. The reason is, because, the suspension, rather than stopping the motor quickly, forwards and backwards, it decelerates the motor and then accelerates in the opposite direction.

SAMANS: *Storing and reusing that energy...*

TILDEN: Exactly right. The energy that's generated back [through the suspension system], in the Robosapien, the reason it gets so much efficiency—do the calculations: how on earth can it be so efficient? Well, when that motor moves backwards, 50 percent of the energy is regenerated because of the 3:1 gear ratio. That energy is stored, as a surface charge, on the alkalines. You can't recharge alkalines, but that surface charge is the equivalent of a 100-farad capacitor. So when he gets up in resonance, and is walking and doing really well, even when he is dancing and things like that, you can see all his symmetric functions, right? This arm is going down while this one is going up, because this is generating half the power that this thing needs, locally, coupled by the stored charge on the battery itself.

SAMANS: *That explains the variations in walking, in terms of walking straight. I did an experiment... and it was pointless. The results were all over the place. He did seem to do better when he "warmed up," for lack of a better term. The longer I did the experiment, the better the results.*

TILDEN: That's exactly what happens, see. A classic example of what I call biomorphic intelligence: walk your Robosapien from linoleum, onto carpet, onto something else, right, and across anything you want. He can walk over Legos. If you know anything about the algorithms normally associated with walking robots, like zero motion point and stuff like that, all of it is based on one thing: you got a flat foot on the ground, and the ground is flat. You'll never see Asimo walking on carpet, you'll never see him walking on an irregular surface. Robosapien? Up to something as deep as 1 inch shag, go go go go go!

If you want sort of predictability, when you actually set him to walking, hold him down solidly by the shoulders, set him to walking, and lightly let him go. Because his initial conditions, that is, the very first step he takes, determines what he'll do eventually. By holding him down, you get the battery up to a certain operational level, and by doing this you get a much greater predictability.

This is a big thing they found with all the girls doing our [quality control] tests. The robot had to sort of operate within certain performance parameters. And many robots were doing things like "oh it walks off, it's obviously defective" and then they'd test it again and be like "No, it walks straight..." I'm sorry, but the robot is based upon a law of indeterminism, which is not wholly measurable in all possible instances.

SAMANS: *In my tests nothing worked, I thought for sure I would see a pattern, and I didn't. I was going to try and figure it out, to tune it, and you can't.*

TILDEN: No, you can't. And the thing is, what are you supposed to do? You gotta remember, at any one particular instance, he only has less than half a square centimeter actually on the ground. He only has both of his footpads on for the amount of time it takes him to rock from one side to the other. And that turns out to be an extremely critical time. The robot is basically like a bottle of ketchup, if you balanced it just on the edge, before it falls over. It's hard to demonstrate on this table. If you've ever taken an empty beer can and spun it slowly so it basically pirouettes… the Robosapien operates on exactly the same principle, but doesn't fall over.

But look at the performance-to-silicone ratio, but also the efficiency, I mean this is something that wound up being one of the major sell points of the toy. It was sold around the world. And people have put some of the worst, crappiest batteries in the feet that you could possible imagine. Carbon cell batteries… you'd be amazed at how much of the world still uses 1970s battery technology. *<Laughs>*

We went up to Tibet and we got the crappiest, cheapest, the worst god-awful batteries you could possibly imagine. And we still got two hours of play out of the Robosapien. So we realized, no matter where this goes, you're going to get two hours of play, that's a good amount of time. The standard RC toy, you have to remember, only lasts 20 minutes. We beat and exceeded that by huge amounts.

Four major things. No matter where this robot went, it ran for hours. No matter where it went, nobody had to worry about English translation. Number three: no laptop required. One of the worst things I always hated, about say, Lego Mindstorms, "laptop not included." You also don't need directions. Four, there are so many things to find out; you can't find them all in one play session. So, standard RC toy, out of the box, forward, back, left and right, crash it into a wall, "Thanks Dad, what's next"? Robosapien is based upon the principle that essentially you always know if you have part of a chocolate bar left over. So you didn't eat it all, you've got that little left over that you can always play with. Robosapien basically has so many things inside of it, that you can't find them all… and that basically turned out to be the fourth. And the big fifth, and this is the hidden fifth, was the fact that not only was it reliable, but it was eminently hackable.

How many times have you tried to hack someone else's technology? Take a look at this stupid camera. Look at that connector! Yeah right! *<Laughs>* It's got wire contacts too small to even see. I hate that. I know somewhere on there is a video out, and there's a power in, probably a couple other lines, but I can't access that. I hate that about modern technology. Give me the good old days, when you know, you and a soldering iron, and a screwdriver, and you own that toy. The bottom line was, you take a screwdriver to that thing, you open it up, everything's color-coded. Everything's labeled. Everything does what it's supposed to do. There's hardly any wires at all. There's always gold-plated contacts, you wouldn't believe how hard I fought to make sure that they were always gold-plated. As soon as you opened it up, the possibilities skyrocketed. For anybody who was like me when I was seven years old…

SAMANS: *I was so pleased to open up the arms and see "Whoa there is a little PCB in here? And it's labeled!?!"*

TILDEN: And socketed. Sorry that the sockets are so cheap, but hey, at least they are there.

It's still too early yet for the major academic guys. Next month, there will be a Robosapien soccer team entered into the international robo soccer competition. Twenty Robosapiens all designed to play soccer. I have no idea what they've done or how they've done it, these are the guys from Carnegie-Mellon University.

For the cost of one Aibo, you can buy 20 Robosapiens. Having that number of interchangeable, exchangeable parts… when you make a mistake; there are standard replaceable parts from the next robot over.

SAMANS: *When I look at hacking the Robosapien I sort of see two schools of thought. There's the bolt-on approach, and then there are the brain replacement guys.*

TILDEN: And then there's enhancement. There are three things. There are people who do things like give it clothes. Weapons, that kind of stuff. They are cute as hell, I really like it. Number two are the brain replacement guys. These guys are nuts! But the fact is, some people have the ego to make it happen. The people that are trying to replace his brains, there are some sophisticated ways of doing that, but there are also some nonsophisticated ways that you can try that don't sacrifice the brain of your robot.

I will give you a circuit, in 12 transistors, that will mimic the complete walking strata of the Robosapien. You can build it yourself and you can add things onto it. One of the things that basically makes me nuts, you have to be able to press the buttons really fast, but you can in fact make the Robosapien walk by basically moving his shoulders at the same time. Unfortunately, we didn't add it, it powered out the motor drive too much, because of the software, but there's no reason why we couldn't have done it, it gave it a lot of personality.

SAMANS: *With a different controller, it is possible to move, say, both arms at exactly the same time.*

TILDEN: It's just a matter of IO limitations and concurrency.... The most important thing is you never start motors at exactly the same time. Always stagger them. Get the legs walking, and then, once the legs are walking, then you move the arms, always at 45 degrees phasing. As soon as the motors start all concurrently, then your power supply drops and you start getting some nasty deep spikes.

We needed seven motors, but let's face it, they are toy grade motors. They're not meant to shoot rapids. The fact that we've gotten as much as 400 hours out of some of our motors, toy-grade motors...

SAMANS: *Four hundred hours continuous?*

TILDEN: Four hundred continuous motion hours. Our biggest problem was things like springs and plastic pieces failing before the motors did. Motor drivers can't take more than 7 volts.... The only reason we don't recommend NiCad batteries is just on the off chance, say, the robot is caught behind the bed, because of their lower internal resistance it might cause a blowout of the drivers. But instances like that are really very rare.

The people that are trying to replace his brains, there are some sophisticated ways of doing that, but there are also some nonsophisticated ways that you can try that doesn't sacrifice the brain of your robot. One of the things people always say is "Oh, when are you giving us a robot with a USB port?" Not until next year, sorry. The brain for the Robosapien costs us 70 American cents. USB, just the interface, is a buck seventy. Just the ability to add USB, not even including all the software, is more than twice the cost of the entire brains of the Robosapien.

The only flat spot on the entire Robosapien is the area on the top of his speaker. And that's where we thought people would mount spare cell phones. Cell phones sometimes have IR ports right on the top of them.... Why is the back of the Robosapien's head IR transparent? So that you can feed him information from something mounted on his back. So you can program a Nokia cell phone, or even a Motorola to control him directly.

Sony Clie, this actually ran one of the hacker IR programs. It was a universal remote control that automatically runs on a Sony Clie, it allows you to program sequences. Set it up as a backpack, a bit of tape, a bit of programming, no modifications required.

We tried for the longest time to find some stable IR platform that we were going to give away software for. But there is no standard! Sony Clie's were great because they have a full-size screen, beautiful interface, already had a programmable this, that, and the other thing, they are based on Palm 3 so there was no license involved, pretty easy to work on, then all of a sudden Sony canceled them. So the software just sort of sat there in limbo. But fortunately some hackers on the web started coming up with their own sort of things. Some people found that a universal programmer worked pretty well. But they weren't sequenceable. People came up with their own blaster technology... The fact is, there is no reason why you couldn't have some sort of programmable, sequenceable controller, recording a Robosapien move and then playing back for hours.

SAMANS: *Using a computer, and a USB IR dongle I got up to like 250 moves before I was kind of worried about overloading the motor drivers.*

TILDEN: One of the things that's cool about the mechanism, if you press something like say, the lean forward, lean backward... there's a point where you can actually press and move the motors faster than the robot does.

SAMANS: *Right, it twitches.*

TILDEN: Hidden secret #13. <*Laughs*> You can, through an IR port, move him faster than he can move himself. We put the IR into one of the only direct interrupts that goes into the processor. So if you are feeding that thing precise controlled IR codes, you can give him much more degree and resolution of motion than he is capable of on his own.

SAMANS: *Which in turn gives him more precision...*

TILDEN: For example, his arms stop here. Why? Because that is exactly the height of an 8-inch step. He is designed to move and manipulate thing around on an 8-inch step that you'd find in your house. You could build him say, his own little disco board, that's the secret number, 8 inches. Give him a little gangster hat. <*Laughs*>

It's still too early for the science. You won't probably see anything until summertime, because right now, a lot of kids are working on Robosapiens for their final school project. But this June, this July, we're going to see a number of hacks, as part of a degree... it's all basically happening right now. It's February, and they are saying, "OK, what can I do with my Robosapien that will get me a grade?" Imagine this; you're taking a standard robot course at any college through North America. And you know what they have there, usually the Rhino arms or some sort of pathetic Meccano-looking carts, or Lego Mindstorms... imagine there you are and everyone is working with these boring robots and you walk in with a Robosapien, with a new brain. Come on! That is Joe Frankenstein. <*in a bad German accent*> "I have rebuilt him! He is mad!"

SAMANS: *That brings up an interesting point about Robosapien's appeal. Look at me, I am relatively nontechnical, but I saw this thing in the press, and I had to have one. And here I am. It has an appeal that I don't even know if I can explain.*

TILDEN: And that's just it. It took me a long time. I tried every bug in the world. Solar rollers, photovores... the problem with building Mars rovers is they just aren't sexy. A full-size Mars rover, it travels a meter a minute. Oooh, now we're really rocking! *<Laughs>*

We had solar roller competitions, where we tried to optimize, you know, efficiency to performance based on limited materials. We had robots that were doing a meter in less than 10 seconds. People solved the problem, but no one ever translated that. The most important thing about a robot is not just its ability to self groom and be tough, but also manage itself from a power effect.

Ever play with an Aibo? Four-minute boot time. It sits there and beeps at you, and I mean no disrespect, but any toy that spends a fifth of its battery life... booting.... *<Shakes head>* Any toy that consumes more power standing up than it does basically even walking... you gotta wonder about that.

I looked at the Aibo, and I recognized the same thing I've seen with more people, people build a legged robot, and this is still a common thing in robot competition today. They do a quick calculation, OK, it's got eight legs, it's about a pound, and the motors can each take like an eighth of a pound... so therefore the robot should be able to, you know, walk. No! The robot should be able to stand. Walking requires that two of those legs are off the ground. Which means that your other motors are going to collapse. And this is why you see an awful lot of walking spiders with like balloons or cables and they can't carry their own batteries.

SAMANS: *Have you seen Ramon the Robot? He is an interesting bipedal design...*

TILDEN: *<mimics Ramon>* Haven't the autistic people of America filed a complaint? I would have thought by now.... obviously it's Rainman.

Ramon is actually pretty interesting—they came in cheaper than us, but they were only able to sell 50,000 last year, and they did so at a massive loss. They basically had a contract that essentially forced them to get something out... same thing, for example, with the original Tomy Omnibot. My big thing was back in the 1980s. In 1982 I got my first Tomy OmniBot. I opened it up and I found out it was mostly empty space. I filled it with a home-built 68000 [an early home automation system based on an 8-MHz processor], and the best visual apparatus I could find. I programmed it from my Atari, I was really hoping I could get this thing to do all this stuff. And I found myself falling into every pratfall that anyone who's ever done artificial intelligence has fallen into. Unless something looks like a man, you cannot tell if it is moving correctly. What sort of body language can you get from a wheel? It's very hard to tell when it is crashing. When Robosapien is in trouble you can tell. Even your dogs can tell. The B.I.O. Bugs were pretty cool, but when a bug is sick no one cares. When a humanoid thing is sick, there is an empathy factor.

▓ ▓ ▓

TILDEN: The new generation robot, Robosapien V2, which is twice the motors...

SAMANS: *Fourteen motors?*

TILDEN: Twelve motors. It can get itself up, roll itself over... it's actually pretty adept. It's exactly one centimeter taller than the Sony QRIO. But it's like 1/1,000th of the cost. The Japanese come out with these new and beautiful things...

My whole career has been based upon one rather exotic premise: I believe that robots are in fact simple and elegant things. I've ALWAYS believed that. Since I was three I was looking at all the problems that people have been having with robots, and saying, you know, what the hell is the problem?

SAMANS: *It flies in the face of everything you think of when you think of robots...*

TILDEN: Let's face it, bottom-up design is not digital. The art of electronics turned into the business of electronics in 1969. And all these beautiful, simple analog solutions were lost under IBM business workings. Why would you want a calculator that gives you a different answer every time? You put up with more things in a robot than you would with a computer. The digital computer has to sit on a table and do something functional. But something that moves, you put up with it. It's one of the contradictions.... Isaac Asimov was a great fiction writer, but unfortunately was a lousy roboticist.

SAMANS: *I see his three laws as... three laws that make a great backdrop to write stories against.*

TILDEN: Exactly right. The problem is everyone read those things like say, detectives read Sherlock Holmes.

SAMANS: *The positronic brain was the worst thing to happen to robotics, ever?*

TILDEN: It really was. It basically said, OK, and a lot of people are still working on this, including some of my friends—one day, consciousness will be reduced down to an equation that you can sell on a t-shirt. Good luck. The fact is, the entire premise of artificial intelligence is based on the idea that human thought is in fact rational and cognitive. You have a law degree... when has this ever been so?!?! *<Laughter>* People act out of spite, emotional responses, and basically caveman primitiveness. This is why Robosapien, as I have said, he is an evolved robot. We didn't try and devolve man. We basically evolved biomorphic primitives, up to a point where all of a sudden they become not just something competent and minimalist, but also extremely robust and hackable.

It took a long time. Check me out, type in Mark Tilden and robotics, and start surfing. 100,000 hits. He's a quack, he's a quack, and so on... yeah, I know his robots work, shut up! *<Laughs>* Completely beside the point!

▧ ▧ ▧

TILDEN: One of the problems with the secret functions is you don't know why the robot needs them. Half of them are designed, basically, for the safety of the robot, the other half are designed for crazy bastards looking into something. How do I explain that? Hi, if you're a crazy bastard who essentially wants to know how to do this, here's what the functions are, here's the modulation characteristics of the eyes....

The Robosapien is the world's first open source interactive robot.

Index